50% OFF Online PMP Prep Course!

Dear Customer,

We consider it an honor and a privilege that you chose our PMP Study Guide. As a way of showing our appreciation and to help us better serve you, we have partnered with Mometrix Test Preparation to offer you **50% off their online PMP Prep Course**. Many PMP courses are needlessly expensive and don't deliver enough value. With their course, you get access to the best PMP prep material, and **you only pay half price**.

Mometrix has structured their online course to perfectly complement your printed study guide. The PMP Prep Course contains **in-depth lessons** that cover all the most important topics, over **700 practice questions** to ensure you feel prepared, and more than **520 digital flashcards**, so you can study while you're on the go.

Online PMP Prep Course

Topics Included:
- Mometrix's PMP Guide for PMBOK 6
    - Project Operating Environment
- Agile
    - Agile Mindset and Common Terms
- Principles
    - Stewardship
- Performance Domains
    - Project Work
- Tailoring
    - What Is Tailoring?
- Models, Methods, and Artifacts
    - Commonly Used Models

Course Features:
- PMP Study Guide
    - Get content that complements our best-selling study guide.
- Full-Length Practice Tests
    - With over 700 practice questions, you can test yourself again and again.
- Mobile Friendly
    - If you need to study on the go, the course is easily accessible from your mobile device.
- PMP Flashcards
    - Our course includes a flashcard mode with over 520 content cards to help you study.

To receive this discount, visit them at mometrix.com/university/pmp or simply scan this QR code with your smartphone. At the checkout page, enter the discount code: **PMP50TPB**

If you have any questions or concerns, please contact them at support@mometrix.com.

Sincerely,

 in partnership with

Online Resources

Included with your purchase are multiple online resources. This includes the practice tests in an interactive format and a convenient study timer to help you manage your time.

Instructions for accessing these resources can be found on the last page of this book.

PMP® Exam Prep 2025 and 2026
3 Practice Tests and PMBOK® 7th Edition Study Guide Book for Project Management [Includes Detailed Answer Explanations]

Lydia Morrison

Copyright © 2025 by TPB Publishing

All rights reserved. No part of this publication may be reproduced, distributed, or transmitted in any form or by any means, including photocopying, recording, or other electronic or mechanical methods, without the prior written permission of the publisher, except in the case of brief quotations embodied in critical reviews and certain other noncommercial uses permitted by copyright law.

Written and edited by TPB Publishing.

TPB Publishing is not associated with or endorsed by any official testing organization. TPB Publishing is a publisher of unofficial educational products. All test and organization names are trademarks of their respective owners. Content in this book is included for utilitarian purposes only and does not constitute an endorsement by TPB Publishing of any particular point of view.

Interested in buying more than 10 copies of our product? Contact us about bulk discounts:
bulkorders@studyguideteam.com

ISBN 13: 9781637754115

Table of Contents

Welcome *1*

Quick Overview *2*

Test-Taking Strategies *3*

Introduction to the PMP *7*

    Function of the Test 7

    Test Administration 7

    Test Format 7

Study Prep Plan for the PMP *8*

Domain I: People *10*

    Task 1: Manage Conflict 10

    Task 2: Lead a Team 11

    Task 3: Support Team Performance 14

    Task 4: Empower Team Members and Stakeholders 16

    Task 5: Ensure Team Members/Stakeholders Are Adequately Trained 18

    Task 6: Build a Team 19

    Task 7: Address and Remove Impediments, Obstacles, and Blockers for the Team 22

    Task 8: Negotiate Project Agreements 23

    Task 9: Collaborate with Stakeholders 27

    Task 10: Build Shared Understanding 28

    Task 11: Engage and Support Virtual Teams 29

    Task 12: Define Team Ground Rules 31

    Task 13: Mentor Relevant Stakeholders 32

    Task 14: Promote Team Performance Through the Application of Emotional Intelligence 33

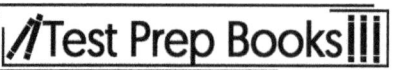

Practice Quiz 35

Answer Explanations 36

Domain II: Process 37

Task 1: Execute Project with the Urgency Required to Deliver Business Value 37

Task 2: Manage Communications 40

Task 3: Assess and Manage Risks 42

Task 4: Engage Stakeholders 45

Task 5: Plan and Manage Budget and Resources 50

Task 6: Plan and Manage Schedule 52

Task 7: Plan and Manage Quality of Products & Deliverables 54

Task 8: Plan and Manage Scope 59

Task 9: Integrate Project Planning Activities 60

Task 10: Manage Project Changes 61

Task 11: Plan and Manage Procurement 63

Task 12: Manage Project Artifacts 65

Task 13: Determine Appropriate Project Methodology & Practices 67

Task 14: Establish Project Governance Structure 70

Task 15: Manage Project Issues 72

Task 16: Ensure Knowledge Transfer for Project Continuity 75

Task 17: Plan and Manage Project/Phase Closure or Transitions 76

Practice Quiz 78

Answer Explanations 79

Domain III: Business Environment 80

Task 1: Plan and Manage Project Compliance 80

Task 2: Evaluate and Deliver Project Benefits and Value 82

Table of Contents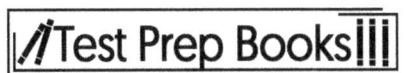

Task 3: Evaluate and Address External Business Environment Changes for Impact on Scope 86

Task 4: Support Organizational Change 87

Practice Quiz 90

Answer Explanations 91

PMP Practice Test #1 .... *92*

Answer Explanations #1 .... *119*

PMP Practice Test #2 .... *139*

Answer Explanations #2 .... *166*

PMP Practice Test #3 .... *184*

Online Resources *187*

Welcome

Dear Reader,

Welcome to your new Test Prep Books study guide! We are pleased that you chose us to help you prepare for your exam. There are many study options to choose from, and we appreciate you choosing us. Studying can be a daunting task, but we have designed a smart, effective study guide to help prepare you for what lies ahead.

Whether you're a parent helping your child learn and grow, a high school student working hard to get into your dream college, or a nursing student studying for a complex exam, we want to help give you the tools you need to succeed. We hope this study guide gives you the skills and the confidence to thrive, and we can't thank you enough for allowing us to be part of your journey.

In an effort to continue to improve our products, we welcome feedback from our customers. We look forward to hearing from you. Suggestions, success stories, and criticisms can all be communicated by emailing us at info@studyguideteam.com.

Sincerely,
Test Prep Books Team

Quick Overview

As you draw closer to taking your exam, effective preparation becomes more and more important. Thankfully, you have this study guide to help you get ready. Use this guide to help keep your studying on track and refer to it often.

This study guide contains several key sections that will help you be successful on your exam. The guide contains tips for what you should do the night before and the day of the test. Also included are test-taking tips. Knowing the right information is not always enough. Many well-prepared test takers struggle with exams. These tips will help equip you to accurately read, assess, and answer test questions.

A large part of the guide is devoted to showing you what content to expect on the exam and to helping you better understand that content. In this guide are practice test questions so that you can see how well you have grasped the content. Then, answer explanations are provided so that you can understand why you missed certain questions.

Don't try to cram the night before you take your exam. This is not a wise strategy for a few reasons. First, your retention of the information will be low. Your time would be better used by reviewing information you already know rather than trying to learn a lot of new information. Second, you will likely become stressed as you try to gain a large amount of knowledge in a short amount of time. Third, you will be depriving yourself of sleep. So be sure to go to bed at a reasonable time the night before. Being well-rested helps you focus and remain calm.

Be sure to eat a substantial breakfast the morning of the exam. If you are taking the exam in the afternoon, be sure to have a good lunch as well. Being hungry is distracting and can make it difficult to focus. You have hopefully spent lots of time preparing for the exam. Don't let an empty stomach get in the way of success!

When travelling to the testing center, leave earlier than needed. That way, you have a buffer in case you experience any delays. This will help you remain calm and will keep you from missing your appointment time at the testing center.

Be sure to pace yourself during the exam. Don't try to rush through the exam. There is no need to risk performing poorly on the exam just so you can leave the testing center early. Allow yourself to use all of the allotted time if needed.

Remain positive while taking the exam even if you feel like you are performing poorly. Thinking about the content you should have mastered will not help you perform better on the exam.

Once the exam is complete, take some time to relax. Even if you feel that you need to take the exam again, you will be well served by some down time before you begin studying again. It's often easier to convince yourself to study if you know that it will come with a reward!

Test-Taking Strategies

1. Predicting the Answer

When you feel confident in your preparation for a multiple-choice test, try predicting the answer before reading the answer choices. This is especially useful on questions that test objective factual knowledge. By predicting the answer before reading the available choices, you eliminate the possibility that you will be distracted or led astray by an incorrect answer choice. You will feel more confident in your selection if you read the question, predict the answer, and then find your prediction among the answer choices. After using this strategy, be sure to still read all of the answer choices carefully and completely. If you feel unprepared, you should not attempt to predict the answers. This would be a waste of time and an opportunity for your mind to wander in the wrong direction.

2. Reading the Whole Question

Too often, test takers scan a multiple-choice question, recognize a few familiar words, and immediately jump to the answer choices. Test authors are aware of this common impatience, and they will sometimes prey upon it. For instance, a test author might subtly turn the question into a negative, or he or she might redirect the focus of the question right at the end. The only way to avoid falling into these traps is to read the entirety of the question carefully before reading the answer choices.

3. Looking for Wrong Answers

Long and complicated multiple-choice questions can be intimidating. One way to simplify a difficult multiple-choice question is to eliminate all of the answer choices that are clearly wrong. In most sets of answers, there will be at least one selection that can be dismissed right away. If the test is administered on paper, the test taker could draw a line through it to indicate that it may be ignored; otherwise, the test taker will have to perform this operation mentally or on scratch paper. In either case, once the obviously incorrect answers have been eliminated, the remaining choices may be considered. Sometimes identifying the clearly wrong answers will give the test taker some information about the correct answer. For instance, if one of the remaining answer choices is a direct opposite of one of the eliminated answer choices, it may well be the correct answer. The opposite of obviously wrong is obviously right! Of course, this is not always the case. Some answers are obviously incorrect simply because they are irrelevant to the question being asked. Still, identifying and eliminating some incorrect answer choices is a good way to simplify a multiple-choice question.

4. Don't Overanalyze

Anxious test takers often overanalyze questions. When you are nervous, your brain will often run wild, causing you to make associations and discover clues that don't actually exist. If you feel that this may be a problem for you, do whatever you can to slow down during the test. Try taking a deep breath or counting to ten. As you read and consider the question, restrict yourself to the particular words used by the author. Avoid thought tangents about what the author *really* meant, or what he or she was *trying* to say. The only things that matter on a multiple-choice test are the words that are actually in the question. You must avoid reading too much into a multiple-choice question, or supposing that the writer meant something other than what he or she wrote.

5. No Need for Panic

It is wise to learn as many strategies as possible before taking a multiple-choice test, but it is likely that you will come across a few questions for which you simply don't know the answer. In this situation, avoid panicking. Because most multiple-choice tests include dozens of questions, the relative value of a single wrong answer is small. As much as possible, you should compartmentalize each question on a multiple-choice test. In other words, you should not allow your feelings about one question to affect your success on the others. When you find a question that you either don't understand or don't know how to answer, just take a deep breath and do your best. Read the entire question slowly and carefully. Try rephrasing the question a couple of different ways. Then, read all of the answer choices carefully. After eliminating obviously wrong answers, make a selection and move on to the next question.

6. Confusing Answer Choices

When working on a difficult multiple-choice question, there may be a tendency to focus on the answer choices that are the easiest to understand. Many people, whether consciously or not, gravitate to the answer choices that require the least concentration, knowledge, and memory. This is a mistake. When you come across an answer choice that is confusing, you should give it extra attention. A question might be confusing because you do not know the subject matter to which it refers. If this is the case, don't

eliminate the answer before you have affirmatively settled on another. When you come across an answer choice of this type, set it aside as you look at the remaining choices. If you can confidently assert that one of the other choices is correct, you can leave the confusing answer aside. Otherwise, you will need to take a moment to try to better understand the confusing answer choice. Rephrasing is one way to tease out the sense of a confusing answer choice.

7. Your First Instinct

Many people struggle with multiple-choice tests because they overthink the questions. If you have studied sufficiently for the test, you should be prepared to trust your first instinct once you have carefully and completely read the question and all of the answer choices. There is a great deal of research suggesting that the mind can come to the correct conclusion very quickly once it has obtained all of the relevant information. At times, it may seem to you as if your intuition is working faster even than your reasoning mind. This may in fact be true. The knowledge you obtain while studying may be retrieved from your subconscious before you have a chance to work out the associations that support it. Verify your instinct by working out the reasons that it should be trusted.

8. Key Words

Many test takers struggle with multiple-choice questions because they have poor reading comprehension skills. Quickly reading and understanding a multiple-choice question requires a mixture of skill and experience. To help with this, try jotting down a few key words and phrases on a piece of scrap paper. Doing this concentrates the process of reading and forces the mind to weigh the relative importance of the question's parts. In selecting words and phrases to write down, the test taker thinks

Test-Taking Strategies

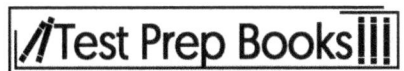

about the question more deeply and carefully. This is especially true for multiple-choice questions that are preceded by a long prompt.

9. Subtle Negatives

One of the oldest tricks in the multiple-choice test writer's book is to subtly reverse the meaning of a question with a word like *not* or *except*. If you are not paying attention to each word in the question, you can easily be led astray by this trick. For instance, a common question format is, "Which of the following is...?" Obviously, if the question instead is, "Which of the following is not...?," then the answer will be quite different. Even worse, the test makers are aware of the potential for this mistake and will include one answer choice that would be correct if the question were not negated or reversed. A test taker who misses the reversal will find what he or she believes to be a correct answer and will be so confident that he or she will fail to reread the question and discover the original error. The only way to avoid this is to practice a wide variety of multiple-choice questions and to pay close attention to each and every word.

10. Reading Every Answer Choice

It may seem obvious, but you should always read every one of the answer choices! Too many test takers fall into the habit of scanning the question and assuming that they understand the question because they recognize a few key words. From there, they pick the first answer choice that answers the question they believe they have read. Test takers who read all of the answer choices might discover that one of the latter answer choices is actually *more* correct. Moreover, reading all of the answer choices can remind you of facts related to the question that can help you arrive at the correct answer. Sometimes, a misstatement or incorrect detail in one of the latter answer choices will trigger your memory of the subject and will enable you to find the right answer. Failing to read all of the answer choices is like not reading all of the items on a restaurant menu: you might miss out on the perfect choice.

11. Spot the Hedges

One of the keys to success on multiple-choice tests is paying close attention to every word. This is never truer than with words like *almost*, *most*, *some*, and *sometimes*. These words are called "hedges" because they indicate that a statement is not totally true or not true in every place and time. An absolute statement will contain no hedges, but in many subjects, the answers are not always straightforward or absolute. There are always exceptions to the rules in these subjects. For this reason,

you should favor those multiple-choice questions that contain hedging language. The presence of qualifying words indicates that the author is taking special care with his or her words, which is certainly important when composing the right answer. After all, there are many ways to be wrong, but there is only one way to be right! For this reason, it is wise to avoid answers that are absolute when taking a multiple-choice test. An absolute answer is one that says things are either all one way or all another. They often include words like *every*, *always*, *best*, and *never*. If you are taking a multiple-choice test in a subject that doesn't lend itself to absolute answers, be on your guard if you see any of these words.

5

12. Long Answers

In many subject areas, the answers are not simple. As already mentioned, the right answer often requires hedges. Another common feature of the answers to a complex or subjective question are qualifying clauses, which are groups of words that subtly modify the meaning of the sentence. If the question or answer choice describes a rule to which there are exceptions or the subject matter is complicated, ambiguous, or confusing, the correct answer will require many words in order to be expressed clearly and accurately. In essence, you should not be deterred by answer choices that seem excessively long. Oftentimes, the author of the text will not be able to write the correct answer without offering some qualifications and modifications. Your job is to read the answer choices thoroughly and completely and to select the one that most accurately and precisely answers the question.

13. Restating to Understand

Sometimes, a question on a multiple-choice test is difficult not because of what it asks but because of how it is written. If this is the case, restate the question or answer choice in different words. This process serves a couple of important purposes. First, it forces you to concentrate on the core of the question. In order to rephrase the question accurately, you have to understand it well. Rephrasing the question will concentrate your mind on the key words and ideas. Second, it will present the information to your mind in a fresh way. This process may trigger your memory and render some useful scrap of information picked up while studying.

14. True Statements

Sometimes an answer choice will be true in itself, but it does not answer the question. This is one of the main reasons why it is essential to read the question carefully and completely before proceeding to the answer choices. Too often, test takers skip ahead to the answer choices and look for true statements. Having found one of these, they are content to select it without reference to the question above. The savvy test taker will always read the entire question before turning to the answer choices. Then, having settled on a correct answer choice, he or she will refer to the original question and ensure that the selected answer is relevant. The mistake of choosing a correct-but-irrelevant answer choice is especially common on questions related to specific pieces of objective knowledge.

15. No Patterns

One of the more dangerous ideas that circulates about multiple-choice tests is that the correct answers tend to fall into patterns. These erroneous ideas range from a belief that B and C are the most common right answers, to the idea that an unprepared test-taker should answer "A-B-A-C-A-D-A-B-A." It cannot be emphasized enough that pattern-seeking of this type is exactly the WRONG way to approach a multiple-choice test. To begin with, it is highly unlikely that the test maker will plot the correct answers according to some predetermined pattern. The questions are scrambled and delivered in a random order. Furthermore, even if the test maker was following a pattern in the assignation of correct answers, there is no reason why the test taker would know which pattern he or she was using. Any attempt to discern a pattern in the answer choices is a waste of time and a distraction from the real work of taking the test. A test taker would be much better served by extra preparation before the test than by reliance on a pattern in the answers.

Introduction to the PMP

Function of the Test

The Project Management Professional exam was developed by the Project Management Institute (PMI) to provide certification and further training in industry best practices. The PMP exam is internationally accredited and abides by the testing practices outlined in the APA's *Standards for Educational and Psychological Testing.* The skills and knowledge assessed in the PMP have been developed and reviewed by project management professionals with their own PMP certifications to ensure that the exam accurately reflects the tasks and responsibilities of the profession.

Test Administration

The PMP exam consists of 180 questions. There will be 5 questions within the 180 that are considered unscored pretest questions used to evaluate questions for use in future exams.

Test-takers are allowed 230 minutes to complete the exam. Two 10-minute breaks will be permitted during the testing period. The first break will begin once the test-taker has completed questions 1-60 and reviewed their responses and the second will begin after question 120 is completed and all answers are checked. Once all responses are reviewed and the break has started, previous material cannot be viewed.

There will be a tutorial section at the beginning of the exam and a survey prompt after the exam is complete. Both the tutorial and the survey are optional and the time used to complete either portion will not be included in the 230-minute testing time.

Test Format

The questions on the PMP exam will be derived from skills and concepts related to the three domains of project management: people, process, and business environment. The following table provides a breakdown of the percentage of questions attributed to each domain:

Domain	Percentage of Questions on Exam
I. People	42%
II. Process	50%
III. Business Environment	8%
Total	100%

The exam may contain multiple-choice questions with single responses, multiple-choice questions with multiple responses, fill-in-the-blank questions, and answer selection questions.

Study Prep Plan for the PMP

1 **Schedule -** Use one of our study schedules below or come up with one of your own.

2 **Relax -** Test anxiety can hurt even the best students. There are many ways to reduce stress. Find the one that works best for you.

3 **Execute -** Once you have a good plan in place, be sure to stick to it.

One Week Study Schedule

Day 1	Domain I: People
Day 2	Domain II: Process
Day 3	Domain III: Business Environment
Day 4	PMP Practice Test #1
Day 5	PMP Practice Test #2
Day 6	PMP Practice Test #3
Day 7	Take Your Exam!

Two Week Study Schedule

Day 1	Domain I: People	Day 8	Task 16: Ensure Knowledge Transfer for Project Continuity
Day 2	Task 4: Empower Team Members and Stakeholders	Day 9	Domain III: Business Environment
Day 3	Task 11: Engage and Support Virtual Teams	Day 10	Task 3: Evaluate and Address External...
Day 4	Domain II: Process	Day 11	PMP Practice Test #1
Day 5	Task 5: Plan and Manage Budget and Resources	Day 12	PMP Practice Test #2
Day 6	Task 7: Plan and Manage Quality of Products & Deliverables	Day 13	PMP Practice Test #3
Day 7	Task 11: Plan and Manage Procurement	Day 14	Take Your Exam!

Study Prep Plan for the PMP

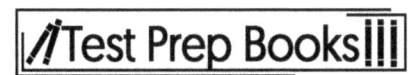

One Month Study Schedule

Day 1	Domain I: People	Day 11	Task 5: Plan and Manage Budget and Resources	Day 21	Task 2: Evaluate and Deliver Project Benefits and Value
Day 2	Task 2: Lead a Team	Day 12	Task 7: Plan and Manage Quality of Products & Deliverables	Day 22	Task 3: Evaluate and Address External Business Environment Changes for Impact on Scope
Day 3	Task 4: Empower Team Members and Stakeholders	Day 13	Task 8: Plan and Manage Scope	Day 23	Task 4: Support Organizational Change
Day 4	Task 5: Ensure Team Members/ Stakeholders Are Adequately Trained	Day 14	Task 9: Integrate Project Planning Activities	Day 24	PMP Practice Test #1
Day 5	Task 6: Build a Team	Day 15	Task 11: Plan and Manage Procurement	Day 25	Answer Explanations #1
Day 6	Task 8: Negotiate Project Agreements	Day 16	Task 12: Manage Project Artifacts	Day 26	PMP Practice Test #2
Day 7	Task 10: Build Shared Understanding	Day 17	Task 13: Determine Appropriate Project Methodology & Practices	Day 27	Answer Explanations #2
Day 8	Task 12: Define Team Ground Rules	Day 18	Task 14: Establish Project Governance Structure	Day 28	PMP Practice Test #3
Day 9	Domain II: Process	Day 19	Task 15: Manage Project Issues	Day 29	Answer Explanations #3
Day 10	Task 3: Assess and Manage Risks	Day 20	Domain III: Business Environment	Day 30	Take Your Exam!

Build your prep plan online by visiting:
testprepbooks.com/prep

Domain I: People

Task 1: Manage Conflict

When managing a team, conflict is inevitable. One of the project manager's most vital roles is to mitigate conflict between team members and stakeholders to maintain positive rapport within the team and ensure that project tasks progress efficiently.

Interpret the Source and Stage of the Conflict

Interpersonal conflict in the workspace can occur for a variety of reasons. In some cases, conflict between team members may even be useful for identifying areas for improvement in the team's processes. In other cases, disagreements can thwart productivity and break down the team's dynamic. It is the project manager's responsibility to analyze the situation and determine the root of the problem so work may resume as usual. Ideally, the project manager should address the source of the conflict before it escalates and impedes project completion. Project managers should remain aware of shifts in group interactions, stalls in collaboration, and other signs of worsening conflict to detect and dispel problems as soon as possible.

Analyze the Context for the Conflict

There are many issues that could spark conflict within a team. Budget or time constraints can increase pressure on team members, while disagreements between team members can impact project deadlines and the quality of the team's work. When the project manager notices a problem brewing, it is important for them evaluate the issue in the context of the team's project plan, circumstances, resources, and work environment. When possible, the project manager should help the team work through blocks, access necessary resources to help with impediments, and work through disagreements to get the project back on track and ensure that each team member feels like their perspective and opinions have been considered.

Further, it is important for project managers to communicate effectively and respectfully with their team as they navigate conflict. Casting blame and revisiting past problems can cause further frustration. Focus instead on creating a positive environment and leading your team to develop a solution to their current conflict together.

Evaluate, Recommend, and Reconcile the Appropriate Conflict Resolution Solution

Project managers should be aware of the best conflict resolution methods to help their teams work through any issue that might arise. Ken Thomas and Ralph Kilmann developed a model that describes six ways to address conflict:

- **Confronting/problem solving.** This style of conflict resolution is employed when the project manager seeks to maintain the relationships between their team members. This method necessitates that all team members have confidence in one another's ability to problem-solve.

- **Collaborating.** This style is used when there is trust between the team members and there is time in the project schedule to reach a consensus on the issue at hand.

- **Compromising.** This style may be used when the team must decide on one of two options. It may also play into power dynamics in the workplace. For instance, one team member may have to agree to use another team member's idea or method in order to resolve the pressing conflict.

- **Smoothing/accommodating.** This style may be used when reaching the team's primary goal is more important than the current conflict. For instance, a sponsor or stakeholder may disagree with other members of the team. Depending on the context and circumstances, the rest of the team may have to accommodate their preferences to complete the project.

- **Forcing.** This style is used when there is no time to collaborate or reach a decision through open discussion and the party with the most power must make a decision for the team to follow. Health and safety issues may require this type of conflict resolution style.

- **Withdrawal/avoiding.** In some cases, it is best to allow the conflict to resolve on its own. This method may be useful if team discussions are heated and require time to cool off, or if a problem arises with an aspect of the project that is not worth challenging.

While each conflict scenario may require different treatment, it is important for project managers to default to the option that will preserve the relationships between team members and foster growth and productivity. Methods that stress the team dynamic, such as forcing, are less desirable.

Task 2: Lead a Team

Showing leadership to a team requires a combination of confidence, skill, persuasion, and compromise. Teams need to have a clearly indicated leader that handles decision making from the top and can direct the team to do the tasks necessary for project completion. However, a leader needs to show that they not only have decision making skills but also people skills.

Set a Clear Vision and Mission

Every project needs to have an ultimate goal in mind. Setting up a vision and mission statement will help teams reach that goal. The vision statement is what the team hopes to achieve in the future. The mission statement is what exactly the team is doing to reach that goal.

There are several key points that need to be addressed at the beginning of the project. The reasons for doing the project, how the team is going to approach finishing tasks and meeting expectations for the project, and how the team and others are going to benefit from the project need to be very clear. Not having a clear vision and mission is like setting off to sea without a map. It is easy to get lost, and there is no clear direction on where to go.

Support Diversity and Inclusion

It is important for teams to include people from different kinds of backgrounds. Diversity refers to race, gender, orientation, religion, culture, and many other aspects. Teams should embrace these different values and utilize each unique member of the team to form a well-rounded group that can handle any situation. This includes the different types of behaviors and thinking styles that teams will encounter. One of the most popular methods of classifying behavior types and thought processes is the Myers-

Briggs Type Indicator (MBTI). The MBTI breaks down people's personalities based on four dimensions. Personalities are assigned a four-letter code, such as ISTJ and ENTP.

Extraversion (E) / Introversion (I): Does this person prefer to be around others or by themselves?

Sensing (S) / Intuition (N): Does this person gather facts or use their intuition?

Thinking (T) / Feeling (F): Does this person look for logical answers or make decisions based on their emotion?

Judging (J) / Perceiving (P): Does this person prefer order and structure or flexibility?

Diverse teams are made up of many different kinds of experts in their field, creating a strong network that the team can access. Hiring is especially important, and emphasis should be placed on acquiring people who can contribute to the team. Everyone on the team needs to feel welcome, and creating an inclusive environment where everyone's opinion is considered is a top priority for project managers.

Value Servant Leadership

Although there is a hierarchy in the team, good leaders understand that everyone contributes to the project. People need to be inspired and led by someone who can prove themselves capable in difficult situations and can provide support to the team members so they can accomplish their tasks smoothly and efficiently. Servant leadership makes the well-being of the team a priority and requires being in the field with the team and working alongside them.

There are several tenets of servant leadership to consider.

- Conceptualization: Leaders can see the big picture and guide the team toward that goal.

- Listening: Leaders actively listen to their team and address their concerns.

- Awareness: Leaders understand how their actions affect others.

- Persuasion: Leaders convince others to willingly follow them by building trust and confidence.

- Stewardship: Leaders take responsibility for what happens to the team and lead by example.

- Commitment to growth: Leaders provide opportunities for their team to improve their skills.

- Healing: Leaders support their team's physical and mental health.

- Empathy: Leaders understand others' feelings and care about their unique situations.

- Foresight: Leaders use their past experience and current information to make predictions on what is most likely to happen in the future.

- Building community: Leaders need to be able to create a community that emphasizes teamwork, inclusion, and friendship.

Determine an Appropriate Leadership Style

Two of the main styles of leadership are directive and collaborative. Directive leaders are confident and unambivalent. They analyze the situation on their own and make the decisions. They are accountable for their own actions and consult the team only when necessary. In contrast, collaborative leaders value their team's opinions and work together with them to make decisions. Directive leaders may appear distant from their team and out of touch with their concerns, while collaborative leaders may take much longer to make decisions and appear too accommodating. With collaborative leaders, constantly needing to consult with the team for every decision and trying to accommodate everyone can make the leader seem unsure of themselves. Sometimes, leaders must make a hard decision and stand by it. For these reasons, the best leaders will balance these two styles.

Inspire, Motivate, and Influence Team Members/Stakeholders

Every member on a team has a reason to be there and is motivated by different factors. A successful team will lay out a team contract, or a list of expectations that every member agrees to. Team contracts are also known as social contracts. Having a team contract gives everyone the chance to work together more cohesively, hold each other accountable, and it provides a foundation for the team to work from. These contracts also provide guidance on communication, meetings, and etiquette.

One big motivation for team members is the reward that they will receive for their contribution. A reward system outlines how contributions will be rewarded and how to create fulfillment. Money, although extremely important, is not always the main motivator. Some may also be seeking fulfillment through satisfying work, advancement, recognition, and a growing sense of responsibility.

Analyze Team Members' and Stakeholders' Influence

Stakeholders should be identified before the start of the project. Doing so will allow their expectations to be considered and to identify potential sources of early conflict. Examples of stakeholders include employees, customers, suppliers, and shareholders. Stakeholders are interested in the project's outcome for a variety of reasons. For example, customers will want to have the best product that the team can develop, and suppliers will want to see that the resources they are providing are being put to good use. Stakeholders have influence over how the project develops over time.

Team members influence the project directly by the quality of their work, their cohesiveness, and their professionalism. Team members need to be aware of stakeholder influence and expectations when completing projects because projects are started for specific reasons. As a part of the team, everyone needs to contribute their skills and knowledge to meet the team's goals and reward the trust that has been placed on them.

Distinguish Various Options to Lead Various Team Members and Stakeholders

Stakeholders have a keen interest in seeing a project succeed. Through their support, the team receives the funding and information to work at an optimal level. It is important to engage with stakeholders in order to understand their expectations. Interpersonal skills play an important role in negotiating with them and helping them to form realistic expectations. These interpersonal skills are also used when interacting with the team. Facilitating a project to meet both stakeholders' and team members' expectations is possible when a leader uses the necessary communication and interpersonal skills.

Task 3: Support Team Performance

Teams need to have a solid support structure in order to function optimally. Creating a supportive environment for teams will lead to better results and increased productivity. Among other responsibilities, there needs to be a way to assess team performance, support growth and development, incorporate feedback, and verify how much a team is improving.

Appraise Team Member Performance Against Key Performance Indicators

Companies utilize key performance indicators (KPIs) to measure how successfully the team achieves its goals and shows improvements. The results from these KPIs are used to identify areas where the team can improve and to address these issues through coaching and mentoring. Implementing these changes allows individual team members to work more effectively together and to improve their performance.

Examples of KPIs used in the industry include:

Human capital value added (HCVA): HCVA determines the financial worth of an employee. It measures how much profit an average employee brings to the company.

Employee engagement level: This KPI measures how much an employee cares about their work and the amount of effort that they put into their work. Engagement surveys can be distributed throughout the company and help to identify potential issues that may cause employees to leave.

Employee churn rate: This measure is similar to the rate of staff turnover. Employee churn rate is taken as a percentage of the number of employees that leave a company over a certain period of time. Turnover is a natural and inevitable consequence of working in a company, but high turnover is damaging for a company and needs to be addressed as soon as possible.

Bradford Factor: The Bradford Factor assesses how impactful an employee's absence at work is for the company. It represents how many unplanned absences the employee has.

Support and Recognize Team Member Growth and Development

Teams are made up of many individuals with their own goals, but all employees need growth, recognition, and development. Rewarding good performances and allowing team members to grow personally and professionally gives them a sense of purpose and increases their appreciation of the company. In order to support teams, there needs to be a growth development plan and resources need to be set aside for this specific purpose. Teams need to have opportunities for professional development through workshops and training, positive feedback and praise for tasks completed successfully, recognition for their contributions, and clear paths to advance their career in the company.

Developing employees and team members is a worthwhile investment. Team members with proper support are able to further develop their skills and contribute to the company. If new technology becomes available, teams will be able to utilize it faster if team members are already highly trained and experienced. Development increases satisfaction and productivity. This productivity leads to better results and engagement. Engagement is particularly important because team members who are not challenged and experience no personal growth become unmotivated and bored. Proper engagement motivates team members and helps them to see the end goal of the project. They are able to handle

Determine the Appropriate Feedback Approach

There are two main types of feedback: positive and negative. Positive feedback encourages a behavior, while negative feedback discourages a behavior. Negative feedback does not necessarily mean the feedback is harsh or condescending. The most important factor to determining the appropriate feedback approach is timing. Feedback needs to be given frequently and at regular intervals. Instead of waiting for the end of a project or an arbitrary timeframe, managers should provide feedback when the opportunity arises, such as when an employee does something particularly well or when employee performance is becoming notably worse. Managers should work on their feedback delivery skills, be specific, and encourage open discussion with employees.

Regardless of how feedback is given to employees, all feedback must be constructive in some way. Constructive feedback shows, in a respectful manner, demonstrable ways to improve performance and is not needlessly hurtful to the employee that receives it. Critical feedback, which is overly harsh and focuses on the negative aspects of employee performance, can damage confidence and self-esteem, which can result in higher team turnover. Maintaining good morale and building a positive, constructive team environment allows constructive feedback to be given in a professional manner. Leaders need to actively listen and address employee worries and concerns.

Verify Performance Improvements

After improvements are suggested, it is necessary to measure how effective those improvements actually were. Several strategies for evaluating the effectiveness of improvements include burnup and burndown charts, self-evaluations, peer reviews, and collecting performance data.

Burnup and burndown charts are used to visualize and track how much work has already been completed for the project. A burnup chart shows how much work has already been completed, while a burndown chart reveals how much work is still needed. Managers can use these charts to estimate how effectively the team is performing and whether or not measures like coaching and training are having an effect on the project timeline.

Self-evaluations are useful because they give employees the opportunity to think critically about their role in the project and how they feel they are contributing to it. The employee can score themselves in a number of different ways, such as stating whether or not they met project goals and deadlines, listing their personal achievements, and if coaching and training improved their performance.

Peer reviews need to be conducted in a respectful manner. Peer reviews are direct feedback given to managers regarding workplace culture, project progress and expectations, and if enough support is provided to the team. Peer reviews are valuable because they give employees a chance to explain their concerns and thoughts on the project.

Performance data is collected through data analysis and can be used to determine team effectiveness. For example, if the project is intended to increase customer retention by 10% in a given time frame, the effectiveness of performance improvements is compared to this goal.

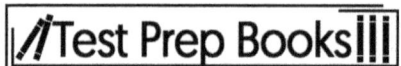

Task 4: Empower Team Members and Stakeholders

Empowering team members and stakeholders means giving them detailed reports about project expectations, assigning them to the tasks that they are best suited for, and allowing them enough independence to finish their work. Team members need guidance from their manager and to focus on deadlines and project expectations. Stakeholders need to be constantly updated on team performance and adjust their expectations from there.

Organize Around Team Strengths

Teams are comprised of many individuals with a diverse skillset. Teams will need to have a general goal that they want to meet, but wherever possible, giving them the autonomy to delegate their own tasks and respecting their professional capabilities are ways to empower the team.

Before starting a project, the strengths and capabilities that the team can offer need to be well documented and carefully considered. This is especially true for new teams that are still getting accustomed to working together. One way to analyze the strengths of the team is by using SWOT analysis. SWOT analysis identifies Strengths, Weaknesses, Opportunities, and Threats. In order to perform a SWOT analysis, there must first be a clear objective in mind, such as whether or not a product should be introduced to the market. Next, the team needs to determine what resources are available to them for completing the project. After this, teams should list their strengths, weaknesses, opportunities, and threats. Examples of what teams could list include:

Strengths: What advantage does our team provide compared to others?

Weakness: What resources are we missing?

Opportunities: Are there new technologies or techniques that we can utilize for the project?

Threats: In what way are our competitors doing better than our team?

Once these categories are listed, teams can begin to develop a plan that incorporates these points and proceed with the project. SWOT analysis is a good way to break down complex problems into more manageable sections and list important factors that teams should consider.

Support Team Task Accountability

Managers need a way to delegate tasks to certain people and make sure that the team knows who is responsible for what. Accountability should be very clear from the start of the project. A RACI (responsible, accountable, consulted, informed) chart is an effective way to handle accountability. Various positions, such as project manager and business analyst, are listed alongside tasks that need to be completed. Their position is then categorized based on their role in the tasks using RACI.

Responsible: This person is responsible for doing the work.

Accountable: This person delegates and reviews the work.

Consulted: This person is asked to provide feedback and advice about the work.

Informed: This person needs to know the outcome of a decision.

Evaluate Demonstration of Task Accountability

After tasks are delegated, managers need to ensure that the work is completed satisfactorily. This involves checking in with team members and making sure that progress is being made.

In an agile environment, there is greater independence, and each team comes together to collectively decide what everyone is doing. Weekly demonstration retrospectives can provide feedback on whether or not tasks are being completed and each team member's responsibility for that task. Retrospectives are meetings done at the end of a work period, or "sprint." At this time, teams can come together and discuss what is going well with the project and what still needs to be done.

The predictive approach to accountability uses milestones and phase gate reviews. Milestones are specific goals that a team needs to achieve, while phase gate reviews analyze previous work cycles before continuing to the next. Managers can assess accountability at each phase of the project before moving on to the next milestone. After this, depending on what information is available, more tasks can be assigned to the team after ensuring current tasks are completed. This progressive elaboration gives the team an opportunity to work on increasingly more complex tasks as the project progresses.

Determine and Bestow Level(s) of Decision-Making Authority

Bestowing decision-making authority to team members is one way of empowering them. It is a way to respect their professional capabilities and to help them make decisions that will help them the most. However, teams can struggle to make decisions that are optimal or that a majority agrees with. Managers can provide overall guidance and as the project progresses, delegate more and more decision-making authority to teams. Decisions need to be made with input from all team members. Several ways of asking the team for their opinion include simple voting, Roman voting, dot voting, Highsmith's decision spectrum, and fist to five.

Simple voting: Each member casts a single vote of either "for" or "against" a decision. Although this is a quick way to determine the team's feelings, it does not allow decisions or ideas to be modified with team member suggestions. This method leaves out other options that may reflect mixed feelings over the decision.

Roman voting: This type of method for obtaining consensus is very similar to simple voting. Instead of casting a single vote, teams use their thumbs and vote simultaneously. A thumbs-up means "agree," while a thumbs down-means "disagree." Some variations also allow members to put their thumb sideways, signifying mixed or neutral feelings over a decision. Members with their thumb sideways can sometimes be asked for their opinion on the matter. Managers count the number of thumbs-ups and thumbs-downs and determine whether or not the decision passes.

Dot voting: In this method, a number of decisions are written on separate pieces of paper and placed for everyone to see. Team members are allocated a certain number of votes, referred to as "dots." Afterwards, team members place dots on their favorite options. The decision with the most votes is implemented.

Highsmith's decision spectrum: Team members are provided with a spectrum showing their feelings about a decision. These feelings can range from "Favorable," to "Mixed," to "Veto." Team members mark where they feel about a decision, and from there managers can take into consideration the overall feelings of the team concerning a decision.

Fist to five: The fist to five method is another quick way of gauging support by having each member hold up their hand and display their support for a decision with their fingers. Feelings can range from having no fingers up (no support) to all five fingers up (full support).

Task 5: Ensure Team Members/Stakeholders Are Adequately Trained

It is important for both team members and stakeholders to receive adequate training because receiving proper training promotes independent working and reduces the need for constant supervision. Although making sure that each team member is working and contributing to the project is important, this constant supervision can take time away from other priorities. Adequate training increases overall performance, promotes independence and autonomy, and can increase the personal satisfaction of team members. Therefore, investing in adequate training is worthwhile because of the increase in project efficiency. It is an important responsibility for project managers to handle.

Determine Required Competencies and Elements of Training

Before training can be provided, project managers and companies should assess what exactly the training needs to provide to team members and stakeholders to be worthwhile. Several techniques, such as a skills gap analysis, surveys, and a SWOT analysis, can be used to help create effective training techniques for project success.

Skills gap analysis: A skills gap analysis is used to determine skills that are desirable to companies and workplaces and compares them to the skills that are actually already present in a workplace. The skills of current employees are directly compared to the skills that are needed in order to achieve organizational success. This technique is useful to determine where gaps in training may exist and what steps are needed to address them. In order to conduct a skills gap analysis, the problem needs to be properly outlined, current skills need to be measured, and action needs to be taken to address any gaps found.

Surveys: Surveys are simple and effective tools to determine what skills and training are desirable for companies. Their anonymity lets participants express their feelings without fear of retribution. Surveys must be designed in a way that ensures that questions are not misleading and attempting to steer participants in answering a certain way.

SWOT analysis: When compared to a skills gap analysis, a SWOT analysis is primarily a reflection of the company's performance and compares it to other resources currently available. SWOT analysis is a broader look at how the company is performing and can help address areas for improvement.

Determine Training Options Based on Training Needs

After determining what skills are necessary for team members and stake holders to have, the company needs to determine what type of training is best for the company. Three types of training are experiential learning, formal training, and informal training.

Experiential learning: This type of training is learned on the job. This can involve mentorship, shadowing, and simulations. Experiential learning is useful because it is very interactive and can be conducted in the workplace, giving learners the chance to see how their work contributes to the overall project. In an agile environment, shadowing and peer mentorship are frequently used to train new members and help them understand the project from multiple viewpoints. Agile environments stress smaller deliverables

Domain I: People

and more frequent updates to finish projects faster. They emphasize transparency, teamwork, and communication.

Formal training: Formal training is structured to train learners on specific, desirable skills. This training can involve online learning, classroom learning, and group training. Formal training provides consistency and a place for new members to ask questions.

Informal training: Informal training is learning that is performed outside of a structured learning environment. Unlike formal training, there is no set curriculum or standards put forth by the company. Informal training can consist of training videos, books, websites, and conferences. Each of these training methods provides knowledge to the participant, and the participant must choose what skills to apply to their workplace.

Allocate Resources for Training

Adequate training is an investment that requires the company to carefully allocate resources to it. This involves developing training courses, paying for necessary supplies, and scheduling training events. Project managers must balance the budget and pay equal attention to training estimates, mentorship and shadowing schedules, and training calendars. Training costs can include venue and food costs, course creation, and instructor salaries.

Measure Training Outcomes

After deciding on the type of training that new members will participate in, the training outcomes need to be measured. Measuring training outcomes provides feedback on whether the training is successful and what needs to be improved upon. For classroom training and online learning in particular, companies can measure effectiveness through exam scores and the average amount of time spent on each course. Data analysis is a useful tool to track training completion and assess training effectiveness. Other ways to measure training outcomes include certificates of completion, training skills gap analysis, and training feedback.

Certificates of completion: These certificates are awarded only after successfully completing training. Companies can require that new members acquire certain certificates before they are able to start working. This also proves to employers that new members can handle the project's workload and have enough working knowledge to provide meaningful contributions.

Training skills gap analysis: This method involves measuring a member's skill level and knowledge before and after completing training. Companies can determine whether members gained useful knowledge after completing the training.

Training feedback: After training, members can answer surveys and provide their opinions about their experience. Companies can use this feedback to improve the training experience for future members.

Task 6: Build a Team

Primarily, a project's success depends on the people that are working on it. Project managers need to consider a wide variety of talents, skills, and personality types in order to assemble the best team to handle project demands. These carefully selected team members solve problems and produce results. Having a team that lacks the necessary skills or knowledge, includes clashing personality types, or

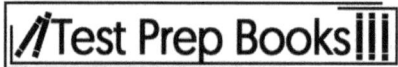

maintains different expectations can slow down project progress. This delays results and could lead to stakeholder and customer expectations not being met. Project managers work with their available resources and are always looking for ways to improve the team.

Appraise Stakeholder Skills

Identifying stakeholders is one of the most important aspects of a project. Internal stakeholders are actively involved in the project and need to contribute their time and resources in order to help the project succeed. They have a vested interest in seeing the project succeed, and appraising their skills is an important step that project managers need to take. This appraisal makes clearer what skills and talents are available for the project and what skills teams still need to complete the project. Several techniques can be used to appraise stakeholder skills, including a skills matrix, surveys, and focus groups.

Skills matrix: A skills matrix makes it easier to visualize a large group's skill level in various areas. It is a table that lists stakeholder names, various skills and competencies, and their level of proficiency. For example, a table may have a list of five people and categories such as communication skills, social media marketing, content management, and data analytics. The team members' skills in each area, as determined by management or a project manager, are listed next to each category. This makes it easier to view an overall picture of what skills the team excels at and what skills need to be improved upon. Training and hiring can be used to fill in any skill gaps in a team.

Surveys: Surveys are a simple data collection method that can be compiled and organized for data analysis. Surveys can be used to assess skills by measuring confidence and familiarity with a subject.

Focus groups: Focus groups function like group interviews in which the group is encouraged to discuss their opinions on a topic. For stakeholders, this is an opportunity to discuss their concerns and display their technical knowledge of the project, which makes it easier to see what specific areas need further improvement.

Agile environments place special importance on having "generalizing specialists" in the workplace. People of this type are skilled in numerous areas and can adapt to the needs of the team. They possess general knowledge of how the company operates and have the technical skills to navigate software and data. They are encouraged to have "T-shaped skills." This means that they have deep knowledge about one topic but also have general knowledge that can be used to help the team.

Deduce Project Resource Requirements

It is always a good practice for project managers to set realistic goals for their team. This ensures that projects do not go over a set budget or become too ambitious and unsustainable. Part of this concept involves analyzing the resources that will be needed to successfully complete a project. Several methods are available to project managers to assist them with this task. These include bottom-up estimating, analogous estimating, parametric estimating, and a resource breakdown structure.

Bottom-up estimating: Bottom-up estimating is one of the most accurate methods available for resource management because of its detailed approach. Resources and costs are considered first at the very lowest level of the project, and the estimation builds upon each level until it reaches management. For example, instead of estimating the cost of selling a product based on similar products, every detail—like the number of available workers, cost of maintenance, and cost of training—is considered. Each small piece creates an overall estimate for the project.

Analogous estimating: As opposed to bottom-up estimating, analogous estimating, or top-down estimating, uses historical data from other similar projects to make a resource estimate. Analogous estimates are quick and can be done with little information.

Parametric estimating: This is a quantitative approach to resource estimating using historical and statistical data. As opposed to analogous estimates, parametric estimates adjust values and use statistics to determine costs. Each resource is listed as a parameter value, and correlated to how much each parameter costs and how long each resource will be used.

Resource breakdown structure: This is a table that lists specific resources that a team needs to finish a certain part of the project. The project is broken down into smaller sections or tasks, and a resource breakdown structure is created for each section. For each smaller section, there is a list of resources and an estimate of how long each resource is needed. Based on this information, companies can adjust their expectations to the workflow and provide more assistance if needed.

Continuously Assess and Refresh Team Skills to Meet Project Needs

Projects are constantly changing, and they demand different skills at different stages. For the predictive approach, it is most important for teams to remain extremely organized and disciplined because they need to meet constant deadlines. The agile approach stresses flexibility, transparency, and adaptability. Teams should constantly look for opportunities that increase their skillset, especially when they need to adapt to a variety of project management approaches. Sometimes, new technology or techniques may be available that require more training to be comfortable using them. Continuously assessing and refreshing team skills ensures that no matter what project the team is working on, everyone is able to meaningfully contribute to it. Training, mentoring, and professional development are all ways to test for and learn new skills. This gives team members a chance for professional growth, increasing their satisfaction and making them more productive members of the team.

Maintain Team and Knowledge Transfer

Communication is key for a successful team. Sharing information between team members fosters teamwork and improves project performance. In a traditional work setting, activities like meetings give everyone a chance to share what they have learned so far and any concerns or problems that they have encountered. Meetings organize the work that the team has already done and help to plan for the future. Constant updates keep teams aware of developments that are taking place. Updates should include progress reports and work that needs to be done.

Agile teams take this a step further and utilize information radiators, or a Big Visible Chart (BVC). This is a highly visible place where all project information is made available to everyone. It helps increase transparency and prevents misunderstandings.

The predictive approach utilizes team meetings, check-ins, review meetings, and phase gate reviews to foster communication. Phase gate reviews are especially important since these meetings determine whether the team has successfully met all of the requirements for stage completion. If the team has not met these requirements, the team will work and communicate to note areas of improvement and discuss problems that must be solved to move to the next stage.

Task 7: Address and Remove Impediments, Obstacles, and Blockers for the Team

Projects do not always progress smoothly. Numerous issues can appear at any stage, and teams need to be equipped to deal with these issues. Impediments, obstacles, and blockers all refer to anything that prevents a team from making project progress. Although project managers will need to play a role in fixing these issues, the best solution to overcoming impediments is by providing teams with the tools they need to succeed. Doing this will develop a well-rounded team that knows how to address issues on their own without excessive micromanagement from the project manager.

Determine Critical Impediments, Obstacles, and Blockers for the Team

Impediments can be identified during team meetings and dealt with accordingly. In order to find impediments, agile teams specifically can find them during the daily standup. Other opportunities to find impediments include Value Stream Analysis and Task Age Analysis.

Daily standup: As an important component of the agile approach, daily standups allow teams to elaborate on what work has been done, plans for the future, and to state anything that is blocking their progress. Teams can support each other and discuss ways to move forward. These daily standups are also progress checks, meaning that a team member who is taking longer on a task can receive help. Additionally, if an impediment is found before the daily standup, the team member should report it immediately and seek advice.

Value Stream Analysis: This analysis primarily deals with what actions are producing value, or progress in a project, and what actions are preventing project progress. By organizing these actions into a chart and stating the project goal, it is easier to identify where project progress is slowing down.

Task Age Analysis: Team members have the chance to update the project's list of tasks whenever they accomplish something. Task Age Analysis emphasizes addressing what tasks have not seen significant updates for some time and determining why these tasks are not progressing.

Prioritize Critical Impediments, Obstacles, and Blockers for the Team

Some impediments are more harmful than others. These can range from minor annoyances to major issues that are preventing teams from making meaningful progress. Teams need to learn how to prioritize which impediments are more important than others. Prioritization helps the team manage their time well and prevents time from being lost on less important matters. Impediments can be found by asking the company and the team for input and can be analyzed purely on the financial damage they are causing. In particular, assigning a financial value based on how much damage the impediment is causing makes it easy to see which impediments are more important than others.

For the company, some impediments are more important than others because the company may have different priorities than individual teams. The company may ask that some impediments be addressed before others, even if this schedule is different than what the individual team may value. This also applies to the team; a team may find an impediment more important than the company does. Teams need to find a balance between the two and work accordingly.

Use Network to Implement Solutions

After teams have identified impediments and prioritized them, the next step is to begin removing them. Teams have numerous resources that they can utilize to help them remove impediments. A network, or a combination of resources and individuals, can help the team when needed. Networking is an opportunity to build up contacts that can address a wide variety of impediments. Some problems can be solved by the project manager or other leadership by using emotional intelligence and discussion. For example, work may be slowing down because not enough team members are skilled in a new technology the company is using. More training and guidance could be offered to address this. Teams may also need to look at their own processes and work methods and adjust them to remove impediments. For example, the ground rules may make it more difficult to voice concerns or request resources. In this case, ground rules can be reviewed and changed if necessary.

Teams should also utilize resources like a project management office (PMO). The PMO maintains company standards for project management and is a central place to seek assistance. The PMO helps with documentation and data analysis and is a good place to network. Before escalating to a PMO, teams need to determine whether their impediment warrants asking upper leadership for assistance. One of the best ways to remove impediments is having each team member resolve their own impediments. Larger team impediments can be addressed as they appear.

In agile environments, the product owner is also a source for solutions. The product owner is responsible for managing the products the team is producing, learning about internal and external stakeholder expectations, and ensuring the company is receiving maximum value from the product being worked on. Therefore, the product owner is usually well connected and has knowledge on common issues that teams face.

Re-assess Continually

Continued maintenance of problem-solving strategies to address impediments is something teams must do in order to ensure that the same issues do not keep reappearing. Solving the same problems repeatedly can waste time and resources. It is best to visualize impediments and to make this knowledge available to everyone. One way of doing this is by using an information radiator, which refers to a large display where teams are easily able to see the project status. The Big Visible Chart is another visualization tool that is helpful in this regard.

Project managers should provide continuous feedback and check with their teams to make sure that their impediments are being addressed. It is helpful to be proactive and willing to help the team with their specific impediments. Frequent data analysis using Value Stream Analysis and Task Age Analysis makes it easier to keep track of whether solutions are working. Finally, team members should try their best to remove their personal impediments in order to speed up their efficiency and give frequent updates to their status during team meetings. This becomes an opportunity to see whether the same impediments are happening frequently.

Task 8: Negotiate Project Agreements

As the project development process continues and team dynamics progress, the project manager must oversee negotiations for project terms and agreements, team values, and guidelines for performance. One way for project managers to take part in this process is by participating in the development of the

project charter, a document that outlines the project plan, defines the team structure, and ensures that all project stakeholders are in agreement on its elements.

The project charter is also the document that officially names the project manager and formally authorizes the team to begin working on the project.

Analyze the Bounds of the Negotiations for Agreement

The first step in compiling and analyzing information for a project charter is to categorize the information into the following groups:

Functional requirements: These requirements define how the product or service should function from the end user's perspective. In other words, these requirements determine how the end user will interact directly with the product or service.

Technical requirements: These requirements define any technical issue that must be taken into account in order for the product or service to be successfully implemented.

Transitional requirements: These requirements are the necessary steps required in order for the product or service to be seamlessly implemented.

Operational requirements: These requirements explain the background operations needed to keep the new product or service functioning.

Once the requirements have been grouped into the appropriate categories, the second step in the process is to ensure that the requirements are defined accurately and detailed properly so everything is identified clearly. If a requirement is not defined accurately, problems can occur and cause a delay in project activity.

Assess Priorities and Determine Ultimate Objectives

The next step is to prioritize all requirements, ranging from the most critical to the "nice to haves." Since budgets are either fixed or limited, the most critical requirements should be considered first. One common method used to prioritize the list of requirements is called **ranking**. Ranking assigns a different numerical value to each requirement based on its importance. In this instance, the number 1 can be used to signify the most important requirement and the number x can be used to signify the least important requirement.

Next, analyze and document the impact that a potential change will have on the project based on these requirements. Understanding the impact of a proposed change, especially its positive or negative consequences, will allow for the proactive development of contingency plans and the ability to handle any issue smoothly.

Verify Objectives of the Project Agreement Are Met

The charter defines the high-level requirements and outlines exactly what the project has to achieve in order to be successful. It also documents the overall goals and objectives, controls scope, and helps manage expectations. The charter is approved by either the project sponsor, stakeholders, or both, and will be referenced throughout the project lifecycle.

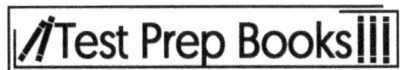

Typically, the charter should not exceed two pages and should include the following sections:

Project Purpose and Definition – this section defines the overall purpose of the project at the high level and describes what the project involves and why the organization has proposed to invest the funds in accomplishing the work to be performed. This includes the project vision, goals and objectives, project scope, and deliverables.

Project Requirements - this section includes the high-level requirements of the project and outlines a clear idea and indication of what the organization is thinking by the creation of the project.

Project Stakeholders – this section includes the names of all the parties involved and their roles and responsibilities. The project sponsor, stakeholders, customers, and key team members may be represented in this section.

Project Plan – this section will provide a general overview of how and when the project will be achieved. This is not a detailed project plan developed by the team, rather the relevant information regarding project strategy, key milestones, deliverables, and acceptance processes.

High Level Risks – this section outlines any known high-level risks that could impact the project and what plans are considered to resolve. The risks identified in this section can be either negative, positive, or both.

Change - this section should define at high level the process around controlling change once the document is approved.

Budget Summary – this section will include a summary of the budget to be used for the project.

Schedule Summary - this section includes the projected start and end dates of the project and any milestones of the project.

Project Manager – this section includes the name of the project manager, their responsibility, and their authority level.

Once the charter has been developed, the next step in the process is to distribute the charter to the project sponsor and any other appropriate stakeholders. The project manager schedules a meeting with the sponsor and stakeholders to review the deliverables produced and referenced in the charter to ensure the deliverables are aligned with expectations. Any changes or updates derived from the review meeting should be updated in the charter. It is at this point the project sponsor will decide if the project will proceed.

If the project sponsor determines the project is approved, the signature of the sponsor is obtained which authorizes the project manager to begin and apply resources to the project activities. The signature also authorizes the project manager to start using the company funds allocated towards the project.

If the project sponsor rejects the charter, he or she must provide the reasons for the rejection and allow the project manager to make the necessary adjustments.

Participate in Agreement Negotiations

The next step in the process is to meet with the stakeholders and settle any issues or conflicts uncovered during the analysis. Conflicting requirements can be developed in three different ways.

One or more of the stakeholders has a misunderstanding of the company goals and therefore leads them to define a requirement which is not in line with the goal and objective.

Two or more stakeholder groups understand the goals and objectives, but each support them in different ways. This generates a difference in the way the needs of each group get prioritized at a company level.

Two or more stakeholder groups have the same goals and objectives, but they disagree over the action to be taken for meeting the goal.

Below are several ways to help resolve conflicting requirements issues.

Set up a meeting with the stakeholder groups and have them reiterate the project goals and objectives.

Set up a meeting with the stakeholder groups with an unbiased mediator who has knowledge geared toward higher level business goals.

Pilot the process with a selected group of people and measure and compare the results.

Create a prototype or mockup of each conflicting requirement issue and conduct a walkthrough with a small user group to determine which works well.

The last step in the process is to analyze the feasibility of the product or service. The feasibility report will determine how reliable and easy the product or service is to use.

Once all of the information gathered has been analyzed, present the written and detailed results report to the stakeholders. Once the report has been reviewed by all respective parties the final step in the process is to obtain sign off from the stakeholders indicating the requirements are precisely reflected and meet their needs.

Obtain project charter approval from the sponsor, in order to formalize the authority assigned to the project manager and gain commitment and acceptance for the project.

Determine a Negotiation Strategy

If discussing the terms of the project charter creates conflict, the project manager may need to employ a negotiation strategy to resolve any questions or disagreements. The preceding examples gave potential solutions to common negotiation scenarios, but project managers should be aware of the communication theories at work behind successful leadership methods.

Domain I: People

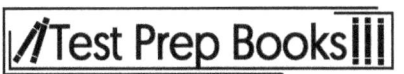

One model of negotiation is Steven Covey's principle of "Think-Win-Win." This model does not only apply to negotiation, but its concepts are helpful in understanding different problem-solving situations and their outcomes. Covey's descriptions of possible interaction outcomes are as follows:

- **Win-win.** Finding a way for disagreeing parties to get what they both desire is the ideal outcome. For the sake of developing project agreements, a win-win solution prevents any party from compromising their desires for the project or the work it entails.

- **Win-lose/lose-win.** This outcome has a competitive element. One party is satisfied, while the other does not. It is important to note that this outcome could impact team dynamics if the "losing" party feels as though they are a martyr and must concede to satisfy the opposing side.

- **Lose-lose.** A negotiation can end in a lose-lose outcome when the disagreeing parties' desire to win overpowers their willingness to collaborate.

In order to achieve the best possible outcome, a win-win solution, the negotiating team members and stakeholders must value one another's opinions, trust that each party has the skills and knowledge to have a valid outlook, and take the opposing party's perspective into consideration when making or debating a decision. The project manager's role in this process is to ensure that these rapport-boosting qualities are present and upheld throughout negotiation so the project can begin on a positive and productive note.

Task 9: Collaborate with Stakeholders

Stakeholder collaboration includes tasks such as project planning, determining requirements, managing expectations, and making important decisions for the duration of the project. Stakeholders may require different levels of interaction or command different levels of influence and authority over the project. It is the project manager's responsibility to appropriately consult and integrate stakeholders whenever necessary or possible.

Evaluate Engagement Needs for Stakeholders

Managing expectations and maintaining communication are critical for project success. It is very important to engage all stakeholders early on in the project, specifically during the planning phase for the purpose of keeping them in the know and aligned with scope, budget, timeline, and resource requirement demands set at the beginning of the project.

Project managers may communicate with stakeholders in a variety of ways, including written methods like progress reports, emails, instant messaging, or brief notes, and verbal methods such as presentations, product demos, and ad hoc discussions. Some forms of communication are considered formal or informal, and it is up to the project manager's discretion to determine which method is appropriate for the situation and shared information.

Optimize Alignment Between Needs, Expectations, and Project Objectives

Collaborating with stakeholders requires consistent and effective communication. A **communications management plan** can help project managers keep track of different stakeholders' needs and ensure that the project continues running smoothly. Stakeholders may have different levels of involvement with and influence over the project. Paying close attention to who receives what information (and in which form) can help project managers keep all stakeholders satisfied and prevent any communication issues from blocking project progress.

Build Trust and Influence Stakeholders to Accomplish Project Objectives

This process of communicating and working with stakeholders not only builds trust, but allows for the development of healthy, credible and rewarding relationships. Often throughout the project lifecycle, issues appear or an unanticipated delay occurs. Painting a clear picture from the beginning of the project, setting clear timelines, and being honest, ensures commitment at all stages, addresses potential concerns, and reassures stakeholder expectations and achievement of project goals. Perform stakeholder analysis using appropriate tools and techniques in order to align expectations and gain support for the project.

Task 10: Build Shared Understanding

Teams are unified by what they want to accomplish. Teams with a shared understanding are better able to find solutions to problems because the solution is related to the project's goals. Strategies like establishing a project vision, a project charter, or project plan are useful tools to establish a shared understanding.

Project vision: A project vision is similar to the final destination on a journey. It establishes where the team is ultimately headed. Problems can be solved in ways that help the team reach the final destination.

Project charter: The project charter is a summary of why the project is important and lists various stakeholders and team members and outlines the project objectives.

Project plan: Similar to a schedule, the project plan lists what tasks need to be accomplished, when the tasks will be accomplished, how long each task will take, and how much these tasks will cost the company.

Break Down Situation to Identify the Root Cause of a Misunderstanding

Root cause analysis helps to identify why a problem occurs. It is an organized system that identifies problem areas and impediments and how the company can address them. Two ways to conduct a root cause analysis include the Five Whys and Fishbone Analysis.

Five Whys: The Five Whys analyze the cause and effect of various aspects of a problem. This method is commonly used in agile teams. The team asks the question "Why?" five times, and each question reveals another aspect of a problem. For example, the main issue could be that customers did not get satisfactory service. Teams ask "Why?" and figure out that the product was faulty. This process continues five times until they reach the root, or main, cause of the problem.

Fishbone Analysis: This is similar to the Five Whys; the main problem is listed first. Then, contributing factors are listed and the team expands on why each factor was a part of the problem.

Survey All Necessary Parties to Reach Consensus

It is important to have everyone's opinion on a decision in order to reach a consensus. Having consensus unites teams and promotes solidarity. Several techniques, like fist to five and Roman Voting, have been discussed previously. For agile teams specifically, planning poker is used as well.

Planning poker: Teams receive cards labeled with the numbers one, three, five, eight, and thirteen. The project manager or another leader describes a situation, and team members pick one card at the same time that represents how much effort that task would take. If opinions differ, team members can elaborate on their choice to the team.

Support Outcome of Parties' Agreement

Teams should refer to their ground rules and team agreement in order to see what is acceptable for the project. Teams need to be unified in their decisions in order to make progress. The project management team should ultimately support whatever decision teams make. Documents like the team charter are useful because they explain what to do when people disagree, or when teams need to decide what kind of project approach to accept.

Investigate Potential Misunderstandings

Misunderstandings and mistakes are a natural part of any project, and teams will need to work together to address these issues. Teams can utilize retrospectives, After Action Review (AAR), and transparency to help teams work through problems.

Retrospectives: In an agile environment, retrospectives are performed after a period of work. This gives a team the opportunity to discuss how much work was finished in this period and what improvements can be made.

After Action Review (AAR): In predictive approaches, this is commonly performed to understand project goals and what was actually accomplished. It analyzes why and what happened, and how people can do these tasks better in the future.

Transparency: Agile environments stress transparency and easy access to information. By maintaining open transparency, team members can easily see what work has been accomplished and what they need to do to finish their tasks.

Task 11: Engage and Support Virtual Teams

Virtual teams are becoming increasingly common, and with these come new challenges. Virtual, or remote, teams became extremely popular during the COVID-19 pandemic. Virtual teams have several benefits that separate them from in-person meetings. Projects teams can easily be expanded with more remote workers, which cuts down on commuting time and costs and allows employees to work in a comfortable environment. However, some team members may feel isolated if they never meet their team in person, onboarding may be slower, and virtual teams become heavily reliant on technology for their work.

Examine Virtual Team Member Needs

One of the biggest challenges for virtual teams is setting a schedule that works for everyone. Some teams have members from across the country or even the world. People can live in different time zones, or they may be in an area with poor internet connection. Without in-person interaction, team members may not be able to see body language and natural cues. Teams need to be flexible and use whatever works in their unique situation. Project managers need to know who is available and make accommodation for people without the best internet connection or those who are not comfortable on camera. Project managers also need to try to develop team culture through events like teambuilding activities. In a virtual environment, teambuilding could involve online games, social hours, sharing stories, and discussing how to solve hypothetical problems.

Investigate Alternatives for Virtual Team Member Engagement

There are two main forms of communication that virtual teams can utilize: synchronous and asynchronous tools. Teams should decide on which platforms they prefer and stick with them.

Synchronous tools: Synchronous communication tools like video conferences, instant messaging, and phone calls allow teams to communicate in real time. These tools mimic in-person meetings with scheduled, real-time interaction. During these meetings, team members can voice their concerns and receive updates on the project. Specific examples include Zoom, Skype, and Google Hangouts.

Asynchronous tools: Asynchronous tools are not scheduled and can be used at any time. These tools store project data and resources, and team members can access these on their own. Team members can message each other when necessary and receive help. These tools are especially useful for teams located in different time zones since the resources can be accessed independently. Specific examples include Slack, Notion, and Microsoft Teams.

In addition to these types of communication, colocation is an option as well. Colocation involves putting all the resources a team might need in one physical location to help them succeed. This works particularly well for in-person teams and includes things like team meeting rooms, break rooms, computers, and documents.

Implement Options for Virtual Team Member Engagement

It can be difficult for virtual team members to build rapport and remain interested in a project. Without the opportunity to directly interact with their team members, virtual team members can feel lonely, bored, and unenthusiastic about completing their work. Project managers need to encourage their team members to take care of themselves and their health and emphasize that lines of communication are always available. Virtual members can contribute in a variety of ways, such as adding to virtual documents and working on projects in small groups. There should also be scheduled meetings and opportunities to spend time with others. Scheduled meetings are a chance for virtual team members to see and hear their team. Virtual team building activities, like games or activities, can be a fun way to solve problems together. Teams should also emphasize that everyone's opinion is valued and give opportunities to express these opinions in team meetings.

Domain I: People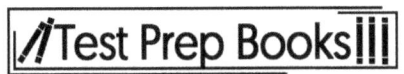

Continually Evaluate Effectiveness of Virtual Team Member Engagement

Team members should have regular checkups to make sure that they are well accommodated. In order to assess remote workers, project managers could send them a simple message asking if they are fine and need anything, or teams can mark their progress through deliverables. One way to do so is by variance analysis, which quantifies actual project results with what was expected. Similar to normal in-person team members, remote workers can engage in surveys and participate in meetings in order to understand what is working and what is not working for the team.

Task 12: Define Team Ground Rules

The basis of any good team starts with rules and structure. Trying to organize a team without rules would be a disaster because everyone would have different opinions about what to do. Ground rules are established to provide uniformity and clear guidance on what kind of behavior is and is not acceptable. This prevents conflicting opinions from appearing and causing confusion for team members. Team members who are uncertain about how to act in certain situations can refer to the ground rules for guidance. There can be any number of ground rules that a group can choose to implement, covering everything from policies regarding online working to taking vacations.

A team charter is a document that usually contains the list of ground rules. In agile teams in particular, this document should be in a highly visible location so that everyone can easily see it. The predictive approach also utilizes this document to great effect. Other names for the team charter include team contract, team agreement, and social contract. The team charter explains a multitude of topics, such as the code of conduct, basic etiquette, procedures for voicing questions and concerns, and types of communication that the team uses. Members can hold each other accountable for the rules since everyone has easy access to the team charter. The team charter consolidates everything into one place and can increase the team's sense of belonging and purpose. It is something that they can always rely on and refer to for assistance.

Communicate Organizational Principles with Team and External Stakeholders

Ground rules should be created with feedback from everyone on the team. Teams greatly benefit from receiving input from people of diverse backgrounds. Project managers need to clearly lay out their expectations for the team and maintain constant communication with the team about rules and updates. Ground rules can always be updated, and the project manager needs to make this clear to everyone. Feedback can be used to improve existing rules.

The ground rules should be clear enough for even external stakeholders to understand. External stakeholders do not work directly with the project but are still affected by the outcomes of the project and therefore have an interest in seeing the project succeed. Project managers can utilize a variety of helpful tools to communicate their expectations and messages, including email, text messages, group chats, and online meetings. Messages should be clear, concise, and respectful. For some stakeholders, simply recapping project information may not be a good idea. Project managers need to understand the audience that they are speaking to and use appropriate language.

Establish an Environment That Fosters Adherence to the Ground Rules

Work environments should be professional and respectful. This kind of environment encourages professionalism and honesty. Project managers should be honest about the project's progress and behave in an ethical manner. This same expectation should also apply to the team and be clearly written in the team charter. This consistency is important to maintaining uniformity and treating everyone fairly. To help teams get used to the ground rules, project managers can refer to the team charter and explain their actions using the team charter. For example, a project manager could communicate to the team that all announcements are posted on a certain message board or that the team charter clearly lays out when all daily meetings are. These are helpful reminders that do not need to be said all the time but are useful if teams are starting to get too comfortable and start to ignore or forget ground rules.

Manage and Rectify Ground Rule Violations

Rules were made to be followed. Project managers especially need to follow the rules and set an example for their team. If violations were constantly unpunished, no one would take the rules seriously. Project managers and team members need to have the confidence and the tact to call out anyone breaking the rules. Calling someone out does not need to be overly harsh or critical. Pointing out rule violations should be respectful. All team members are working professionals and should be treated as such.

Teams should treat the ground rules as their own personal team's code of conduct. This encourages team enforcement because the ground rules were created with input from the whole team. Project managers can accomplish more when the team is helping them to reinforce the rules. The project manager needing to handle every case is an inefficient use of their time.

Ideally, after someone has been called out for a rule violation, this person would learn quickly from their mistake and not do it again. Consequences for breaking ground rules include removal from the team and being reprimanded. However, continued violations or problematic outbursts can be solved with mentoring and guidance. This also applies to underperformance. Team members who are underperforming should be informed and given time to fix their mistakes. Repeated underperformance is an issue, however, and it may fall to the project manager to determine whether that person should be removed from the team.

Task 13: Mentor Relevant Stakeholders

As a team develops, the project manager may notice areas where team members and stakeholders can improve their performances and contributions to the team's goal. It is essential that project managers learn how to recognize ways for each member of their team to improve and take advantage of opportunities to help them.

Allocate the Time for Mentoring

In addition to organizing appropriate training, project managers should make the time to mentor stakeholders to ensure that their individual needs are met. In order for each team member to function independently, they must feel as though they receive adequate support from the project manager. If the project manager notices an area for improvement, they should provide the team member with timely, helpful feedback and discuss performance concerns in one-on-one meetings to prevent a hold on progress and encourage individual and team growth.

Recognize and Act on Mentoring Opportunities

Mentoring opportunities can take various forms. It is imperative that project managers pay close attention to team members' performances to monitor for changes, interruptions, or even direct requests for guidance on new or challenging tasks. Each team member will respond differently to mentoring and feedback, so it is helpful for project managers to consider which methods or approaches may be most effective for the individual and situation at hand.

While there may be opportunities to mentor multiple team members at once if a common skill needs further development, it is important to note that most people receive constructive criticism better when it is discussed privately.

Task 14: Promote Team Performance Through the Application of Emotional Intelligence

Emotional intelligence is an important and often overlooked aspect of someone's ability to work and be a part of a team. Emotional intelligence is the ability to understand one's own emotions and the emotions of people around them. This also means that team members need to control their own emotions and learn how to work with their team. There are several concepts that make up emotional intelligence, including self-awareness, self-regulation, motivation, empathy, and social skills.

Self-awareness: It is important to recognize one's own emotions and how they affect others. Being acutely aware of one's emotions improves decision making because people are able to recognize how their actions affect both themselves and others.

Self-regulation: People need to be able to control their emotions, especially negative ones like anger. Respect is extremely important in a working environment.

Motivation: Motivation gives people a reason to do something. Team members who can find a reason for improving themselves and working well in a team will be successful. With motivation, people look for opportunities to improve their skillset.

Empathy: Empathy is the ability to relate to others. People with empathy can recognize how others are feeling. This diversifies viewpoints because the same problem can be looked at from multiple angles.

Social skills: Since projects are heavily team based, having great social skills is extremely important. Social skills are based on how well someone can communicate and interact with others. People with great social skills make great leaders and are easier to work with due to their ability to easily fit into different team environments.

Assess Behavior Through the Use of Personality Indicators

There are a variety of personality types that can be measured through assessments like the famous Myers-Briggs Type Indicator (MBTI), Keirsey Temperament Sorter (KTS) or DISC assessment. They function similarly and are introspective self-assessments that can give people an idea of what kind of personality they have and how it affects their behavior. Another model that can be used to assess behavior is the Merrill-Reid model, which breaks down personality into four categories: Analytical, Amiable, Driver, and Expressive.

Analytical: These people are intelligent and require data and facts to justify decisions. They follow rules and are careful but may overanalyze situations.

Amiable: Amiable people are relaxed and emphasize order and harmony. They will try not to upset others and prefer a slower routine, which may be an issue in hectic work environments.

Driver: Drivers have a strong and dominating personality. They are disciplined and will get work done but may come across as stubborn or unfriendly.

Expressive: Expressive people are sociable, friendly, and fun. They work well with others but may need extra guidance and set schedules.

Analyze Personality Indicators and Adjust Accordingly

In order for the team to function, everyone's personality needs to be considered, especially key project stakeholders. To do so, project managers should use their best judgement to optimize their team by utilizing everyone's personality in an efficient way. This means working with their faults and playing to their strengths. For example, Expressive personality types will be friendly but need guidance and reminders to stay on task. Drivers will get the work done but need help in compromising with others and fostering good team relationships. Knowledge of emotional needs of team members and stakeholders can allow for structuring team assignments and tasks for employee satisfaction and efficiency.

Practice Quiz

1. Teams should have a vision statement before they begin a new project. What is the purpose of a vision statement?
    a. It lists the different personality types on the team.
    b. It lists the names of the project manager and product owner.
    c. It lists the goal that the team or company is ultimately trying to achieve.
    d. It lists the resources that a team will use to achieve its goals.

2. During a team meeting, one member says that he greatly appreciates leaders who support the team's physical and mental health. Which type of leadership is being described?
    a. Listening
    b. Healing
    c. Stewardship
    d. Empathy

3. A project manager decides to gather a large group of potential stakeholders and evaluate their skills all at once. What is this method called?
    a. Skills Matrix
    b. Surveys
    c. Peer reviews
    d. Focus groups

4. A stakeholder explains one of her suggestions to the team, and the team later complains that the suggestion makes it more difficult for them to pursue their own interests for the project. What should the team do?
    a. Teams should work to meet the expectations of the stakeholder.
    b. Teams should wait until another work cycle to consider the suggestion.
    c. Teams should treat the suggestion as an impediment and work to remove it.
    d. Teams should ignore the stakeholder's suggestions and update the stakeholder at a later time.

5. Which of these is NOT an aspect of emotional intelligence?
    a. Motivation
    b. Social skills
    c. Empathy
    d. Foresight

See answers on the next page.

Answer Explanations

1. C: Vision statements are important because they explain what the team or company is trying to attain in the future. It helps to give teams a bigger picture of the company and its goals. Choices A, B, and D are incorrect because they are not the main purpose of vision statements.

2. B: It is important for leaders to take care of their team's physical and mental health, especially in chaotic work environments. Choice A is incorrect because listening is the ability to attend to other people's opinions. Choice C is incorrect because stewardship means being responsible and working alongside the team to accomplish work. Choice D is incorrect because empathy means understanding other people's emotions and being sensitive to their feelings.

3. D: Focus groups are a way to assess the skills that stakeholders possess and function like a group interview. Choice A is incorrect because a skills matrix is a chart that displays various skills and whether the team has them or not. Choice B is incorrect because a survey is a series of questions that participants answer. Choice C is incorrect because peer reviews involve teammates rating and analyzing each other's performance.

4. A: Stakeholders have influence over the project because they have a personal interest in seeing it succeed. Teams need to accommodate stakeholder expectations because they help to provide resources and guidance to teams. Choices B and D are incorrect because they take too much time and do not consider stakeholder concerns. Choice C is incorrect because impediments stop team progress, while stakeholder concerns are a way to suggest improvements to the project.

5. D: Emotional intelligence refers to how well a person can understand their emotions and the emotions of others around them. Foresight is an aspect of leadership with which leaders are able to make predictions with information that is available to them. Choices A, B, and C— social skills, empathy, and motivation—are incorrect because they are aspects of emotional intelligence.

Domain II: Process

Task 1: Execute Project with the Urgency Required to Deliver Business Value

Project managers must measure the performance of the project and take corrective actions when necessary to realign the project with its objectives. Project performance is measured by comparing the actual costs and schedule against the planned costs and schedule.

Assess Opportunities to Deliver Value Incrementally

Performance Measuring and Tracking Techniques

Earned Value Measurement

Earned value (EV) is the value of the work that has been completed on a project. It is used to show the progress that has been made on a project in relation to the project's total budget. The EV is found by multiplying the total budget, or *budget at completion (BAC)*, by the percent of the project that has been completed to date.

$$EV = BAC \times \%\ Complete$$

For example, if a project has been allocated a budget of $200,000 and 50% of the work has been completed, the earned value for the work is $100,000. Earned value measurement compares the earned value against the *planned value (PV)* and the *actual cost (AC)* of the work completed to date. Earned value measurement reveals variances in the performance of the project to date and can help to forecast future performance to determine if corrective action must be taken to maintain the schedule and the planned BAC.

Planned value (PV): The work that was scheduled to be completed to date and the budget allocated for the work.

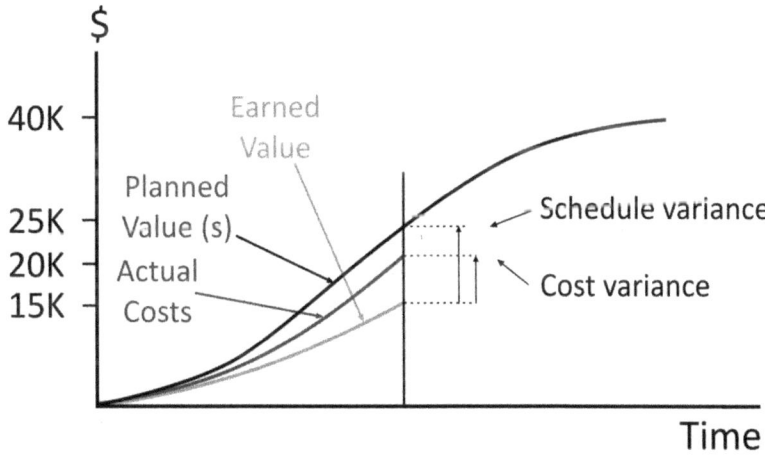

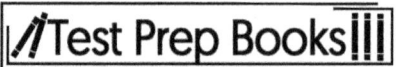

Domain II: Process

Examine the Business Value Throughout the Project

The following tools and techniques are used to calculate a project's performance and find variances in performance that might require corrective action.

Cost Analysis Techniques

Cost Variance (CV) is calculated as the actual costs subtracted from the earned value using the equation:

$$CV = EV - AC$$

For example, if the project budget is $200,000 and 30% of the project work has been completed, the earned value is $60,000. However, the project manager had to spend $65,000 to complete the work, so the cost variance is $5,000.

Schedule Variance (SV) is the difference between how much of the work of the project was planned to have been completed and how much of the work has actually been completed using the equation:

$$SV = EV - PV$$

If the project was planned to be 50% complete after six months, the planned value after six months is $100,000. However, if only 30% of the work is complete after six months, the earned value is $60,000, so the schedule variance is -$40,000.

Cost Performance Index (CPI) is the amount of work completed per dollar spent. The CPI is calculated using the equation:

$$CPI = \frac{EV}{AC}$$

For example, if the earned value is $60,000, but the actual cost is $65,000, the CPI is 0.92, meaning the project loses $.09 for every dollar spent, which will result in a total loss of $18,000 if the project continues at the same performance rate.

Schedule Performance Index (SPI) is the measurement of how closely the project is following the planned schedule. The SPI is calculated using the equation:

$$SPI = \frac{EV}{PV}$$

For example, if the earned value is $60,000, but the planned value is $100,000, the SPI is .6.

Estimate at Completion (EAC)

The *Estimate at Completion (EAC)* is a projection of how much the project will cost to complete based on the current project performance. EAC is calculated using the formula:

$$EAC = AC + \left(\frac{BAC - EV}{CPI \times SPI}\right)$$

Using the values from the previous examples:

$$EAC = \$65,000 + \left(\frac{\$200,000 - \$60,000}{0.92 \times 0.6}\right)$$

$$EAC = 318,623.19$$

The *To Complete Performance Index (TCPI)* predicts whether the project can be completed within the planned budget based on the current performance or whether it can be completed at the new EAC. The two equations to measure the TCPI follow. If the value for either equation is greater than 1, the project is unlikely to be completed within the budget or at the new EAC.

Determine if the project can be completed within the planned budget:

$$TCPI = \frac{BAC - EV}{BAC - AC}$$

$$TCPI = \frac{200,000 - 60,000}{200,000 - 65,000}$$

$$TCPI = \left(\frac{140,000}{135,000}\right)$$

$$TCPI = 1.04$$

Determine if the project can be completed at the new EAC:

$$TCPI = \frac{BAC - EV}{EAC - AC}$$

$$TCPI = \frac{200,000 - 60,000}{318,623.19 - 65,000}$$

$$TCPI = \frac{140,000}{253,623.19}$$

$$TCPI = 0.55$$

The *Estimate to Complete (ETC)* is the estimate of how much money will be required to complete the project under the current conditions. The equation to calculate ETC is:

$$ETC = EAC - AC$$

$$318,623.19 - 65,000$$

$$ETC = 253,623.19$$

Flawed Estimates

When the cost to complete the project is higher due to flaws in the original cost estimates, incorrect assumptions, or other unexpected additional costs, a change request is made to include the new ETC in the project plans. In this case, the previous equation provides the most accurate ETC.

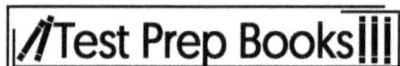

Anomalies

When the additional time and money spent to complete the work to date is due to a single event or circumstance such as a mistake or environmental interference, the following equation is used to calculate the ETC:

$$ETC = (BAC - EV)$$

Typical Variances

When the variances in project performance are expected to continue throughout the lifecycle of the project such as workers requiring more time to complete work due to lack of competence or training, or due to frequent rework, the following equation is used to calculate the new ETC:

$$ETC = \frac{BAC - EV}{CPI}$$

Variance at Completion

At the end of the project, calculate the *Variance at Completion (VAC)* using the equation

$$VAC = BAC - EAC$$

Support the Team to Subdivide Project Tasks

To bring the project work back into alignment with the project plan, change requests are made to take corrective actions to account for variances. Corrective actions include shifting the schedule, re-assigning workers, re-allocating resources, repairing defects, etc. These corrective actions are communicated to and, in some cases, approved by stakeholders and applied by the project manager.

In some cases, project managers may have to break down the project tasks further to allow team members and stakeholders to complete their work.

Task 2: Manage Communications

A communications management plan can help project managers assess and carry out stakeholder communication. Stakeholder needs may vary depending on their respective roles, so it is important for project managers to employ the correct communication methods and take stakeholder feedback into account throughout the project life cycle to achieve the best possible outcome.

Analyze Communication Needs of All Stakeholders

The first step to successfully managing the communications of any project is to identify possible stakeholders. In project management, stakeholders can be thought of as any individual or group that may affect or be affected by the outcome of a project. Depending on the kind and size of the project—as well as what stage the project is in—there can be many different stakeholders, and it is perhaps best for project managers to consider ways of categorizing the different kinds. One major distinction that can be drawn immediately is how close a specific stakeholder is to the project. For example, members of the organization can be thought of as internal stakeholders, whereas the end users of a product can be thought of as external stakeholders.

Stakeholders that are closely related to the project, such as the customer or end user of the developing product, are easy to identify. Stakeholders that are indirectly related to the project's work may be harder to recognize or categorize.

Determine Communication Methods

Features of a stakeholder's role—such as power, impact, expectations, influence, and proximity to the project—can help project managers determine the method of communication and level of detail that is most appropriate. Proper communication can ensure that all stakeholders stay informed and invested in the project's progress, so project managers should take care to build and maintain a positive rapport across all mediums.

Project managers may utilize different forms of communication depending on context and circumstances, but it is important to recognize the three main categories and their purposes:

- **Push communication** is a one-way communication method that allows the project manager to share information with stakeholders without receiving immediate feedback. This method is useful for quick updates. Examples include emails, memos, status reports, and voice mail. It is not recommended to share information that might have a significant impact on the stakeholder's perception of the project this way to prevent damaging the working relationship.

- **Pull communication** is information that stakeholders seek out themselves through conducting research or asking questions. This method allows the project manager to note any issues or concerns that the stakeholder may have about the project without having to ask them directly.

- **Interactive communication** is true engagement. Meetings, phone calls, conversations, and product demos are examples of ways that project managers and stakeholders can communicate back-and-forth and receive feedback on one another's thoughts and ideas.

Communicate Project Information and Updates Effectively

Once a stakeholder analysis is completed and the communication needs of stakeholders have been appropriately prioritized, the actual process of engaging with stakeholders can begin. Depending on the stakeholder and their beliefs, interests, and influence, a project manager may decide it is best to communicate in a number of different ways. Stylistically, project managers can consider the format of their communications—whether it's verbal or written—as well as the degree of formality, with methods ranging from briefings to progress reports to emails to simply just having conversations. It can also be helpful for project managers to categorize the type of communications that may occur. The term *push*, for example, describes any one-way communication used to inform stakeholders, such as a memo or an email blast. A *pull*, on the other hand, describes any information that is sought out by the stakeholder. Often, the best communication methods involve more than just a push or a pull, with interactive methods allowing for an exchange of information and quick feedback loops that can ensure all stakeholders are adequately informed and heard.

Confirm Communication Is Understood and Feedback Is Received

As a project continues, it may be important for the project manager to contemplate more formalized models to help streamline communication and ensure that all communications are understood. Particular models that may be investigated include Alistair Cockburn's model, which considers communication channels along scales of both effectiveness and richness, and cross-cultural models, which consider the backgrounds and cultural predispositions of both the sender and the receiver. It may also be helpful for project managers to take into account metrics that may indicate failures in the communication pipeline. For example, a significant number of pulls may indicate that stakeholders are not being appropriately informed. Therefore, it is essential that project managers monitor the flow of communication, ensuring that engagement is interactive and responsive for all stakeholders in a project. There are a number of specific tools a project manager may consider using to ensure communications are being received in both directions. Phase gates—prescheduled checkpoints that help signal the finishing of one phase of a project and the beginning of another—can be a great time to get feedback from stakeholders. This is especially true if the stakeholders of a project are likely to change as the project progresses because these phase gates may be the last place for stakeholders leaving a project to voice their opinions.

Task 3: Assess and Manage Risks

Throughout the course of the project, continuously monitor the risks identified on the risk register to determine if the probability and impact of risks have changed. This continuous risk monitoring process improves project performance by focusing only on the risks that continue to impact the organization and by identifying unknown risks that could be negatively impacting the work and performance of the project.

Determine Risk Management Options

Risk monitoring involves assessing the current response strategies established in the Risk Management Plan to ensure they are still effective in mitigating and preventing risks, as well as benefiting from the opportunities identified in the planning process and any new opportunities that arise.

The risk monitoring process begins with the Risk Management Plan that defines the process for identifying risks, the metrics against which to measure the impact of risks, and the overall strategy for analyzing and planning risk management. The risk register identifies specific risks, the root causes of the risks, the likely impact of each risk, and the strategies to respond to specific risks or types of risks. Work performance data offer insight into issues within work activities that could result in new, greater, or increased risks.

The process of risk monitoring includes the following:

- Verify risk response strategies are being implemented as outlined in the Risk Management Plan
- Evaluate current strategies to determine whether they are appropriate and effective
- Verify assumptions upon which projects plans have been made
- Monitor the conditions that could trigger exposure
- Determine whether impact of identified risks have changed
- Determine whether existing exposure to risks has changed
- Confirm policies and procedures are carried out properly by the project team or whether failure to carry out policies has resulted in new risks
- Evaluate Risk Management Plan to ensure the plan is adequate and appropriate to identify, measure, and respond to risks
- Assess whether contingency funds, schedule reserves, and fallback plans are sufficient to deal with identified and potential risks

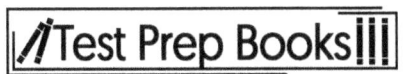

- Update risk register and project documentation to reflect changes
- Document new risks in the risk register

The following tools and techniques are used to monitor risk and evaluate risk response strategies:

Earned value analysis indicates the current performance of the project. If the project fails to meet the planned or expected costs, schedule, and quality targets, this could indicate the project has been negatively impacting by unidentified risks or inefficient response strategies, and the project cannot perform as planned until the risks are appropriately managed.

Periodic Risk Reviews should be scheduled regularly to ensure all risk and project documents are up to date and accurate at every stage of the project.

Data analysis techniques are used to identify gaps or inaccuracies in the risk management plan, risk monitoring process, and risk-related project documentation. These techniques include the following:

Technical performance analysis used to evaluate the team's competence and success using the technology, equipment, and material required to complete the work of the project. This information is compared to the project schedule and quality of the deliverables to determine whether or not the team is performing to expected standards. This reveals potential risks that could result from lack of training or competence, and poor product quality.

Reserve Analysis is used to evaluate the funds, time, and resources set aside in a contingency reserve to offset risks or issues that impact the project scope, schedule, and budget, as well as the performance of the project team and quality of the deliverables.

Risk Response Audits should be conducted regularly to examine how well the risk response strategies have been planned in the Risk Management Plan, how effectively they have reduced the impact of risk, and how well they have been executed by the team members responsible for risk management activities.

Iteratively Assess and Prioritize Risks

The outputs of the risk monitoring and assessment process include the following:

Work and process performance information: Insight into the performance of team members conducting risk response activities, effectiveness of the processes used to respond to risk, and the impact of past risks on the project cost and schedule.

Change requests: Requests to change risk response strategies and processes, perform corrective action to lessen or offset the impact of past risks, increase or decrease contingency funds, etc.

Project documentation: Updates to the project management plans to account for changes to the project schedule, risk management plan, cost management plan, risk register, issues log, lessons learned, etc.

Identify high level risks, assumptions, and constraints based on the current environment, organizational factors, historical data, and expert judgment, in order to propose an implementation strategy.

One of the key tasks performed during project initiation is the identification of high-level risks, assumptions, and constraints on the project.

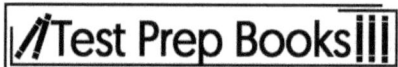

A **high-level risk** is something which could potentially block or prevent project completion. Risks should be identified early on in the project to remove any surprises later on. An example of a high-level risk is a situation in which the legacy system is not stable and data is not clean. Understand that risks can positively or negatively impact the project.

An **assumption** is something which has not been fully proven or tested and will be true for the future of the project.

An assumption is based on some knowledge or experience and should be documented on the risk management plan.

An example of an assumption is all the resources requested will be available to you.

Constraints

A **constraint** is something which restricts or limits the actions of the project team to move forward with the project and will impact the scope, timeline, quality, cost, and resources. Constraints must be balanced in order to achieve project success.

An example of a constraint is a **fixed budget** or an organizational constraint to share resources with another department.

While it may be quite easy to identify known risks, assumptions, and constraints of the project, it is imperative to consider the current state of the business environment, organizational factors, historical data, and expert judgment during the identification process.

Let's take a look at the business environment and organizational structure. Businesses operate in what is called an **environment** and include both **internal and external factors.** A business environment is the total of both internal and external factors and organizational structure is the overall framework that is used to summarize the communication process within the company. Both of these must be considered carefully in the identification process and can impact the business as well as project success.

Internal factors are factors which can impact the success of the business's day to day operations. Managing these factors and recognizing the strengths and weaknesses they may have on your project, will help eliminate any risks and delays moving forward. Some examples of internal factors are company leadership, the size of a company, leadership style, structure, and approaches as well as the strength of the employees. All of these need to be taken into consideration when identifying the risks, assumptions, and constraints within the project.

External factors are factors which can impact the businesses objectives and strategic goals. The economy is one of the biggest external factors that can affect the business as it relates to global market fluctuations. Another external factor can be financially related in regard to interest rates and types of loans that have been secured in order to fund the project. Certain laws, trends, and infrastructure can also negatively affect the business if the product or service becomes outlawed. These external factors must be considered in the identification process of potential risks, assumptions, and constraints and most cannot be controlled.

Next, let's take a look at historical data. Historical data is significant as it can help assess the likelihood and consequence as it relates to the identification of risk, assumptions, and constraints. It often includes events within the business environment and situations that have occurred in similar environments. Having access to this documented data from prior projects will allow for the prediction of the future state on the current project based on similar experiences.

Domain II: Process

Last, is expert judgment. Expert judgment requires an expertise that has been acquired in a particular knowledge area and discipline. Although judgment may be attainable by project team and project lead, it is often common for a business or organization to bring in consultation of an external group with this relevant skill set. Seeking external support allows experts to make unbiased and accurate decisions. These decisions and opinions are considered when identifying risks, assumptions, and constraints and will help reduce impact to the project.

Task 4: Engage Stakeholders

Managing expectations and maintaining communication is critical for project success. It is very important to engage all stakeholders early on in the project, specifically during the planning phase for the purpose of keeping them in the know and aligned with scope, budget, timeline and resource requirement demands set at the beginning of the project.

This process of communicating and working with stakeholders not only builds trust, but allows for the development of healthy, credible and rewarding relationships. Often throughout the project lifecycle, issues appear or an unanticipated delay occurs. Painting a clear picture from the beginning of the project, setting clear timelines, and being honest, ensures commitment at all stages, addresses potential concerns, and reassures stakeholder expectations and achievement of project goals. Perform stakeholder analysis using appropriate tools and techniques in order to align expectations and gain support for the project.

Analyze Stakeholders

Stakeholder analysis is the process in which information is consistently gathered and analyzed throughout the project to determine, address, and align expectations. This process consists of three steps. Identify the stakeholders, interview the stakeholders to assess their interest and influence, and record the collected information which will be used to create a communication plan for each stakeholder group. The outcome of this analysis generates support and structure, identifies potential risks, singles out negative stakeholders in the group, establishes the key people to keep informed, and improves the quality of the overall project's success.

The **first step** in performing a stakeholder analysis is to identify who the stakeholders are. While stakeholder identification is primarily performed as soon as the project charter is created and approved, this process is continual throughout the project lifecycle. As the project moves forward new stakeholders may be introduced and old stakeholders may drop off.

The best tool to identify stakeholders is a *brainstorming session* which includes both team members and experts. Brainstorming sessions can be easy and exciting as they enable and encourage all members to participate.

Categorize Stakeholders

The stakeholders should be placed into group categories based upon their interest level in the project, as defined below.

Primary Stakeholders - the people or groups affected directly, either positively or negatively, by a change in time, scope, or budget activity on the project. These people are generally considered the beneficiaries or recipient of all efforts performed on the project.

Secondary Stakeholders - the people or groups affected indirectly, either positively or negatively, by a change in time, scope, or budget activity on the project. These people are generally considered those directly responsible for the beneficiaries or recipient of all efforts performed on the project. Some of these individuals may overlap with those in the primary category.

Key Stakeholders – the people or groups that may or may not belong to either the primary or secondary group and may not be affected by a change, but yet still have an interest and are willing to work to influence the outcome.

Interest/Importance is the priority given to satisfying the overall need and interest of each stakeholder.

Influence is the power each stakeholder has to either expedite or block the achievement of the project's goal or objective.

It is suggested to map out the interest and influence of each stakeholder group by creating a **stakeholder matrix** and place each stakeholder name into the appropriate box according to their impact.

Example of a Stakeholder Matrix

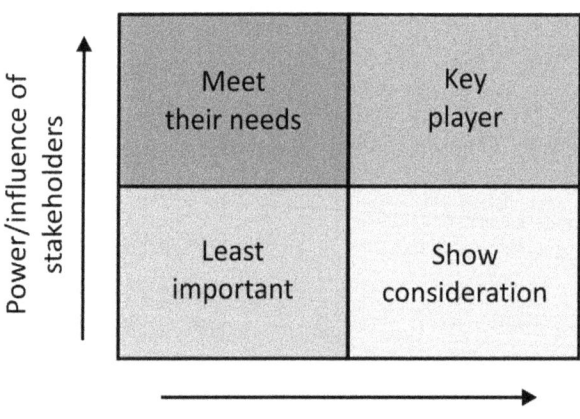

Meet their Needs – are stakeholders who are helpful in formulating opinions and decisions and should be engaged on interest level. They are considered high importance and low influence.

Key player – are the stakeholders who are involved in the decision making and should be engaged regularly throughout the project as they are most critical. Key players are of high importance and high influence on the project.

Least important – are stakeholders who are non-supportive and have a low importance and low influence on the project.

Show consideration – are stakeholders who should be engaged and kept informed in the low-risk areas of the project. They are of low importance and high influence.

The **third step** is to interview a sample of these stakeholders and record the notes from the interview. The outcome of the interview is to find out what they know about the project, their goals and objectives, and any concerns they may have around the project. These face-to-face interviews allow the project manager to gain insight and a perspective of what each stakeholder expects from the overall project as well as uncovering any critical issues that require special attention.

Engage Stakeholders by Category

The last task in the planning phase of the project is to create a **Stakeholder Management Plan** that describes the strategies to engage key stakeholders and manage their expectations. The purpose of the Stakeholder Management Plan is to identify the needs and the attitudes of the stakeholders in order to satisfy their needs within the scope of the project.

The Stakeholder Register often includes information such as the stakeholders' expressed needs and expectations or the project while the Stakeholder Management Plan examines their unspoken or implicit needs and expectations. This is a confidential document that expands on the information detailed in the Stakeholder Register with additional insights collected about each stakeholder. These are insights into the stakeholder's current level of engagement compared to the level of engagement the project manager considers ideal. A stakeholder's level of engagement can be unaware of the project, resistant to the goal or the result of the project, neutral to the project, supportive of the project, or leading the efforts to successfully execute the project.

The plan includes information about the stakeholders' current levels of resistance or support for the project, as well as the potential positive or negative impact the completed project will have on the stakeholder that influence their attitude during the project. It may detail the stakeholders' underlying motivations for the success or failure of the project.

To establish the positive or negative influence stakeholders have over other stakeholders, the project manager often examines the functional, organizational, and social relationships between stakeholders and project team members.

Develop, Execute, and Validate a Strategy for Stakeholder Engagement

These insights can assist the project manager to devise strategies to manage stakeholders tailored to their individual needs, attitude toward the project, and level of influence over other key stakeholders. The plan details strategies for how to increase or decrease level of engagement for each stakeholder, how to decrease resistance and increase support, and how to engage influential stakeholders to assist in garnering support for the project.

The project manager might also devise strategies for how to limit the influence of negative stakeholder. They might also include strategies to communicate with each stakeholder based on their individual preferences and even how to limit communication to stakeholders who could cause disruptions to the project.

Tools and Techniques
The tools and techniques to organize and classify stakeholders to inform these strategies include a stakeholder engagement matrix, a power-interest grid, a salience model, and a social network analysis.

Stakeholder Engagement Matrix

A stakeholder engagement matrix organizes stakeholders by current (C) and ideal (I) level of engagement.

Stakeholder	Unaware	Resistant	Neutral	Supportive	Leading
Stakeholder 1	C			I	
Stakeholder 2			C	I	
Stakeholder 3				I C	

Power-Interest Grid

A power-interest grid classifies stakeholders based on their level of power and their level of interest, which helps to identify the best approach to communicate with each group.

Power-Interest Grid

	Low Interest	High Interest
High Power	Keep Satisfied — *Pull*	Monitor Closely — *Interactive/Push*
Low Power	Monitor — *Least Effort*	Keep informed — *Marketing*

Salience Model

The salience model also classifies stakeholders, though it is more complex than the Power-interest grid. This model is based on the intersections of three factors (power, legitimacy, urgency) to identify eight unique groups of stakeholders.

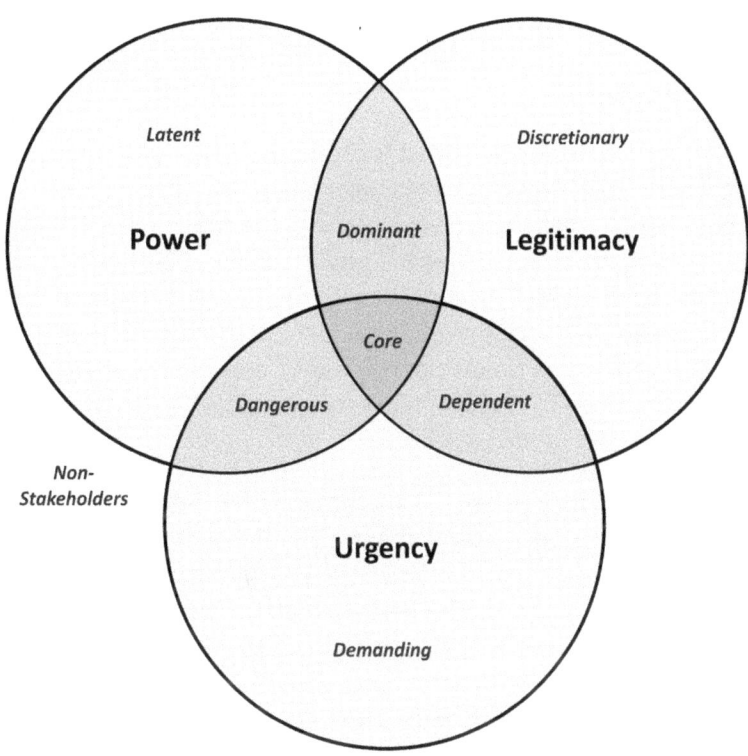

Social Network Analysis

A social network analysis can detect functional, organizational, and social links between stakeholders to identify stakeholders that have a lot of influence over other stakeholders, even if they do not hold power in the organization or the hierarchy of the project.

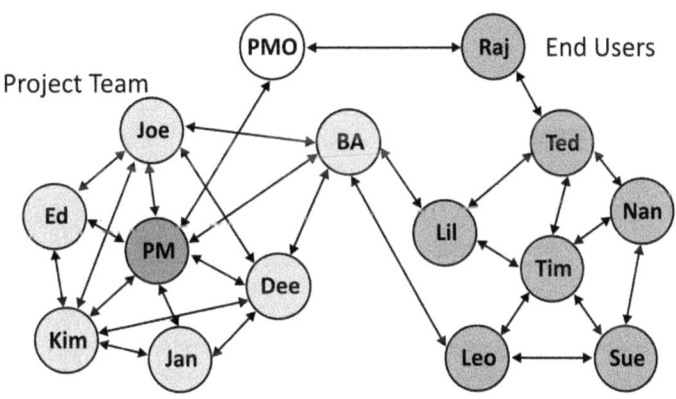

Task 5: Plan and Manage Budget and Resources

Properly planning and allocating the project's budget and resources is one of the most important aspects of project management. Budgetary restrictions and availability of necessary resources are common blockers, so proper management of both features is essential for the project to run smoothly and remain on track with its established schedule.

Estimate Budgetary Needs

Before actual work can be started on any project, it is essential to estimate the project costs. In estimating costs, the first concern of any project manager should be ensuring that all potential categories of cost are considered. Depending on the scope of the project, there may be multiple categories of cost, ranging from the direct cost of the raw materials going into the project deliverable to costs associated with information technology requirements and potential service fees. In addition, project managers should make sure to incorporate both indirect costs, such as any management overhead, as well as a contingency fund for unexpected costs. In many cases, when estimating the scope of the project and the budgetary needs, project managers will consult with a project charter, which lists the preapproved financial resources of the project.

One particular project artifact that may be helpful in estimating budgetary needs is a lessons learned register. A lessons learned register is any document in which members of the project team record and relate their project experience. There are a number of reasons why this document may prove particularly valuable. One reason is that a lessons learned register may often relate previous budgetary estimates, which can be helpful to compare to the actual costs to gain a better sense of where the estimations may be incorrect or not accounting for a particular factor. In addition, a lessons learned register may contain useful cost-saving information, either by providing an example of what to do or what not to do. Finally, as a result of its anecdotal nature, a lessons learned register may contain valuable tacit knowledge, which would otherwise be difficult to transmit between members of the project or organization.

Anticipate Future Budget Challenges

It is one thing for a project manager to estimate budgetary needs but another thing entirely to anticipate all potential budgetary challenges that may be encountered during the project process. These challenges can stem from many different factors—so many so that it may be more helpful for a project manager attempting to anticipate potential budgetary challenges to monitor certain project measurements that may indicate problems with the budget. As an example, project managers should always be sure to keep themselves abreast of both project and industry trends. As the names imply, project trends are any metric associated with a project that may indicate some sort of novel and potentially unwelcomed change. For instance, an increase in the number of missed deadlines may be an indication that certain project groups or individuals are not receiving adequate resources. Industry trends, although not always as directly informative as project trends, can also provide useful information for project managers, particularly as it applies to industry-specific budgetary concerns.

Moving beyond general data trends that may help project managers anticipate future budget challenges, it might also be useful for project managers to consider and keep track of specific systems and registers that may provide useful information as it pertains to future budgetary challenges. For example, a project manager may want to use the stakeholder register as a means of assessing the budget requirements for different kinds of stakeholders. This can be especially helpful if new stakeholders are introduced to a project after the initial budget and register are created. Similarly, a project manager may turn to an assumptions register when dealing with budget challenges. Assumption registers are project artifacts used to log project assumptions—any non-verified piece of information on which project decisions are made. Because the validity of these assumptions is in question, it may be a good place for project managers to start identifying the underlying causes of budget challenges. Finally, monitoring team member performance and any sort of change log can assist the project manager in identifying which areas of a project need more budgetary assistance and which ones do not.

Monitor Budget Variations

Although project managers should always be aware of and vigilant about any sort of budgetary variations, it is inevitable that, at some point, the actual costs will exceed the budgetary allotment. For the most part, small variations either way (meaning the estimates either slightly undershot *or* overshot the actual costs) are acceptable and even expected. All the same, it is a diligent project manager's responsibility to record and monitor these variations wherever they occur, unless a number of smaller variations add up to an unacceptable variation for the total project budget. One common tool for project managers that can assist in the monitoring of budget variations is a cost baseline table. Cost baseline tables are approved budgets that are structured temporally, which allow users to see when certain payments and costs are expected. Although these tables are clearly useful in and of themselves, it is also common practice to use the cost baseline table to create a graph, with total costs along the *y* axis and number of weeks since the project began along the *x* axis. The resulting graph, commonly referred to as an *S-curve graph*, allows for easy visualization of budget variations, with a project manager simply having to sum up the current expenses to see if the project is over or under budget. Depending on which it is, there may be a number of potential causes and solutions for the governance team to consider.

Plan and Manage Resources

Resources consist both of physical resources and team resources. Physical resources can include the equipment or materials needed to design and/or construct a project deliverable or the facilities or infrastructure needed to store and transport other forms of resources. Team resources, also referred to as *personnel,* consist of the human elements of a project. It is the responsibility of the project manager to ensure that both physical and team resources are considered and accounted for throughout the duration of the project. In the planning phase, this can be achieved most easily through the creation of a resource management plan, which should contain information regarding the categorization, allocation, management, and scheduled release of all project resources.

Once the management plan has been created, there are a number of different methods a project manager may want to consider to successfully manage the movement and usage of resources. For example, if there is a problem with resources not being sent out to the appropriate parties at the right time, a project manager should contemplate shortening their planning horizons to ensure that each step of the project is receiving the attention and care it needs. It may also be helpful for project managers to think about how their physical resources and team resources will work together and how certain changes may improve this connection. For some projects, depending on their scope, it may be best for them to have all of their physical and team resources in the same location, whereas for other projects this may not be ideal or even feasible.

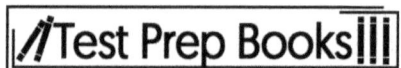

Task 6: Plan and Manage Schedule

Planning and managing the project schedule ensures that the team and relevant stakeholders stay on task and ensures that the project is completed in a timeframe that works for all involved parties. Project managers must help the team and stakeholders develop a plan that is achievable and profitable/productive. After the schedule is established, it is the project manager's responsibility to look out for signs that the project is being completed at the correct rate and intervene when progress slows or the established schedule poses a problem for project completion.

Estimate Project Tasks

In order to estimate the time needed to complete a project, the project tasks should be outlined and an expected timeline for their completion should be drafted. Project managers can measure the project's progress via checkpoints and deliverables that compare the project's actual completion with its planned schedule.

A **milestone** is a specific check point within a project marking a stage of a major accomplishment or the end of a phase. Milestones are the actual task activities that have a fixed date assigned to them, have zero duration, and do not impact the project schedule. They are identified and created to track and report progress of completion and are used as inputs for review. Defining activities and milestones are part of the project team responsibilities during planning and scheduling phases within the project. They are not part of the initiation phase.

Dependencies are tasks that are interrelated, or that depend on other tasks to be completed. There are four types of dependencies:

- **Mandatory dependencies** are required by contract or by the type of project at hand. Most of the time, these dependencies cannot be changed.

- **Discretionary dependencies** are based on industry best practices or preferences.

- **External dependencies** pertain to the relationship between project activities and other external influences. These usually cannot be changed.

- **Internal dependencies** are tasks that rely on other project tasks to be completed.

Dependencies can affect the project timeline, but some may be harder to anticipate than others. During the planning stage, the team may be able to identify mandatory, discretionary, and internal dependencies based on available information. External dependencies may be harder to predict.

During the planning phase, team members can help the project manager develop **story points** that estimate the effort and time needed for a particular task. Story points take the complexity, risk potential, and overall effort involved in a task into account, which provides a more complete picture of how long it could take to complete.

Milestones, dependencies, and story tasks contextualize the project and its tasks and help the project manager estimate its length and phases. While circumstances can change throughout the duration of the project, these features help project managers understand the moving parts of the project and get all team members and stakeholders involved in schedule planning.

Utilize Benchmarks and Historical Data

In addition to considering the time necessitated by project tasks, benchmarks and historical data can provide context on industry trends and performance data that may impact the project schedule.

Project managers may compare the estimated project tasks and timeline with those from previous projects or industry standards. This process can help determine project and task length when the team cannot decide or provide context for unexpected stalls if the established schedule proves to be insufficient.

Prepare Schedule Based on Methodology

Commonly, project schedules are developed using an adaptive methodology such as agile project management. The goal of agile management is to save time and reduce wasted resources while maximizing output and efficiency. Some methodologies that follow these principles include Kanban and Lean.

Adaptive scheduling uses incremental planning, which relies on multiple "iterations" that break down project sections into features and tasks. With each iteration, value is delivered. Adaptive approaches may also use timeboxes, which organize tasks picked from a prioritized backlog. In this approach, the team estimates how much they can get done within the timebox and provides a tentative completion time. At the end of the timebox, the team reports on what they have completed. From there, the project manager may give the team new goals or reconsider the prioritized backlog.

Measure Ongoing Progress Based on Methodology

All scheduling approaches must take into consideration both effort and duration. Some effort-driven tasks can be completed sooner if more people are assigned to work on them. Other tasks may have a fixed duration, such as testing or training. The project manager must take these factors into consideration when creating or editing the project schedule. If the task allows, the project manager should consider how changes in assignments or resource allocation could help the team complete tasks more efficiently.

Project managers may also compare actual and planned start and finish dates, feature completion rates, and schedule variance when determining progress. **Schedule variance** is the difference between the earned value at the time of assessment versus the planned value. These figures enable the project manager to visualize how the current project status compares with its projected status and directly assess the impact of schedule changes on measured performance.

Modify Schedule as Needed Based on Methodology

When the project manager observes an issue with the planned schedule, they may need to adapt their plan to ensure that all project objectives are completed on time.

If the estimated schedule goes beyond the desired end date, the project manager may use **schedule compression** methods to reduce the project timeline. The following methods may be applied when necessary:

- **Crashing** is a method that shortens the project timeline for the least additional cost. This may be performed by adding additional team members to a particular task or implementing overtime.

- **Fast tracking** pushes tasks that are normally completed in succession to be completed at the same time. Fast tracking may require adding leads and lags to the network path. A **lead** requires that the second task in a series is started before the first task is completed, while a **lag** requires delaying the second task.

Schedule constraints may also be employed to get a task completed before its estimated end date.

Coordinate with Other Projects and Other Operations

In order to keep the project on track, project managers may need to maintain communication with leaders of other projects or teams. In some cases, external dependencies may require close interaction between two organizations. Project managers should be prepared to consider these external influences in their own project timeline to avoid mismanaging time or resources.

Task 7: Plan and Manage Quality of Products & Deliverables

The *Control Quality* process ensures the deliverables for the project meet the expectations of the stakeholders and the standards of quality outlined in the Quality Management Plan. The Control Quality process is applied throughout the lifecycle of the project to identify and repair defects in deliverables, as well as eliminate the root causes of defects to prevent more rework that could impact the project cost and schedule.

Determine Quality Standard Required for Project Deliverables

The inputs for the Control Quality process are the same as those for other areas of the monitor and control domain and include the following:

Project Management Plan: Project Management and component plans including the Quality Management Plan that establishes the metrics to measure and respond to quality results.

Tests and Evaluations: Results of tests and evaluations used to analyze the current quality of the deliverables and determine trends in defects or variances.

Performance Data: Data used to determine the quality of the work performed by the project team compared to the key performance metrics established in the Project Management Plan.

Project Documents: Documents relevant to project standards that can help determine the quality of the deliverables compared to the established project standards.

Deliverables: Completed deliverables to be evaluated for quality.

Project Management Information System: Quality control software, physical filing system, or other system specific to the enterprise environment that is used to organize quality control processes, procedures, policies, industry standards, regulations, etc.

Organizational assets: Policies, procedures, and standards for quality control required by the organization.

Tools and Techniques to Control Quality

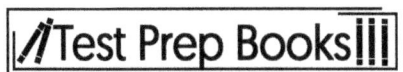

Domain II: Process

The following techniques are used to examine and evaluate the quality of the project deliverables and the processes outlined in the project management plans:

Data gathering is used to collect data about defects or variances in the quality of the deliverables. The tools and techniques to gather data vary depending on the type of deliverable and the specifications for quality control specified in the Quality Management Plan. These tools and techniques include the following:

- *Check sheets*, or tally sheets, to identify the frequency of quality control metrics using check marks or tallies

- *Statistical sampling* to evaluate a sample of deliverables or processes from the complete batch to determine if the variances fall within the *upper* and *lower control limit* or below the *tolerance threshold*

- *Inspections* to physically examine the components of the deliverable

- *Testing and evaluation* of the deliverables to determine if they meet the requirements and quality standards of the product.

Upper and Lower Control Limits: Data points within which results must fall to remain in control. The control limits and the mean, or average, of results within the control limits are typically represented in a control chart.

Mean: Average of variance in between the upper and lower control limits.

Tolerance Threshold: Maximum allowable variation in quality considered within the control limits, after which the results are considered unacceptable.

Variances in quality are expected and can take the form of random variances; predictable or known variances that are the result of characteristics of a product or service; variances inherent to any process such as human error, machine malfunctions, environmental factors, etc.; and special cause variances that are the result of unusual circumstances and are not common to the deliverable or process.

Data representation tools are used to visualize the results of data gathering. These tools include the following:

Control charts display the variances in quality of a deliverable or process over time to determine if the variances are in control, falling between the upper and lower limits of performance, or out of control, falling outside the upper and lower limits.

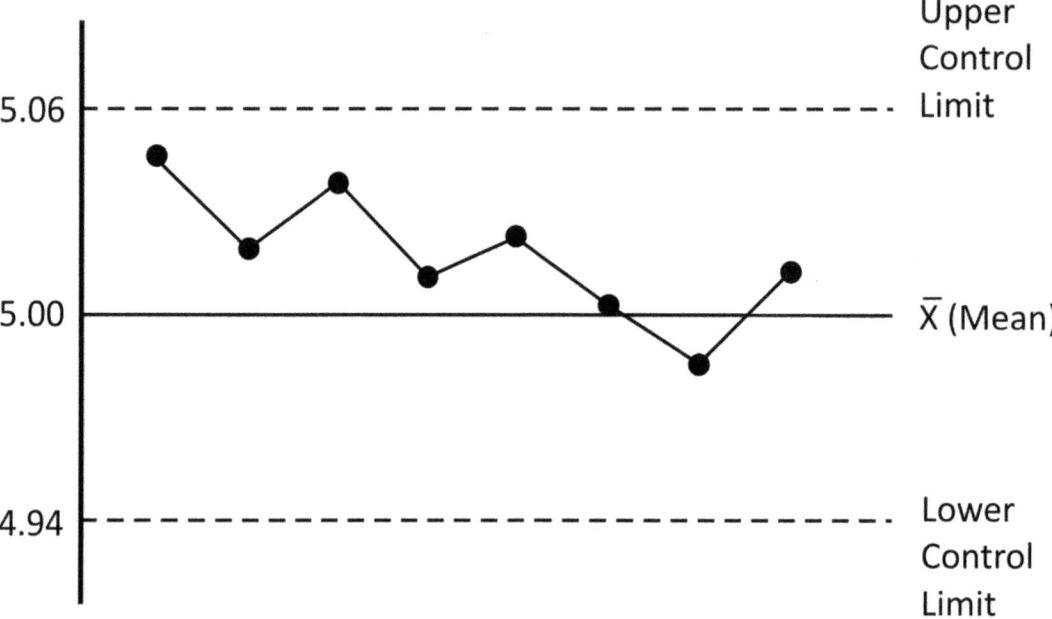

Pareto diagrams, or histograms, display the top causes of quality variance in order of importance by frequency over time. Pareto diagrams are named for Pareto's theory that it is more beneficial to spend the majority of time fixing the most important problems, rather than trying to fix them all. In the example, the most important problems are represented by bars while the cumulative percent of the problems appear as a circle on a line.

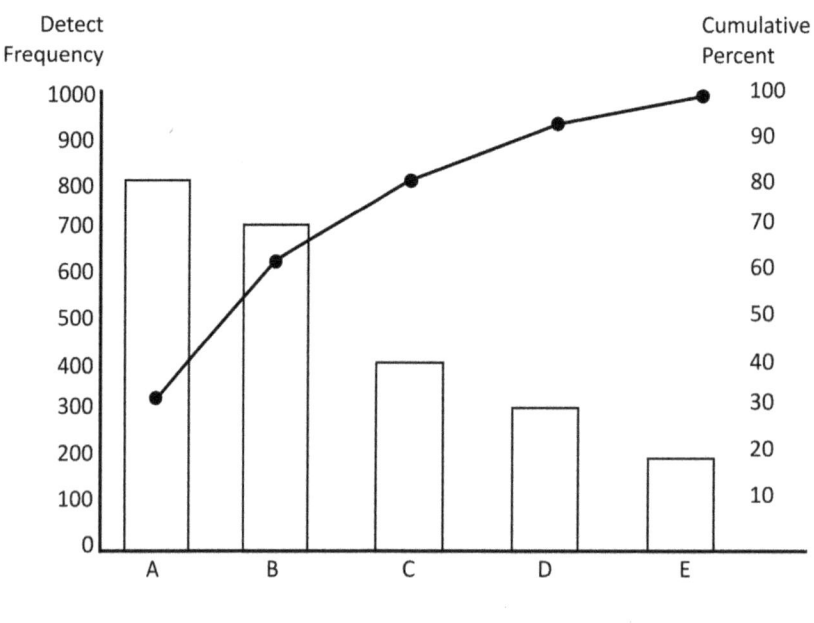

Scatter diagrams, or correlation charts, are used to establish a cause-and-effect relationship between an independent variable on the x-axis and a dependent variable on the y-axis. For example, use time spent working on a deliverable on the x-axis to find a correlation to the quality of the deliverable on the y-axis. The closer the data points resemble a diagonal line on the diagram, the greater the correlation between the two variables.

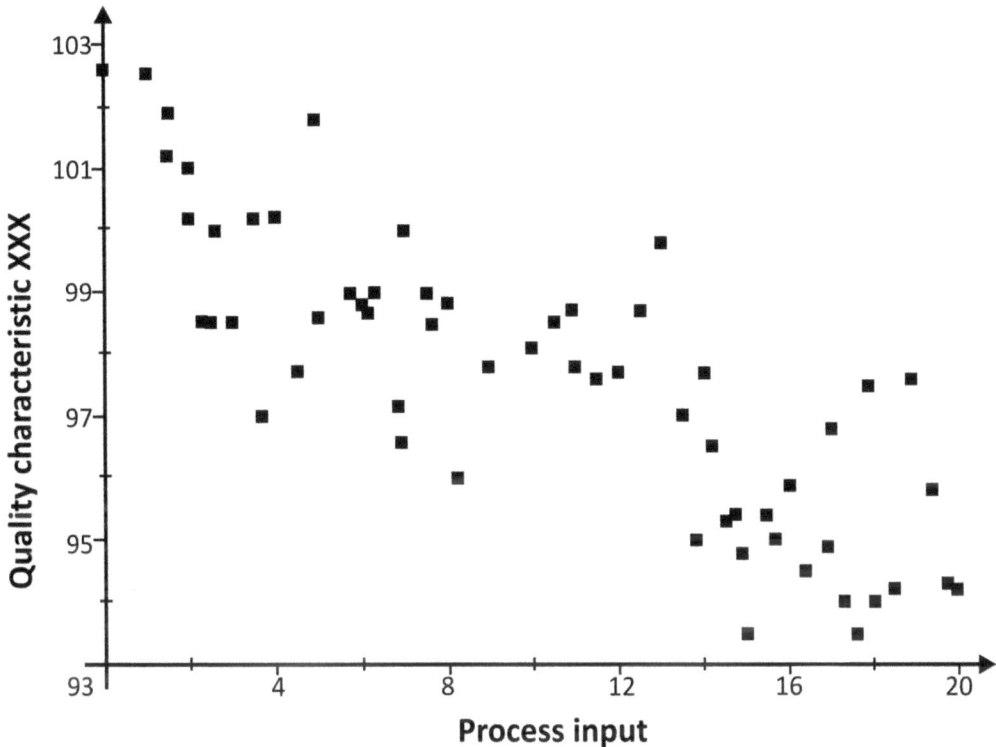

Trend Analysis

Trend analysis uses results from previous tests and evaluations to predict performance in the future. The results of the trend analysis can be used to identify the common causes of variances in technical performance, cost, or budget, so the project manager can take corrective action to eliminate these causes and prevent future variances.

Process Analysis

Process analysis is used to identify problems, inefficiencies, or non-value-added activities within the project or organizational processes in order to determine how these processes can be improved. The following tools and techniques are used to analyze the processes of a project or within an organization:

Gap analysis examines the complete process used to perform activities; the inputs into the project that guide and determine how and why each activity is performed; the output of the activity; and the human or material resource that is used to perform the activity. This analysis reveals the gaps in each element, such as dependencies being missed in the input, inaccurate instructions in the guide, defects in the output, or inexperience of resources.

Value-added analysis examines each activity in the process to determine if they add value to the project by contributing to the project goals in order to eliminate activities that do not directly contribute to the project or that cost unnecessary time and money.

Root cause analysis is described in Domain II: Planning. This type of process analysis uses a diagram to identify and define the causes of problems in the process.

Recommend Options for Improvement Based on Quality Gaps

Lean *and* efficient principles are used to eliminate inefficiencies in processes that use unnecessary time, money, and resources.

Six Sigma uses data analysis to prevent quality variance. The Six Sigma *Lean* process analysis technique examines processes to determine where and why rework is occurring in the process, where activities are being duplicated during the process, and what is causing bottlenecks in the process in order to identify how to improve the process to be leaner and more efficient.

The **Kanban** technique also applies lean and efficient principles to optimize processes. It uses visual models to identify the flow of work, typically in the form of sticky notes on a whiteboard that identify the work to do, the work in progress, and the work that has been completed as in the following example:

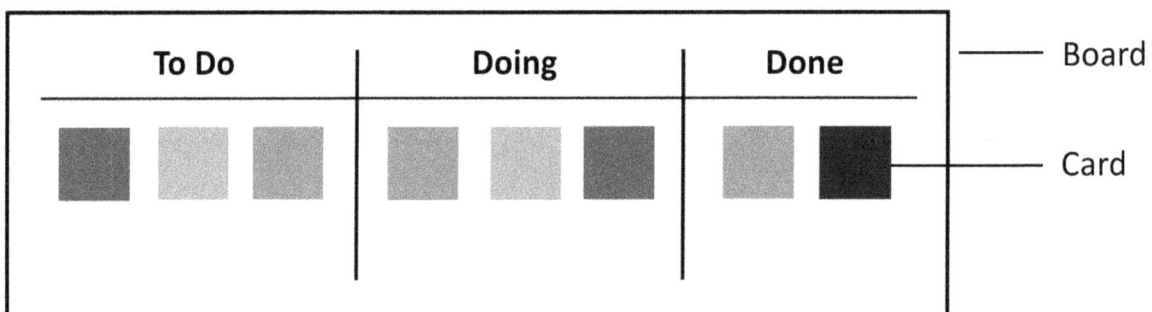

Continually Survey Project Deliverable Quality

Consistently monitoring the quality of project deliverables is the best way to measure the effectiveness of improvement interventions. The quality control process results in the following values that can be used to measure improvements in quality and record management interventions for future analysis:

Quality control metrics: Metrics against which to compare deliverables and processes

Quality deliverables: Deliverables that meet the requirements of the project goals with minimal variance in quality

Work and process performance information: Insight into the performance of the activities to produce deliverables, as well the performance of the processes during which the activities are performed

Change requests: Requests to change processes to improve efficiency, and requests to perform corrective action to repair defects or take preventive action to prevent future defects and other variances

Project documentation: updates to the project management plans to account for changes in processes, etc.; and updates to issue log, lessons learned register, risk register, test and evaluation results

Task 8: Plan and Manage Scope

Project scope is the total of the products, services, or results that make up the project. Scope can be defined during the planning phase, but it may change over time as the project evolves.

Determine and Prioritize Requirements

To determine the project scope, the project manager should outline the deliverables of the project as well as their criteria. Project managers can develop a **scope statement** that lays out this information.

While defining and prioritizing deliverables is important, the project manager should ensure that the team completes this portion of scope definition late in the planning stage. This way, changes to the project's scope result in as little wasted time and resources as possible.

Break Down Scope

Project managers may also break down scope into finer detail using a **work breakdown structure**, or WBS. A WBS further defines the total scope of the project's work as a hierarchy ranked by the deliverable's value and the estimated work it will require.

It may also be useful to organize project deliverables by themes using an agile approach or product hierarchy. Deliverables can be grouped together by determining a shared value—such as their function or the sources they derived from—presented as **user stories,** or descriptions of a planned outcome. The project manager should guide the team in creating **epics**, or large groupings of user stories that cannot be completed in a single iteration, that can be broken down into **features**, or the set of requirements that must be met to complete the tasks.

Monitor and Validate Scope

Throughout the project's duration, the project manager must remain aware of the project's estimated scope and ensure that the project's execution reflects the team's plan. One way for the project manager to stay on top of the project scope is to monitor the completion of deliverables. This can be done in multiple ways:

- **Acceptance or completion criteria** must be met for a project's completion. Project managers can use these markers to determine project progress.

- **Technical performance measures** are specifications for a task or product that may be defined by other documents, but they can also be added to the project's WBS.

- **Definition of done** is a phrase used in adaptive management approaches that refers to a checklist of criteria that must be completed for a project to be considered complete or for a product to be considered ready for use. This form of scope management is often used in software development projects.

It is important to note that these benchmarks can change depending on environmental or industry pressures, introduction of new standards and criteria, or other project updates. Project managers should be prepared to guide their teams through shifting deadlines and changing terms, which may be stressful or frustrating for team members and stakeholders.

Task 9: Integrate Project Planning Activities

While the project planning phase will ultimately end so work can begin, project managers must continue to employ project planning principles throughout the duration of the project to keep their teams on track and account for any changes.

Consolidate the Project/Phase Plans

Project managers may choose to consolidate sections of the project plan to simplify tasks or to group related tasks together. Examples of project phases are listed below:

- Plan
- Design
- Build
- Test
- Deploy
- Close

While each project phase has its own requirements for completion and must meet certain criteria before the team can move on to the next phase, different development approaches may involve different phases and orders. Predictive, iterative, incremental, and adaptive development approaches may organize project phases in different ways that ultimately affect the outlook of the project life cycle. For instance:

- A **predictive** development approach typically completes one project phase before the next begins. In most cases, the phase would be completed once and it would focus on one type of work. Changes to the project may require that phases be added or repeated, but most planning is completed early on.

- An **incremental** approach may include multiple iterations of phases compiled in a set, such as three iterations of Plan-Design-Build. Each iteration would divide the project into smaller but fully functional sections.

- An **iterative** approach may design the project life cycle much like the incremental approach would, but each iteration would build upon the last iteration's work.

- An **adaptive** approach also organizes project phases by iterations. At the end of each iteration, stakeholders review the project and provide feedback that helps the project manager reprioritize the plan and make necessary changes to be enacted in the next iteration. New tasks will also be chosen from the backlog to complete during each iteration.

Assess Consolidated Project Plans for Dependencies, Gaps, and Continued Business Value

Regardless of which project phases or management approach is used, the project manager must assess the project plans and account for dependencies, gaps, and performance.

Dependencies may influence the order and number of project phases, while gaps in the project process may require that the project plan be reconsidered to eliminate potential error. In order for business value and performance to reach or maintain a desired level, the project manager may also find it necessary to overlap project phases when possible to minimize time and resources.

Collect and Analyze Data to Make Informed Project Decisions

The format of the project life cycle impacts how planning takes place. Project managers can assess project performance at different stages in the project life cycle and utilize the appropriate development approach to improve project outcomes.

Depending on the development approach and life cycle of a particular project, problems like risk may be handled differently. For instance, a predictive approach may add phases for additional testing and documentation that could resolve risk and ensure that the product meets relevant standards. An iterative approach may release a product based on initial projections, receive feedback, and then address and correct problems in the next project phase.

Determine Critical Information Requirements

Ongoing project planning requires more than just choosing an effective project development approach and analyzing its effects at different points in the project's life cycle. Project managers can use the information gained from observing these processes in tandem with stakeholder responses to determine requirements for future project tasks.

The project manager should evaluate the project's performance at each phase and record areas for improvement. These areas may inform future requirements that can be documented and presented to stakeholders for review and acceptance. These types of changes are most common in incremental, iterative, and adaptive approaches where performance can be easily measured at multiple points throughout the project.

Task 10: Manage Project Changes

Anticipate and Embrace the Need for Change

While the goal of the project manager is to prevent the root causes of issues or circumstances that require formal changes to the project, changes are likely to occur throughout the project lifecycle. The changes that require change requests to execute are typically those that affect the project scope, schedule, or cost estimates. These changes include corrective action to adjust the project schedule for performance variances, repairs to correct defects in deliverables, changes to vendor contracts, and changes to the cost to complete estimate for the project.

To ensure the project remains on track and in alignment with the project goals, the project manager must make changes that impact the project using integrated change control processes.

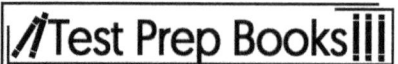

Domain II: Process

Integrated Change Control is the process of managing changes to the project plans and documents, vendor contracts, schedule, policies and procedures, and deliverables while remaining aligned with the goals of the project. This approach to change control focuses on accepting or rejecting change requests based upon how the change will impact all other areas of the project plan; communicating the change to the team; implementing the change; and evaluating the results of the change.

Determine Strategy to Handle Change

The integrated change control process includes the following steps:

- Identify the need for a change within the project.
- Submit a change request.
- Update the change log with request information including:
- Change request Identifier
- Date submitted
- Category of change requested
- Description of change
- Submitted by
- Status of request
- Disposition of request
- Measure the impact of the change on all areas of the project.
- Present the requested change to the Change Control Board that approves or denies the change.
- Communicate the disposition of the change request to the requester and approved requests to the team members who will be impacted by the change.
- Update the impacted project plans and documents.
- Execute the change.
- Verify the change has been made during the quality control process.

Execute Change Management Strategy According to the Methodology

Any changes made to a single area of a project can affect the other areas of the project, so the integrated control process focuses on thorough analysis to determine if the change will impact the goals and plans for the project, how it will impact the project, and to what extent.

In order to measure the impact of the change, the project manager must have an accurate and realistic project plan against which to measure the following potential impacts:

- Requirements to implement the change
- Risks to the project related to the change
- Effect the change will have on the project schedule and milestones
- Cost to reject the change and cost to approve the change
- Response the project team will have to the change
- Roles and responsibilities of team members and stakeholders with respect to the change

Determine a Change Response to Move the Project Forward

For smaller projects or organizations, the project manager might have the authority to review and authorize changes to the project plan, but often the project manager is responsible for facilitating the review and analyze steps of the integrated change control process. For larger projects or for projects in which the project manager lacks the authority to approve or reject changes, a *Change Control Board* is responsible for making decisions regarding changes to the project while the project manager is responsible for measuring the impact of the change, presenting the results to the board, and providing recommendations regarding the change. The change control board is often made up of stakeholders, subject matter experts, project sponsor, team leaders, the project manager, etc.

Task 11: Plan and Manage Procurement

As the project progresses, the project manager administers contracts and coordinates procurements to ensure vendors are performing as expected so the materials required to complete the work are available when they are needed. The project manager must be familiar with the contract requirements and terms, as well as the metrics against which to measure vendor performance to determine if they are meeting the requirements, maintaining quality, and remaining on schedule.

Define Resource Requirements and Needs

In some cases, project managers may be able to define the necessary resources for a project at its outset. In other cases, resources may be determined while working on the project as new information is discovered or changes are required. Ease of resource planning and management is a great motivator for project managers to develop a clear project plan and scope early on in the process.

Project managers should pay close attention to the difference between a project's planned resource utilization and its actual resource utilization, as well as the differences in cost for both values. Since resource planning is closely related to budget planning, project managers should be aware of possible budgetary restrictions resulting from unclear resource requirements and mismanagement.

Communicate Resource Requirements

Throughout the project, the project manager acts as a contract administrator. In this capacity, the project manager is responsible for monitoring the terms of the contract to ensure all parties are fulfilling their obligations to each other. This helps to prevent disagreements that could cause delays in the schedule or cause the work to stop completely in the event of disputes over violations of terms or failure to perform to the standards specified in the contract.

To perform contract administration, the project manager requires the following input:

- Procurement documentation, including the statements of work for each contract, the contracts themselves, the specs, drawings, or plans for the work to be performed, quality metrics, policies and procedures, etc.

- Project schedules, including payment schedules to ensure the work performed is paid according to the terms of the contract when the vendor fulfills their obligations

- Vendor performance evaluation that indicates how well the vendor performed under the terms of the contract

- Change requests that pertain to procurement such as changes to the terms of contracts, addendums, and changes in the work requirements, the project or procurement schedule, the prequalified vendor list, etc.

Manage Suppliers and Contracts

Vendor performance is measured against the terms of the contracts, which are based on the statement of work, the requirements for the product or service, and the production schedule. The project manager is responsible for maintaining control over the project schedule and budget by ensuring vendors are completing the deliverables completed in a timely manner to the quality specifications outlined in the contract. The vendor's performance determines if the work meets the standards required for payment, if the vendor is owed incentives, or if the work must be redone.

To monitor vendor performance, the project manager or a third party might visit the vendor site to perform physical inspections of the deliverable during the vendor's production process; conduct quality audits to determine whether the vendor is performing the work correctly and on time and is following any required policies and procedures; or complete performance reviews based on predetermined metrics. Performance reviews may be required by the accounting department before payment can be rendered.

To measure the performance of the vendor over the course of the project, the project manager analyzes the results of inspections, quality audits, and performance reviews using data analysis techniques that measure the quality of project deliverables.

Plan and Manage Procurement Strategy

The project manager must maintain accurate and complete records of procurement documentation, including what work was planned, what work vendors performed, when they performed it, when they completed deliverables, if the deliverables had to be redone, if contracts were disputed, and when the work was paid. These documents include items such as purchase orders, invoices, receipts, open and closed contracts, any correspondence or communication related to procurement activities and contracts, change requests, results of audits, inspections, and performance reviews and any analyses performed.

The records should be included in a procurement file for the project and maintained regularly to ensure the information is accurate and complete. In the case of a dispute with a vendor or other third party, accurate records protect the vendor from unfounded claims and ensure the buyer has the appropriate documentation and evidence in the event they make a claim against a vendor, and vice versa.

In the event the buyer or vendor contests the terms of the contract, the project manager is responsible for monitoring, documenting, and maintaining records related to claims. If the parties are unable to agree on the terms of the contract or claims another party has failed to meet the terms of the contract, the parties can settle the dispute outside of court through *alternative dispute resolution (ADR)* methods such as *mediation* or *arbitration*.

Mediation: During mediation, an independent third-party attempts to guide the parties involved in a dispute to negotiate a mutually beneficial agreement. Mediators use communication techniques to engage the participants in open discussion in order to create empathy and understanding, rather than hearing the arguments and rendering a decision as in other dispute resolution methods.

Domain II: Process

Arbitration: In the event the parties failed to settle the dispute through mediation, the parties can enter arbitration. Arbitration may be voluntary, or it might be included as part of the contract in a dispute resolution clause. During an arbitration hearing, each party presents their arguments to an arbitrator, the independent party that will make the final decision to settle the dispute. The decision made by the arbitrator is legally binding and enforceable in court.

Develop a Delivery Solution

The procurement processes should result in closed procurement documents that include formal or informal acceptance from the project manager as established in the Procurement Management Plan or as required by the organization. The closed procurement documents are added to the project documentation along with any changes to the procurement plan such as change requests to void contracts, perform corrective action, alter the project schedule, etc.

Task 12: Manage Project Artifacts

Determine the Requirements for Managing the Project Artifacts

Project artifacts can consist of templates, documents, outputs, and/or project deliverables. Clearly, there are many different kinds of documents that could be considered project artifacts, and artifacts are often highly unique to the specifications of the project and the organization. In order to effectively manage this kind of project, it may be helpful for a project manager to take into account, during the planning phase, the types of artifacts they may encounter rather than try to delegate who is responsible for each one. In general, the project manager should assume responsibility for all artifacts created specifically as a result of the project. Other artifacts may be the responsibility of other members of the project team, depending on their particular areas of expertise. A project manager may think about categorizing the artifacts by what stage or phase of the project they occur in, or they may define artifacts by what they represent or how they represent it. It should be stated once again that project artifacts should largely be defined by a project manager and for a specific project. Therefore, the following is not and should not be considered a comprehensive list, nor should it be used in totality.

Considering the project chronologically, the first kind of artifacts a project manager may want to contemplate are strategy artifacts. Strategy artifacts are any documents created before or at the start of the project that address the strategic and business goals. Project managers may consider further defining and developing their strategy artifacts during the start of the project, but strategy artifacts typically do not change beyond then. Many, if not all strategy artifacts, present high-level information about the project. For example, a project roadmap will present high-level information in a timeline format, whereas a project vision statement will do so in a more concise manner, with the intention of inspiring the project team. Similar to strategy artifacts, plans are any artifacts that offer a proposed means of accomplishing something. Plans may concern individual aspects or a phase of a project, or all that information may be combined into one all-encompassing project management plan. It is important to note that plans merely represent *proposed* means, and therefore plans represent only the precursor to another type of project artifact, baselines. *Baselines* are the approved versions of either a plan or a work product and are used primarily to measure the gap between expected performance and actual performance. A budget would count as a baseline because it is an approved estimate for the project.

Moving beyond artifacts more typically identified and developed at the start of a project, there are a number of artifact types a project manager may want to think about developing over the course of a

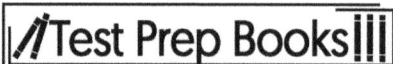

Domain II: Process

project. Logs are project artifacts used to record information about aspects of the project that may need to be updated continuously. Other common terms for logs include *registers, risk registers,* or *risk logs.* Specific kinds of logs that project managers may want to consider incorporating into their projects include assumption logs, which include all factors thought to be true for a certain project or aspect of a project, and a lessons learned register, which catalogs the knowledge gained on a project for the advancement of future projects. Like logs, hierarchy charts are usually updated over the course of a project, but whereas logs typically do not attempt to depict high-level information, hierarchy charts begin with high-level information. Then, as the project goes on and more information is gained about specific processes, the chart is filled in with lower levels of information. For example, a work breakdown structure (WBS) chart breaks down all the work to be carried out on a project hierarchically, starting with the most high-level conception of project work and increasing in specificity and detail as the project commences. Although contracts are certainly not as work intensive as logs or hierarchy charts, they can be thought of similarly because they may need to be drafted or signed at any point in a project.

Finally, there are the types of artifacts a project manager may primarily encounter toward the end of the project process. First, there are many different types of reports that may be written as different aspects of the project wrap-up. Reports usually present information on the summary level, with the intended audience being stakeholders perceived as interested in the project status. Particular examples of report artifacts that may be of interest to a project manager include quality reports, which summarize the findings of quality control activities, and risk reports, which summarize information regarding the level of project risk. In addition, visual data and information made be used alongside or independently from reports to help present raw data in a more digestible format. Visualization artifacts are often especially helpful in the decision-making process, and the kinds of visualization artifacts a project manager chooses to use will largely depend on the kind of data they are gathering and what they wish to represent. Any form of chart, graph, or diagram can be considered a visualization artifact by the project manager.

Validate that the Project Information Is Kept Up-to-Date and Accessible

Unfortunately, it is rarely sufficient for a project manager to simply worry about determining what type of project artifacts need to be gathered and how they should be managed. In addition, it is the project manager's responsibility to ensure that information contained within artifacts is accurate and kept up-to-date and that they are made accessible to the pertinent stakeholders. One of the most effective ways for project managers to ensure these details are effectively managed is through the use of version control. Version control, which is usually included as a function of most project management software, allows for project managers and other relevant personnel to track changes to project artifacts. There are numerous benefits to using version control, including allowing for easy consolidation of files and preventing unapproved versions of documents from being sent to the wrong stakeholder. Speaking of stakeholders, version control and other aspects of project management software can assist in the managing of stakeholder communication because different stakeholders may require access to different documents and even different versions of the same document.

Continually Assess the Effectiveness of the Management of the Project Artifacts

As with many other tasks and responsibilities of the project manager, it is not enough simply to set up the system by which project artifacts may be managed. In addition, project managers are responsible for ensuring that the system functions and continues to function over the entire course of the project. There are many different ways a complex system can fail, so it may not be helpful for the project manager to try to be overly proactive. Instead, the best way to ensure project artifacts are being effectively managed is often just to maintain an awareness of the process as a whole. For example, instead of trying to anticipate where errors may occur in the system, project managers may be better off recognizing system malfunctions and correcting errors where they occur. This process can also be made simpler through the use of project management software, which can automate processes and clarify confusion.

Task 13: Determine Appropriate Project Methodology & Practices

Effective project management relies on proven methodologies to organize and direct project work. The project manager, along with their team members and relevant stakeholders, must determine the appropriate methodology and development approach to follow for their particular project's needs and goals.

Assess Project Needs, Complexity, and Magnitude

The chosen development approach and affects many aspects of the project's execution, including its life cycle, schedule, and phases. Before the project manager can choose an appropriate approach, they must closely consider the project itself and the product, service, or result that it is aiming to produce.

Depending on the larger organization's industry, the project manager may first consider standards, regulations, and requirements that would impact the timeline of the project. Does the organization and industry allow for multiple releases of a product or result that can be subsequently tested and improved, or do they require that the project's scope encompass all necessary research and testing so that the product is complete when the project resolves?

Further, project managers should consider the complexity of the project and its tasks and the scale in a large organizational or industrial context. Does the project's final goal rely on several other smaller goals to be completed? Do other departments or organizations rely on the project's completion, or does the project depend on external sources to be completed?

These initial questions can help project managers and other stakeholders determine the actions that need to be included in the project plan and the correct approach for organizing them.

Recommend a Project Execution Strategy

When the project manager and their team determines the objectives and requirements of their project, they must then decide on an execution strategy for carrying them out.

In most cases, a project execution strategy will depend on the availability of funds and resources. Closely estimating and responsibly monitoring the expected costs and profitability of the project will help the project manager properly plan the project budget.

In the event that the project manager's team does not perform all the functions required for the project, they may need to contract another organization or individual to complete the tasks that they cannot. Project managers should choose an appropriate source to contract based on the amount of work needed, the scope of the work, and the risk level assessed and tolerated by their organization. In the event that work must be contracted, all information regarding the contracted work and the vendor will be included in project documentation and the vendor will be considered a project stakeholder.

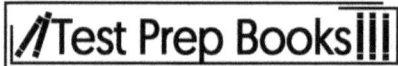

Recommend a Project Methodology or Approach

The project manager must choose a development approach that is appropriate for the project and its projected tasks. Predictive, adaptive, and hybrid approaches are the three most common.

A **predictive approach** is used when the project's requirements and objectives can be clearly defined at the beginning of the project. This approach helps the team reduce risk and resource waste, which makes it most appropriate for projects with high investments and high risk levels. This is also referred to as a "waterfall" approach.

An **adaptive approach** is used when the project's requirements and objectives are uncertain or likely to change throughout the project's duration. As with the predictive approach, the project's features are defined at the beginning of the project, but the adaptive approach allows for the details to be changed in response to feedback or unforeseen circumstances. Often, this approach breaks down the project into multiple iterations, or groups of project tasks, that allow for feedback and reorganization between each transition.

Hybrid approaches share qualities with both predictive and adaptive approaches. This type of approach is utilized when the project's deliverables can be divided as individual goals or be completed by other teams. Hybrid approaches are often either incremental or iterative. An **incremental approach** is useful for producing a product throughout a series of iterations, in which each iteration adds functionality. An **iterative approach** is useful for producing a product in an earlier iteration that could be considered usable before the end of the project.

Use Iterative, Incremental Practices Throughout the Project Life Cycle

After determining the best approach for the project at hand, the project manager must determine the best ways to manage the project's tasks. The first step of the learning management process is to identify the experiences from which lessons were learned that could offer guidance and insight in the future. The tools and techniques to identify and collect lessons learned are similar to those of the other areas of project planning used to identify needs, risks, issues, etc.

To solicit insight from the team members and stakeholders, the project manager should offer a public forum in which everyone involved can discuss the work performed to date and what they experienced. The forum might be a wiki on the company intranet, an online chat session, web meeting, or conference call. The method to engage the team to participate often depends on the company culture, the preferences or limitations of the stakeholders, and the enterprise environmental factors such as the availability of online tools and the distance between team members and stakeholders. Often, project managers and team members prefer to hold in-person sessions in which all the stakeholders and team members can brainstorm and learn from each other.

Regardless of the method used to engage team members, asking questions can help to identify what experiences should be included on the lessons learned register. These questions might arise based on the business needs of the project or the stakeholders, or they might include some of the following basic questions:

- What happened?
- What went well?
- What could have gone better?

- What challenges did they face?
- What shortcuts did they find?
- What was wasted?
- What was scarce?
- What lessons could help solve or avoid problems in the future?
- What lessons could help team members improve processes or activities in the future?
- Who was involved?
- Were any special circumstances involved?
- Did the people involved impact the work in positive or negative ways?
- Did the right stakeholders get involved at the right times to solve problems or lessen negative impacts?
- What could be done better next time?
- How should it be done?

Some of the tools and techniques to facilitate the success of lessons learned sessions include providing a template for team members to share their thoughts ahead of time so important information isn't missed in the session or sending a survey to team members to record and compare specific information the project manager or stakeholders want to collect. Organizing lessons learned into categories can help to keep the sessions focused and simplified. Depending on the nature of the project or organization, some of these categories might include the following:

- Processes
- Resources
- Designs
- Materials
- Requirements
- Communication
- Technical
- Quality
- Third parties
- Testing
- Record Lessons Learned

For the project manager, team members, and future project teams to benefit from the lessons learned in the past, the lessons identified in the previous step must be recorded and maintained. As previously mentioned, these lessons are recorded on the lessons learned register, in the case of a single document, or entered into and maintained in the lessons learned repository, in the case of a database.

Depending on the expectations of leadership or stakeholders, the lessons learned from each session are provided to leadership in a brief summary report of the strengths and weaknesses of the project, major gains and serious setbacks, issues and proposed solutions, explanations of special circumstances or persistent concerns, or other information important to the project or stakeholders.

To make the most of the lessons learned, the register should be analyzed regularly to ensure it is useful to the team and future teams. This analysis includes prioritizing and organizing lessons so they can be found by the people who need them when they need them, checking that the information is still relevant and accurate, determining whether information is missing or duplicated, etc. The register should be revised and updated to eliminate any gaps, duplicates, discrepancies, inaccuracies, or outdated entries.

The lessons learned register should be stored in a repository that other team members and project managers can easily access and that the contributors can update as needed. The risk register might be a single spreadsheet organized by category and stored on a file sharing site, a simple database, a physical document library, an addition to PMIS software with other project documents and assets, or a robust repository on an online knowledge management system.

However the lessons learned are stored, the team must be able to retrieve them. If team members are unable to access and reuse the lessons learned, the previous steps might as well not have been performed at all. Though lessons learned can be helpful to provide progress reports or project summaries to stakeholders or leadership, the primary purpose of the lessons learned is to provide wisdom and support for project managers planning a project and team members executing the project.

The more organized, relevant, and complete the lessons learned repository, the easier it is to retrieve and use them. The most effective methods to store lessons learned to ensure team members can find what they need when they need it include repositories that use keywords and standardized formats to enable search.

To ensure the recording, storing, and retrieving steps of the process are as efficient as possible, evaluate the repository regularly. The project manager should evaluate the way information is stored, organized, structured, and categorized in the repository, and the repository itself, whether it is a knowledge management system, a shared file, word of mouth, or a handful of SMEs.

The questions asked to identify lessons learned as well as lean and efficient principles and data analysis can be applied to the learning management process to determine how the steps in the process can be more effective, more efficient, and more beneficial to the project and future projects.

Like any process or management tool, lesson management can be improved to make the process more efficient and effective, less time consuming, and more beneficial to the stakeholders. In this step, project managers seek to improve lesson management by transforming the backwards-facing lessons learned into a proactive tool through which team members and stakeholders can foresee problems, issues, setbacks, and opportunities before they happen.

Task 14: Establish Project Governance Structure

Determine Appropriate Governance for a Project

Governance refers to the organizational or structural arrangements designed to influence organizational members' behaviors. These arrangements are present at all levels of an organization and require both careful consideration of individuals, roles, and policies, as well as providing feedback and oversight. Governance should be distinguishable from management; whereas management should tackle the question of how work on the project is completed, governance should tackle the question of what work should be completed on the project. It is recommended that all project managers incorporate organizational project management (OPM) strategies into their governance structure. OPM provides guidelines for the aligning of portfolio, program, and project management practices with the existing objectives and strategies of the organization. It is important to clarify that the OPM governance framework is only part of the overall OPM implementation strategy, and any project manager looking to incorporate OPM strategies into their governance structures should ensure that they are adhering to all aspects of the OPM framework.

Focusing specifically on project governance, it may be helpful first to define what project governance is, given what is known about project management and governance strategies. One way to define project governance is that it consists of both the framework and specific processes used to direct project management activities to create a unique product or result while meeting organizational standards and goals. Requirements for proper project governance should be weighed in light of the project environment and the larger organizational environment, with the goal of integrating these two distinct environments. In order to properly consider and tailor governance policies and expectations for the organization in question, it may first be helpful to contemplate who the representatives of these different environments are. Clearly, the project environment is best represented by the project manager, but who best represents the organizational interests may be more variable. For this reason, it is often best for a project governing body to be established, with members generally consisting of the upper management of the organization, project sponsors, and other key stakeholders.

Once a project framework has been established, with the project manager working with and being responsible to the project governing body, project managers can begin the vital work of tailoring the project governance structure to the organizational and project environment. In doing so, there are several specific considerations project managers may want to take into account. The first, and perhaps most obvious, is how exactly the governing body should be involved in the project. As opposed to the project manager, who handles the management of the project, the project governing body is generally responsible for the decision-making process as well as providing oversight to the project. However, there are other ways beyond being involved in decision making for the project governing body to assist the project process. The governing body, as a result of their position in the organization and the industry, may often possess useful organizational or functional expertise, which they can provide for the project manager and project team. In addition, it is often helpful and essential for organizational change to occur as a result of the project, either as a result of the project's outcomes or so that progress may be more effective. In these cases, it is another responsibility of the governing body to support and promote organizational change.

Define Escalation Paths and Thresholds

As previously stated, the role of the project manager can best be summarized as managing the project process, whereas the project governing body is responsible for decision making. This type of arrangement, although effective, does require some further planning. As an example, given their varying levels of direct involvement in the project, there is going to be a significant knowledge gap between the project manager and the governing body, specifically as it relates to the day-to-day work of the project. Therefore, it is ultimately up to the project manager to know what to bring in front of the governing body and when—an arrangement that can cause difficulties for both parties if not handled properly. In order to clarify and streamline this process, it is common practice for project managers to establish so-called escalation paths. The ultimate goal of any escalation path is to shorten the amount of time between a decision needing to be made and that decision reaching the appropriate individual or group.

It is best practice for project managers to at least begin the establishment of escalation paths early in the planning stages of the project. The first step any project managers should take is simply to establish the categories of decision making for which escalation paths are required. These categories can include but are not limited to finance, staffing, tools, and technical features. In all of these categories, notably there is a gap between the personnel and the environment in which these categories of decision first arise—usually during the project process—and the individuals or groups ultimately responsible for making those decisions. Noticing this gap may be another way for a project manager to decide what categories of decision making need to have escalation paths.

Once the project manager feels satisfied that they have determined all the potential categories of decision making, the next step in creating escalation paths is to determine the starting point. It may be helpful for the project manager to think of this step as answering the following question: What is the source of problems that need an escalation path to be resolved? Almost always, the answer is found at the lower levels of the organization. This is for two reasons. First, individuals at this level are more likely than higher-level individuals to be involved in the functional work of the project in which most questions arise. Second, due to their position as lower-level members of the organization, they do not always possess the expertise or authority necessary to effectively make a decision like this, creating the environment for a breakdown in the decision-making process. Because these individuals are not part of the decision-making process, it may also be helpful to streamline the process further by having the project manager—in accordance with the project governing body—select certain thresholds that will serve as an automatic indication that this information should be brought up to individuals responsible for decision making. As an example, a project manager may set an escalation threshold on how much over budget a particular phase of a project can be before an escalation path is triggered or may do the same if the project is too far behind schedule.

After a project manager has successfully identified the starting point, it is then up to them to determine the appropriate ending point. Naturally, this will most likely be either an individual in the upper management of an organization or an individual with a particular expertise. As stated earlier, it is essential for the project manager to start the process of defining escalation paths as early as possible, and this is especially true when it comes to identifying these individuals. Without their identification, no decisions can appropriately be made. The final step for the project manager is to review the escalation plans with the project governing body. Although it is ultimately up to them to either approve or reject escalation paths, the project manager should also ensure that there is buy-in at all levels of the project and organization.

Task 15: Manage Project Issues

Inconsistencies between what occurs during the course of a project and what was planned can create issues in a project. Issues occur frequently throughout a project lifecycle. To keep track of these issues, the project manager must maintain the project *issue log,* the record of all the issues that have arisen during the work of the project. The issue log includes information such as the nature and description of the issue; the cause, if known, of the issue; the owner assigned to resolve or oversee the resolution of the issue; and how the issue should be resolved.

The project manager must understand how to review and update the issue log when new issues arise, when past issues are resolved, or when current issues have changed.

Recognize When a Risk Becomes an Issue

Issues and risks share similar characteristics, and the methods used to identify them, measure their impact, and mitigate or resolve them are often the same. Both issues and risks represent the potential for negative impacts to all areas of the project, such as inconsistencies in the project plans, delays to the schedules, increases in cost, failures within processes, injuries to workers, or defects in the deliverables. They differ in several ways.

Issue management is usually reactive. Issues often take the form of *risk events*, discrete events that cause a negative impact. These can be conflicts, problems, gaps, inconsistencies, delays, lost funds, etc. Issues are typically unexpected, and when they are identified, it is because they are already negatively impacting the problem and require an immediate resolution. Often, the team has not seen the issue before and has no predetermined strategy or solution. The team member responsible for addressing the issue may be obliged to come up with a creative solution if they cannot find a possible solution in the *lessons learned repository*, the organization's policies and procedures, or from experts with experience solving similar issues.

Risk management is usually proactive. Risks represent the potential for exposure to negative impact, rather than an existing condition or occurrence. If the organization is exposed to a risk, an issue may arise, but risks do not necessarily result in a negative impact. Risks may also represent a benefit to the organization if the potential for gain is greater than the potential for negative impact. When risks are identified, the project manager and team members can plan a response strategy to prevent, transfer, or mitigate the negative impact.

For example, if a worker falls ill and must take a week off work, this is an issue. If potential exists for workers to be injured due to inherently hazardous work conditions, this is a risk.

Attack the Issue with the Optimal Action to Achieve Project Success

The issue log, also called an *issue register,* is a component of the Communications Management process. It's used as a tool to communicate issues identified by team members, project managers, or the customer to the appropriate stakeholders, as well as to assign issues to the team members responsible for addressing each issue and track issues until they are neutralized or resolved.

The issue log can help the project manager manage stakeholder expectations, ensure transparency in processes, and prevent greater risk from lack of reporting in the event of a serious exposure incident.

Updating the issue log

The issue log is often maintained as a spreadsheet, a database, or within a project or issue management software. Whatever tool is used to create and maintain the log, it should be accessible to stakeholders and relevant team members, and a method to communicate changes to the log should be included in the Communication Management Plan.

Components of the Issue Log

Though the components of the issue log may change depending on the requirements of the organization or the project, the following information is typically required:

ID: Name, number, or identifier of the issue. This may be a ticket number in case the issue log is maintained in a ticketing system.

Type: Category of the issue as defined in the project management documentation. This might be in the risk register, the Communication Management Plan, in a separate glossary or database of terms, or the issue log itself, depending on the assets of the organization (ex. content management systems). Types of issues might include technical, resource, vendor, environmental, hazard, etc., depending on issues typical to the industry or organization.

Reported by: Name of the team member, stakeholder, customer, etc. who identified and raised the issue.

Reported date: Date the issue was reported or added to the log, depending on the policies of the organization.

Description: Explanation of the issue including all relevant information such as the areas of the project it is impacting or is expected to impact if it is not resolved.

Priority: Criticality of the issue based on its impact or nature. This is often expressed as critical, high, medium, or low, or as numeric values, depending on the preferences of the organization.

Owner/Assigned to: Name of the individual or group responsible for addressing the issue by resolving it or assigning it to another team member.

Date of target resolution: Date the issue is required or expected to be resolved.

Status: Progress of the issue to date. This can include labels such as open, claimed, reassigned, in progress, closed, etc., depending on the preferences of the organization.

Disposition: Description of the solution that was used to resolve the issue, description of circumstances that neutralized the issue, explanation of why the issue was not resolved, etc.

When changes are made to any of these components, the project manager should update the issue log.

Corrective Action

As issues represent a present impact on the project, corrective action should be taken quickly to resolve the issue and realign the work with the project goals.

Collaborate with Relevant Stakeholders on the Approach to Resolve the Issues

The techniques to determine whether the project manager must take corrective action to resolve the issue include the following:

- Determine whether the issue is temporary, is related to timing, will resolve itself, or is permanent and cannot be resolved
- Determine whether the issue will delay milestones critical to the success of the project
- Determine whether the issue can be resolved by performing alternative activities to the activities the issue has caused to be delayed or blocked
- Determine whether sufficient contingency reserves can offset the loss of time or money caused by the issue
- Determine whether the issue will remain until corrective action is taken

If the project manager is unable to discover an alternative to corrective action, they must initiate the corrective action through a change request. When this occurs, the issue log should be updated to indicate when the request is made, when the solution is in progress, and when the issue is resolved.

Task 16: Ensure Knowledge Transfer for Project Continuity

Discuss Project Responsibilities Within the Team

As with any other process, the first step to ensuring an effective transfer of knowledge for any project is for the project manager to define what is meant by *knowledge*. Generally, it can be helpful for project managers to separate and consider the two kinds of knowledge, specifically *explicit* and *tacit* knowledge. Explicit knowledge—concepts or ideas that can be easily represented by words, data, or pictures—is usually the simpler of the two forms of knowledge to recognize and transfer to others, whereas tacit knowledge—concepts or ideas that are more personal, such as insights and experiences—is much more difficult for individuals to recognize and share. Despite the difficulties inherent in both collecting and transmitting tacit knowledge, there are also benefits that tacit knowledge provides that explicit knowledge does not. One benefit is that tacit knowledge can provide the context that explicit knowledge often lacks. Therefore, it is essential for the project manager to be aware of these differences and explore avenues to ensure that knowledge of both kinds is being gathered and shared. It is also essential that, from the earliest stages of the project, the project manager and other project team members begin the discussion of who is responsible for which aspect of knowledge transfer. One project artifact that may be helpful in delineating these responsibilities is an RACI matrix, which lists the responsibilities or positions of project members in relation to all project deliverables. The acronym RACI provides the four components/roles included in the matrix—which parties are Responsible, Accountable, Consulted, or Informed on the status of a project deliverable.

Outline Expectations for Working Environment

In terms of changes that can be made to a project to ensure that proper knowledge transfer occurs, perhaps the single most important change is the establishment of an atmosphere of trust (if one is not already present in the organization). Regardless of any technique used or practice implemented, knowledge will not be properly transferred on any project if members do not trust the project environment enough to share their knowledge. This is especially the case for tacit knowledge because it can really only be communicated by the individual who possesses it, and this individual cannot be forced to share the knowledge if they feel uncomfortable. Therefore, establishing a trusting working environment in which no one is blamed or shamed for speaking up is vital to ensuring that the transfer of knowledge is as unrestricted as possible. Project managers should therefore first and foremost be exemplars of the practices that lead to a trusting work environment—namely, listening to all members of a team and ensuring that they all have a place to voice their knowledge.

Confirm Approach for Knowledge Transfers

Once this environment has been created, a project manager can much more easily think about and manage the actual tools and techniques that go into the process of knowledge management. Here, it can be helpful to try and categorize the kind of knowledge that is being brought to a project. Doing so can also help clarify the goals of the knowledge management process. In general, knowledge used in a project will either come from some preexisting source or be created over the course and as a result of the project. By considering the sources of knowledge for their project, project managers can naturally see why it is the goal of any knowledge management process to contribute not only to the current project at hand but to all subsequent projects and to organizational learning and knowledge in general. In doing so, they allow for the transfer and continuity of knowledge to flow not just within their own project but throughout the larger organization and into future projects.

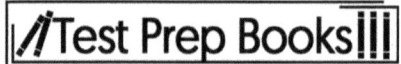

Particular preexisting sources of knowledge that are commonly used by project managers in knowledge management systems include any project document, such as a lessons learned register from previous projects and a stakeholder register. Experts in the project area of interest or in knowledge management in general can also be identified, with the tool of *expert judgment* allowing for the inclusion of tacit knowledge. In addition, techniques such as group workshops or focus groups can allow for the creation of new knowledge, which is created by allowing people to connect and work together. Finally, information management tools can be used to gather more explicit knowledge, with examples ranging from the aforementioned lessons learned register to simple web searches. At the end of the project, the project manager should ensure that the knowledge gained and used is properly recorded, whether through the lessons learned register or the creation of an entirely new process asset.

Task 17: Plan and Manage Project/Phase Closure or Transitions

Determine Criteria to Successfully Close the Project or Phase

As with many aspects of the project management process, it is essential that, in the earliest stages of the project, the project manager defines the criteria that will serve as the signal to close a phase or transition from one phase to another or to close the project. These criteria are also referred to as *deliverables* and can be defined as any unique or verifiable result or product that is required to successfully close a project or phase. The latter part of that definition is crucial to understand. Deliverables are identified to help actualize the stated goals of the project or that phase of the project. In general, *project life cycles* consist of a series of *project phases,* which consist of *project activities* that have the completion of a deliverable as their end goal. In this way, deliverables are critical to the project life cycle, and a clean and thorough investigation and determination of what should be considered a project's deliverables should be one of the first steps any project manager takes in regard to the project life cycle and how the project will proceed. Specific factors they may want to consider include the timing and frequency of project deliverables (referred to as *cadence*); the developmental approach (whether the means are predictive, adaptive, or a hybrid of the two); and factors regarding the product and the organization.

Validate Readiness for Transition

Although the deliverables identification process will certainly alleviate many of the issues a project manager may encounter with planning and managing project close and/or phase transitions, it is also important for them to understand that simply establishing deliverables is only half the battle. Depending on a variety of factors, there may be additional steps a project manager and their team may need to take to ensure project deliverables are sufficient for the project to either transition or begin the process of closure. These factors can range from matters concerning the deliverables or aspects inherent to the project or even the organization. For example, as previously discussed, depending on the deliverable selected, there may be a number of different delivery cadences. An organization seeking to rework a particular process may only have a single deliverable toward the end of the project, whereas clinical trials often have multiple deliveries as different trials commence and finish. In some cases, more longtime delivery cadences may be needed, and deliveries can also be made continuously in markets and situations in which this kind of response is necessary. In considering project variables, it may be important for project managers to take into account the needs and involvement of stakeholders as well as constraints that may or may not exist on scheduling and funding. Contemplating organizational variables may entail looking at aspects of organizational structure, culture, capability, and size. In order to simplify the process of considering all these distinctive variables, many project managers institute phase gate reviews (sometimes called a *stage gate*), which serve to check that the desired criteria that signal the project to move to the next phase have been reached.

Conclude Activities to Close Out the Project or Phase

Once criteria for project closure and/or phase transition have been successfully determined and it has been properly validated that the criteria have been successfully met, the process of actually closing out the project/phase can begin. As with almost every other phase of a project, there are many different factors that may impact how project/phase closure proceeds. Therefore, instead of considering all the specific steps a project manager may or may not take, it may be helpful to reflect on the modes in which these activities occur. To put that another way: Who/what are the likely targets of these steps? Taken this way, there are three general categories that can be defined, and they are nearly identical to the factors listed previously. First, there are aspects specific to the project that need to be updated. Most specifically, a project manager should ensure that a lessons learned register is updated with pertinent information at the end of any project so that knowledge acquired on the project may contribute to future projects. Agile projects may instead use a retrospective, conducted during a meeting of the project team. In addition, the organization may acquire these assets as a final report and the benefits that stem from having their organizational processes updated as a result of the project. Final reports summarize overall project performance, including information about the scope, quality, and cost of the project. Depending on the scope of the project, there may have also been a need for procurement—the acquiring or purchasing of resources from outside the project group or organization—and project managers should ensure that all matters related to procurement are settled. Finally, there are the direct benefits of the deliverables, which can perhaps best be seen (where applicable) in the experience of the customers and other stakeholders. After all, there is certainly no better way to judge the effectiveness of a project than by looking at how it affects those for which it was created.

Practice Quiz

1. In project management, what is meant by the term *procurement*?
   a. Procurement refers to any process in which products, services, or results are being acquired or purchased from somewhere other than the project team or organization.
   b. Procurement refers to any process in which physical resources are acquired or purchased.
   c. Procurement refers to the stage of the project life cycle in which the project deliverable is first made available to the desired audience.
   d. Procurement refers to the stage of the project life cycle in which the project deliverable or a function or part of the project deliverable is first made available for internal testing.

2. Which of the following is a benefit of a lessons learned register?
   a. Lessons learned registers often have valuable tips that can save precious time, money, and resources.
   b. Lessons learned registers often contain estimates made by previous project teams, which can improve the current team's ability to make accurate estimations.
   c. Lessons learned registers often contain tacit knowledge, which is not possible to attain in many other forms of data collection.
   d. All of the above are benefits of a lessons learned register.

3. Which of the following project management tools would be MOST helpful in assessing and managing risk?
   a. Root cause analysis via a fishbone diagram
   b. Lessons learned document
   c. Stakeholder analysis
   d. Probability and impact matrix

4. Which of the following is NOT true regarding version control systems?
   a. Most project management systems contain some form of version control.
   b. When a file is changed, the file is automatically saved and given a new version number.
   c. Version control allows project managers to select which parts of a document are visible to which stakeholders, allowing multiple different versions of a document to be sent at once.
   d. Any changes made to a document are identified with the name of the user who made the change as well as a time stamp.

5. A social media app releases a new update on the first of every month. What kind of delivery cadence is this?
   a. Single delivery
   b. Multiple deliveries
   c. Periodic deliveries
   d. Continuous delivery

See answers on the next page.

Answer Explanations

1. A: *Procurement* specifically refers to any situation or process in which a vendor or supplier outside of the project group or organization is being used.

2. D: Lessons learned registers are used to document and preserve knowledge gained during the project process. They are useful for many reasons: They can contain cost-saving tips; they include the calculations and estimations made by previous project teams; and team member stories can provide valuable tacit knowledge.

3. D: A probability and impact matrix is a table that combines both risk probability (the chance that the issue occurs) and risk impact (the severity of the consequences of the issue occurring) for both project threats and opportunities. The other three answer choices, although all certainly helpful in identifying potential risks, do not play as much of a role in the active assessment and management of risks.

4. C: Version control systems record and track changes to a file and can be used to retrieve previous versions and to see who made changes to a document and when those changes were made. Because version control is simply a storage system, there is no functionality added that allows it to be used in sending multiple versions of the file to stakeholders at once.

5. C: Delivery cadence refers to how project deliverables are released over a project life cycle. Deliverables that are released on a fixed schedule are referred to as periodic deliveries.

Domain III: Business Environment

Task 1: Plan and Manage Project Compliance

Compliance means defining the company's goals and ensuring that projects are meeting these goals. Project compliance means that whatever work is being done on a project meets the company's standards. These standards may include the company's own guidelines as well as legal standards. Compliance can act as a form of quality control and as a measure of how effectively the company is operating. Project managers work with other members of the team to ensure that aspects like budget, time management, and products are consistently meeting targets. This involves regular review of the work teams are doing and engagement with the company to observe how it handles projects.

Confirm Project Compliance Requirements

Project compliance requirements are usually first discussed during planning. This discussion should clearly lay out the expectations that need to be met as the project progresses. It is in the company's best interest to meet these requirements because there may be consequences, such as fines and legal action, for not following compliance rules. Companies must have a process in place to handle various issues that may have specific requirements such as security, health and safety, and regulatory compliance. These practices should be documented and compared with industry standards to determine whether or not the requirements are sufficient.

Companies can test their processes in these categories by asking the following questions.

Security: How do we handle sensitive data? How will we ensure that our data is kept safe and confidential? How will we handle a data breach?

Health and safety: What are we doing to ensure a safe working environment? How do we handle concerns over safety?

Regulatory compliance: How are we meeting industry standards? How are we complying with applicable laws and regulations?

A compliance framework can help companies meet these requirements. This framework is a set of guidelines that summarizes and clarifies all the requirements a company needs to meet. Some examples of compliance frameworks are the Health Insurance Portability and Accountability Act (HIPAA) and the Federal Risk and Authorization Management Program (FedRAMP). HIPAA focuses on protecting patient data, while FedRAMP is concerned with data security for cloud-based services.

Classify Compliance Categories

Compliance is broken down into categories to help with organization and structure. These categories depend on the industry that a company works in, but general categories include health and safety, diversity, ethics, data security, environmental risk, and social responsibility.

Health and safety: This deals with worker safety and handling workplace injuries.

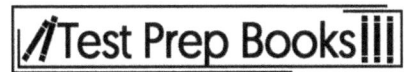

Domain III: Business Environment

Diversity: It is increasingly important to have a diverse team full of different opinions and viewpoints. This category challenges companies to scrutinize their hiring practices and consider how to approach and appeal to new diverse team members.

Ethics: Companies must know how to conduct business ethically and fairly. Ethics compliance creates a professional and trusting working environment.

Data security: Since many companies handle sensitive information like customer demographics, this category trains them to address security issues and understand how to handle breaches.

Environmental risk: A company should also assess the effects of its work on the environment. Some ways to create products are faster or more efficient but cause pollution or waste. Companies must balance productivity with its potentially harmful effects on the environment.

Social responsibility: Companies are not only working for themselves but also for others. Companies should use their vast resources to benefit their community and the world in general.

Determine Potential Threats to Compliance

Compliance is not an easy task, and numerous roadblocks can make it difficult to meet all of the requirements. Dedicated teams within the company should work to minimize the damage of threats against company compliance. Three of the most common threats are ignorance, changes in regulatory laws, and errors in product testing.

Ignorance: Companies should responsibly research compliance requirements for their company and work during the planning phase of a project. This is especially true when working with compliance in other parts of the world. For example, compliance laws in the United States may differ from compliance laws in Europe and Asia. Lack of awareness can jeopardize a company's work.

Changes in regulatory laws: new laws that change regulatory requirements force companies to adapt to them. Something that was acceptable before may not meet the new requirements. A company's corporate counsel plays a pivotal role in monitoring changes to compliance laws. The legal team will conduct research into existing laws and advise the company on its best course of action. Companies must adjust their products and practices to ensure that they are in compliance with new laws. One example of a regulatory requirement that needs to be assessed for changes concerns monitoring laws, which give employers permission to monitor their employees' workplace activities.

Errors in product testing: False data obtained from product testing is dangerous because the company may believe it are in compliance when in actuality it is not. Equipment may fail or be incorrectly calibrated, or an employee may miss an. Every phase in product testing needs to be checked for potential errors.

Use Methods to Support Compliance

Depending on the project management style, there are a few ways to support the team's compliance. In a traditional work environment, compliance is measured through tools like deliverables status and risk reports. In an Agile environment, teams can use tools like product roadmaps and Kanban boards to document compliance. Product roadmaps and Kanban boards work similarly because they both present an overall plan of how the project will proceed. In addition to using these tools, companies should conduct regular audits and product tests to analyze the effectiveness of their practices.

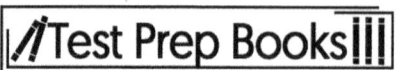

Analyze the Consequences of Noncompliance

Consequences for noncompliance range from minor to severe. The most obvious result is financial penalties for breaking the rules, but punishment can also mean damage to reputation and status or the loss of certifications necessary to continue working in an industry.

Companies should create a detailed plan that outlines various company operations to analyze where compliance is needed. The quality management plan is one tool that specifies necessary quality objectives. Details in the plan include the level of quality the company is looking for, quality standards that will be used, individual responsibilities, and a list of product deliverables.

Determine Necessary Approach and Action to Address Compliance Needs

Being organized and proactive is the key to ensuring company compliance. In addition to the quality management plan, there are several steps a company can take to remain organized and move forward with addressing compliance. First, create a framework that lists compliance obligations, including risk management and legal requirements. Next, perform a risk assessment that analyzes the risks in each phase of project development and the probability that these risks would become an issue. After this, companies can incorporate practices that ensure they are meeting requirements and adjust those practices as needed. Throughout the process, companies should document their findings and regularly report on the company's compliance status. This documentation is especially useful for external and internal audits.

Measure the Extent to Which the Project is in Compliance

Compliance is a team effort. Companies can measure to what extent the project is in compliance by following a series of steps. After researching compliance requirements, companies assess the quality of their practices and identify flaws and places for improvement in project development. External and internal audits, as well as regular project reviews, can verify these practices. Finally, companies confirm their compliance and take action if it is not met.

Task 2: Evaluate and Deliver Project Benefits and Value

Project managers must conduct a benefits analysis with relevant stakeholders to validate project alignment with organizational strategy and expected business value.

Investigate that Benefits Are Identified

A project benefits analysis is a technique used to evaluate and compare the project's cost with the dollar value of expected benefits the project will produce. The benefits analysis is conducted during the initiation phase and the results determine whether a project should move forward. If the project quantifiable benefits outweigh the project cost, more than likely the project will be approved and is viewed as a good investment for the organization. Otherwise, if the project cost outweighs the expected quantifiable benefits, it is likely the project will not be approved.

Document Agreement on Ownership for Ongoing Benefits Realization

Business performance is affected by a variety of changes in the organization's market. For this reason, many organizations are seeking better ways to demonstrate their value and contribution to benefits realization.

Project managers can express their commitment to business performance by communicating with leaders and stakeholders not only about current tasks, but also about strategies for taking on better and more profitable projects. In the same vein, project managers can also track their teams' resource consumption to minimize waste and phase out processes that do not meet evolving efficiency and productivity standards.

In addition to these management tasks, project managers can also work on business performance by changing their interactions with team members and stakeholders. Taking part in recruitment processes and making an effort to retain talent can help build and develop better teams with better outcomes.

Verify Measurement System is in Place to Track Benefits

The project manager is responsible for conducting the analysis and the results conclude whether the project is worth the investment to produce or if it makes more sense to buy the product or service.

Below are the steps the project manager will use take to conduct the benefits analysis:

- Identify costs – Identify and quantify all costs associated with the planned project. Both monetary and non- monetary costs need to be taken into consideration.

    - Monetary – Costs associated with the implementation of the project and throughout the project life. Examples: Licenses, materials, start-up fees, subscription fees, wages or salary etc.

    - Non-monetary – Costs that are likely to be absorbed throughout the project life cycle. Examples: Time and effort, costs incorporated with research, insurance, or bank loans etc.

- Identify benefits – Identifying the expected benefits on a project is more of a forecasted cost determination. The benefit is determined by weighing out future value of the project once it has been completed.

- Identify benefit to cost ratio – Once the costs have been identified for the project and a cost has been assigned to each benefit, the following calculation can be performed from the total benefit of the project and the total cost of the project which will determine the benefit to cost ratio:

$$\frac{\text{Benefit}}{\text{Cost}} = \text{Ratio}$$

Example of Benefit Cost Analysis:

Project ABC will charge $100, 000 (cost) and generate $150,000 in value (benefit).

$$\frac{150{,}000}{100{,}000} = 1.5$$

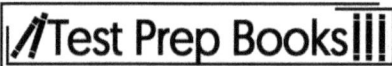

Domain III: Business Environment

*This project will be **approved** by the organization because the benefits outweigh the cost it takes to produce.

Project XYZ will charge $150,000 (cost) and generate $100,000 in value (benefit).

$$\frac{100,000}{150,000} = .66$$

*This project will be **rejected** by the organization because the benefits outweigh the cost it takes to produce

Organizations may also perform the following advanced calculations to determine the value of a project. These calculations determine profit over a specific period of time.

Return on investment (ROI) measures the return on the cost invested. Below is the formula used to calculate ROI.

$$\frac{\text{Net Profit}}{\text{Investment}} \times 100 = \text{ROI}$$

Example: Project DEF will charge $100, 000 (cost) and generate $150,000 in value (benefit).

$$\text{Net profit} = \$150,000 \text{ (benefit)} - \$100,000 \text{ (Cost)}$$

$$\frac{\$50,000 \text{ (net profit)}}{\$100,000 \text{ (cost)}} = 0.5$$

$$0.5 \times 100 = 50\%$$

The ROI for this investment is 50%, which means that the investor made their initial investment back plus 50% of that investment.

Present Value (PV) formula tells you the value of future cash flows. In other words, what is the current worth of a future sum of money. Organizations base project approvals by using this calculation in terms of whether the investment today will be worth more in years to come. Below is the formula used to calculate PV.

$$PV = \frac{FV}{(1+i)^n}$$

PV = present value

FV = future value

i = interest rate or internal discount per the time measure being used (such as an interest rate for money received in a certain number of months)

n = number of time period from today (based in the same time measure used in determining i)

Example: Project GHI invoices a client $1,000 now and the client wants to wait three years and pay a $300 late fee for a total of $1,300. We can use the present value calculation to determine if this is a good deal or not. For this example, the organizations cost of capital is 15% (.15).

$$PV = \frac{1{,}300}{(1 + .15)^3}$$

$$PV = \frac{1300}{(1.15)^3}$$

$$PV = \frac{1300}{1.52}$$

$$PV = \$855.26$$

Although you receive an extra $300 later, $144.74 is lost in present value under the proposed deal. It is not worth waiting given the current rate of return.

Net present value (NPV) measures the difference between the cash inflows and outflows over a period of time.

This calculation is used to compare revenues to cost in arriving at the value of a project.

NPV = PV benefits− PV investments (both over the flow of time)

Example: Let's consider a case where an organization can purchase an already developed product from Company A for $17,000 with some cutover support costs charged upfront.

Company B is proposing they can develop the product from scratch and is willing to accept equal payments over the life of the project totaling $18,000.

Interest Rate or cost of capital is 1.5 percent each month.

Company B PV	$ 17,393
Company A PV	$ (16,567)
NPV	$ 826

The calculation shows that spreading out the payments does not offset the higher price of Company B and by selecting **Company A the NPV is $826.** The smarter choice for the project is to buy the already developed product and not develop in house. NPV allows for the time value in money.

Evaluate Delivery Options to Demonstrate Value

Evaluating the value of a project can be achieved by comparing the planned benefits delivery to the actual benefits deliver. In some cases, this information can ensure the continuation of a project by demonstrating that the project is on track to produce the value that it promised. In other cases, this measurement can help organizations cancel projects that are not profitable.

A related measure is the calculated return on investment, or ROI. This value reports the financial return in relation to the project's cost. ROI is usually calculated at the beginning of the project to help the organization decide whether or not they want to accept it, but it can also be reevaluated at different points in the project's life cycle to help the organization determine if they want to continue the project.

Appraise Stakeholders of Value Gain Process

One way to appraise stakeholders' input on the value gain process is by measuring their satisfaction. Determining how likely stakeholders are to recommend the organization's products or services, tracking responses to project updates, and measuring turnover are methods that can provide observable and trackable metrics on stakeholder satisfaction.

Task 3: Evaluate and Address External Business Environment Changes for Impact on Scope

A business environment refers to all external and internal factors that affect a business. Internal factors are those that the business controls and that have an effect on its performance, such as company policy, culture, and business practices. External factors are outside of a business's control, and include market performance, competition, and customers. Any changes to a business environment can either help or hinder its success. It is the business's responsibility to adapt to changes and proceed with its operations.

Survey Changes to External Business Environment

Changes to the external business environment come from outside the organization. These include changes to regulations, technology, geopolitics, and the market. Project managers should keep these factors in mind when leading their projects. They need to understand these changes and find opportunities within them to help their team develop.

Regulations: Similar to compliance, regulations dictate what a company can or cannot do. Changes to regulations may mean overhauling company policies and practices to adhere to these new regulations.

Technology: New technology is especially important to the external business environment. This includes new software, communication tools, and services. Innovation creates more opportunities for success because there is a new way to approach projects and business. Companies should embrace new technology and provide training to employees, so they are prepared to use the new technology efficiently.

Geopolitical: Companies work within the politics of their location and should navigate the political system to ensure that they are following the law. Geopolitical changes can mean new policies regarding the economy, labor, and the environment.

Market: Market shifts and customer demand affect the kind of products companies develop. The market can be volatile, so companies need to monitor market changes and plan their business strategy accordingly.

Assess and Prioritize Impact on Project Scope/Backlog

Although many external factors affect how companies operate their business, some factors play a larger role than others. For example, perhaps there is a new law restricting the materials available for a project, or new software is available that is expensive but efficient. Companies need a way to prioritize which external factors to address to analyze how they will affect projects.

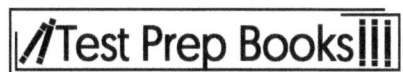

Domain III: Business Environment

Project scope is a list of tasks and goals that teams need to accomplish before the project is successfully finished. It provides a comprehensive overview of how the entire project will proceed. The project backlog is similar to the scope but is more concerned with finishing a list of tasks within a certain time period. The backlog is especially important for Agile teams. In an Agile environment, tasks and deliverables are listed and ranked according to priority. The product owner, a member of the Agile team, determines which tasks are most important based on customer and stakeholder needs. This helps the team know which areas to focus on for maximum efficiency.

One of the best ways companies can assess and prioritize external factors is to use change control boards. Change control boards handle all aspects of the project regarding change, such as reviewing and recommending changes to teams. For example, suggestions are given to the board to review, and the board then determines the scope and impact of these changes on the project. From there, project managers can compare these changes to the project's tolerance levels. Tolerance levels describe a project's ability to incorporate change before requiring approval. For example, project managers can set a limit on the acceptable amount of time that a project can run late. If this limit exceeds acceptable standards, upper management must be contacted for approval.

Recommend Options for Scope/Backlog Changes

Changes regarding aspects like schedule and budget should be made with careful consideration and collaboration. For example, project costs can change during the lifetime of the project. In more traditional work settings, change control boards are responsible for evaluating suggested changes and relaying their suggestions to the project manager. If the project manager accepts these changes, they adjust the project's scope and list of deliverables and explain the changes to the team in a meeting.

In Agile environments, product owners handle schedule and budget changes and make any adjustments to the project roadmap. The roadmap is a timeline of deliverables and an overview of how a product will change over time.

Reviewing External Business Environment for Impacts on Project Scope/Backlog

Companies should proactively monitor changes, both good and bad, that can affect their projects. For example, if the economy is undergoing a recession, companies need to have a plan put in place to maintain operations, or there could be changes in the political landscape, like new trade restrictions against a country, which also need to be monitored. For most work environments, a steering committee supports the project and gives advice when change or challenges happen.

For agile environments, the product owner will be most concerned with the external environment because they prioritize stakeholder and customer expectations. They can present their findings to the team throughout each work period and advise on potential changes to the project's scope and backlog.

Task 4: Support Organizational Change

Adaptability is an important quality for project managers to have. Organizations must constantly change to meet with the demands of the environment that they work in. The organization's structure and the way it operates need to be understood before organizational change can happen. These factors include how teams are organized, what the opportunities for advancement are, what the organizational mission and vision are, and more.

Assess Organizational Culture

Organizational culture consists of the beliefs and practices that an organization follows. It is an expectation of what to do and how the organization operates. Culture plays a role in how team members respond to issues, or how a team reacts to the adoption of new technology. Assessing organizational culture involves looking into various aspects of the organization and determining whether or not they promote a healthy working environment. These aspects include onboarding, incentive programs, communication, transparency, and team interactions. Simple surveys, along with interviews and team discussions, can be used to ask workers how they feel about the company culture.

Organizational structure can reveal some aspects of culture as well. Different types of structures include functional, projectized, and matrix.

Functional: People are divided into different departments, and departments handle specific projects. Project managers do not play a large role. Instead, functional managers oversee projects and the department.

Projectized: Projects are the main focus, and project managers play a significant role.

Flat: Employees have a lot of independence and can make decisions for themselves.

Matrix: This is a combination of functional and projectized structures in which people perform both project-based and department work. People frequently perform multiple different jobs.

Evaluate Impact of Organizational Change to Project and Required Actions

Organizational change can be a tumultuous period. Shifts in operating procedure take time to adjust to. Sometimes organizations can suffer from a loss of productivity, and not all change is good. It is important to evaluate the effect that change has on an organization. After evaluating a change, organizations can determine how to address shortcomings or issues. Calculate the net present value and the return on investment and compare productivity levels to gain useful information about the organization's health.

Net present value: This value is used to determine how much money an organization will gain or lose with an investment or change. It shows the current value of an investment.

Return on investment: A simple way to calculate this is to divide the projected benefits of a change by the cost of implementing it. Organizations can determine whether or not this change is worth implementing based on the gained cash flow and profitability.

Productivity levels: Productivity is how much work or how many products an organization produces. This can include the number of products made, the amount of work employees finish, and the amount of time spent on tasks.

Evaluate Impact of the Project to the Organization and Required Actions

Change control boards are one of the main tools that a company uses to evaluate the impact of a project or change. The board assesses the costs and risks of a project and presents their findings so management can take action. Another way to analyze the impact of change on a company is to use a rollout plan. Every project eventually produces a workable product, and the rollout plan is a document that predicts how this product will affect customers and stakeholders. Rollout refers to the process of introducing a new product or change into the market. Rollout plans include sections such as expected outcomes, threats to product success, steps to take if the rollout period is unsuccessful, post-launch support, and what performance metrics the company will use.

Performance metrics are especially useful because they allow a company to measure the success of the product or change. These metrics include sales, profit, customer satisfaction, return on investment, and much more. Companies can use this information to determine what needs to be done to support the project and meet customer and stakeholder demands.

Practice Quiz

1. A new company is concerned with how they will create and maintain a sanitary working environment for their employees. Which category of project compliance does this condition fall under?
    a. Geopolitical
    b. Regulatory
    c. Data
    d. Health and safety

2. After expanding its operations to Canada, a U.S.-based company continues to use materials that are approved for use in the United States. The company assumes that the material has no issues for its Canadian operations. What threat to compliance does this fall under?
    a. Ignorance
    b. Errors in product testing
    c. Market shifts
    d. Changes in regulatory laws

3. Which of the following factors affect the internal business environment?
    a. Market performance
    b. Customer culture
    c. Company culture
    d. Competition

4. What term refers to how flexible a project can be when handling change or setbacks, such as with a project running late?
    a. Project scope
    b. Compliance
    c. Tolerance
    d. Productivity

5. Expensive new technology is available for a company to use in its projects. Management is interested in this technology's potential future cash flow. The company estimates the benefit of implementing this new technology by dividing its projected benefits by the cost of implementation. What does this formula calculate?
    a. Net present value
    b. Return on investment
    c. Productivity levels
    d. Functional organizational structure

See answers on the next page.

Answer Explanations

1. D: Health and safety, Choice *D*, is the responsibility for companies to provide safe, sanitary working conditions for their workers and is the correct answer. Choice *A* is concerned with the effects of government and politics. Choice *B* concerns industry standards for compliance, such as with environmental laws. Choice *C* handles data security and keeping customer information safe.

2. A: Ignorance of compliance laws does not excuse a company from not following compliance laws for different countries. Compliance can be challenging when working with other countries. What works in one country may not work in another. For example, one country may have laws against a certain material used in a product. Companies need to research all relevant compliance laws before they begin work in another country. Choice *B* is a threat to compliance because errors in product testing can give false data. Choice *C* affects companies and their business practices through the current demands of the market. Choice *D* is the term for when a country changes a law, and companies must adapt to it.

3. C: Business environment refers to how the company operates itself. Internal and external factors can affect the business environment. Internal factors like company culture, Choice *C*, are controlled by the company itself. Choices *A*, *B*, and *D* are external factors that the company does not have direct control over.

4. C: Tolerance is usually determined by a project manager and refers to how flexible a project can be with deliverables and progress. Choice *A* is a part of project planning and lists project goals and a timeline for deliverables. Choice *B* is when companies need to adhere to laws and rules of their industry. Choice *D* is a measure that companies can use to analyze how change is affecting them.

5. B: Companies use different metrics to measure how change affects them. The return-on-investment metric, Choice *B*, estimates future cash flow and is concerned with profitability. Choice *A* measures the current value of an investment and not the overall profitability. Choice *C* is a measure of how much work employees accomplish at a company. Choice *D* is a type of organizational structure that a company can utilize.

PMP Practice Test #1

1. The team is impressed by a new project leader because she leads by example and takes responsibility for her actions. What tenant of leadership is this project leader displaying?
    a. Persuasion
    b. Stewardship
    c. Awareness
    d. Foresight

2. During a survey, most of the team members answered that they like leaders who take time to listen to everyone's opinion and make decisions with the rest of the team. Which style of leadership is this?
    a. Conceptualization
    b. Extroverted
    c. Collaborative
    d. Directive

3. After taking the Myers-Briggs test, a team member gets ENTP as a result. What does the *T* stand for in this result?
    a. Thinking
    b. Tenacity
    c. Timeliness
    d. Torpor

4. What is a disadvantage of the collaborative style of leadership?
    a. Collaborative leaders do not understand their team well.
    b. Collaborative leaders can appear unfriendly or distant from their team.
    c. Under collaborative leadership, only one person makes decisions.
    d. Under collaborative leadership, making decisions can take a long time.

5. A project manager notices that their team's productivity has been going down and that team members are becoming dissatisfied by the slow progress of their careers. How can the project manager address this?
    a. Ask the team to engage in team building activities.
    b. Provide opportunities for professional development.
    c. Remind the team of their responsibility to project stakeholders.
    d. Refer team members to the team contract for advice on what to do.

6. Which key performance indicator measures the financial worth of an employee?
    a. Human capital value added (HCVA)
    b. Employee engagement level
    c. Employee churn rate
    d. Bradford Factor

7. What effect does positive feedback have on a behavior?
    a. It has no effect on the behavior.
    b. It decreases the frequency of the behavior.
    c. It eliminates the behavior.
    d. It encourages the behavior.

8. During a personal meeting with a team member, the project manager focuses only on the drawbacks of the team member's performance and does not offer advice on how to improve. Which kind of feedback is the project manager giving to the team member?
    a. Negative feedback
    b. Positive feedback
    c. Constructive feedback
    d. Critical feedback

9. Which of these statements is an example of constructive feedback?
    a. "You haven't done anything right."
    b. "I see that you've been missing project deadlines. I wanted to see if there was anything I can do to help you reach your goals."
    c. "Great work on the project, I have nothing else to add."
    d. "How much more work is left for this project cycle?"

10. When would a burnup chart be used?
    a. During a team meeting to show the amount of work already done
    b. After surveying customers to obtain their feedback on a product
    c. After completely finishing a project
    d. When discussing with stakeholders how many resources a project will need

11. Which key performance indicator would be used to measure the effect an employee's absence has on a company?
    a. Employee engagement level
    b. Employee churn rate
    c. Bradford Factor
    d. Human capital value added (HCVA)

12. A team member wants to know if their new suggestion is helping the team and decides to ask their colleagues to rate his performance. What is this method called?
    a. Peer reviews
    b. Self-evaluations
    c. Burnup
    d. Critical feedback

13. When is the best time to give feedback on team performance?
    a. During a yearly performance review
    b. At regular intervals
    c. Whenever the project manager has time in their schedule
    d. After a project has finished

14. What is the problem with a team only performing quarterly or yearly performance reviews?
    a. Employees are less likely to have time available for a performance review.
    b. Feedback should be given at irregular intervals, not after a fixed amount of time.
    c. Too much time has passed since the project started.
    d. There has not been enough time to gather data.

15. What does the *S* in SWOT analysis stand for?
    a. Surveys
    b. Strengths
    c. Stakeholders
    d. Skills

16. Which question is an example of the *O* in a SWOT analysis?
    a. What advantage does our team provide compared to others?
    b. What resources are we missing?
    c. Is there any new technology or techniques that we can utilize for the project?
    d. In what way are our competitors doing better than our team?

17. A project manager wants to improve project performance and suggests using a RACI chart. What is the main purpose of a RACI chart?
    a. To determine task accountability
    b. To chart the amount of work that needs to be done
    c. To discuss feedback with employees
    d. To map out the resources that a project has

18. A project manager lists a computer engineer as an *I* in a RACI chart for a deliverable. What is the purpose of this?
    a. The computer engineer is primarily responsible for working on the deliverable.
    b. The computer engineer needs to determine whether or not the deliverable is acceptable for the project.
    c. The computer engineer needs to provide feedback and assistance for this deliverable.
    d. The computer engineer needs to know the progress of this deliverable.

19. In an agile environment, when is an appropriate time to determine whether tasks are being delegated and worked on satisfactorily?
    a. At the end of a sprint, or work period
    b. After the project ends
    c. After a stakeholder gives feedback on the work that needs to be completed
    d. At the end of the year

20. Before a project starts, a company determines that a rival company is outperforming its teams and wants to find a solution to this. Which component of a SWOT analysis does this best represent?
    a. S
    b. T
    c. O
    d. W

21. In order to make a teamwide decision, the team decides to write down all of the options available and asks team members to place a small mark on their favorite decision. What is this decision-making technique called?
    a. Simple voting
    b. Roman voting
    c. Dot voting
    d. Fist to five

22. What is a disadvantage of using the simple voting technique to make a decision?
    a. It takes a very long time before results are seen.
    b. Mixed opinions are not included in this voting technique.
    c. This voting technique is not normally used in agile environments.
    d. This voting technique is available only after a project ends.

23. In Roman voting, what does a sideways thumb indicate?
    a. Agreement with a decision
    b. Mixed feelings on a decision
    c. No opinion on a decision
    d. Disagreement with a decision

24. Effective training programs can be created by first using what technique?
    a. Human capital value added (HCVA)
    b. RACI chart
    c. Fist to five
    d. Skills gap analysis

25. New hires for a company are required to complete classroom training before they can start working on a project. What type of training is this?
    a. Formal training
    b. Experiential learning
    c. Agile learning
    d. Shadowing

26. What type of training is mentorship?
    a. Formal training
    b. Classroom training
    c. Experiential learning
    d. Informal training

27. A passionate young employee is determined to learn as much as they can to develop their skills and to work on a project. They look up information online, attend private workshops, and read books for self-improvement. How would this training be classified?
    a. Agile project management
    b. Informal training
    c. Experiential learning
    d. Mentorship

28. What is a component of allocating resources for training?
    a. Determining instructor salaries and venue costs
    b. Analyzing what skills a team needs to succeed
    c. Providing feedback after a work period
    d. Performing a SWOT analysis

29. A project manager is rushing to build their team and decides to take on a new hire immediately. The new hire is not doing well with the team, and the project manager discovers that the new hire is unfamiliar with the technology the company uses. What should the project manager have done first?
    a. Made a decision with Highsmith's Decision Spectrum
    b. Held a team meeting to determine the resources the project needs
    c. Appraised the potential employee's skills
    d. Asked the team to participate in Roman voting

30. The team is talking to a new member and is impressed by his deep knowledge of computer technology and his general knowledge about different aspects of the project. In an agile environment, what is this individual classified as?
    a. T-shaped individual
    b. S-shaped individual
    c. L-shaped individual
    d. W-shaped individual

31. Why is a skills matrix useful to project management?
    a. It functions like a group interview and helps teams decide what skills they are missing.
    b. It creates an organized list that makes it easier to determine what skills the team excels at.
    c. It is a type of formal training that companies can utilize.
    d. It helps to create individuals that are "generalized specialists."

32. As opposed to analogous estimating, what does bottom-up estimating excel at?
    a. Using historical data to determine future project costs
    b. Listing different project resources and determining how much each resource costs
    c. Estimating the skills that a team needs to acquire to succeed
    d. Determining project costs by examining smaller tasks and combining results

33. A project manager has not been assessing their team's skills because it takes too much time. What kind of problem could this team face in the future?
    a. Funding will not be available for training sessions.
    b. A Big Visible Chart (BVC) will not be effective in this team environment.
    c. The team will not be prepared for new projects that require new technology.
    d. Too many "generalized specialists" will be on the team.

34. Which estimating technique can be done with very little information?
    a. Analogous estimating
    b. Bottom-up estimating
    c. Parametric estimating
    d. Resource breakdown structure

35. When should an impediment be addressed?
    a. When a new hire is introduced to the team
    b. During a daily meeting
    c. Immediately
    d. During yearly reviews

36. Although a team is facing an impediment at work, the company determines that a different impediment in another department needs to be addressed first. Why would a company prioritize another impediment first?
    a. It gives project managers a chance to determine how their team would work with impediments.
    b. It makes it easier to determine future project costs using historical data.
    c. It creates a better opportunity for developing new training methods.
    d. It helps to reduce time lost on issues that are not as important at the time.

37. Team members have the chance to update their progress on the project whenever they complete something. If a task has not been updated in a long time, what is the next step?
    a. Perform a value stream analysis.
    b. Perform a task age analysis.
    c. Perform a skills gap analysis.
    d. Perform a SWOT analysis.

38. How could a project management office (PMO) assist a team?
    a. Assign financial values to impediments.
    b. Organize resources into a Big Visible Chart (BVC).
    c. Provide guidance on company standards for project management.
    d. Address individual team members' impediments.

39. What is the best thing that a team member can do when they encounter an impediment?
    a. Try to resolve the impediment on their own as soon as they can.
    b. Wait until the end of a work period to address it.
    c. List the impediment on the Big Visible Chart (BVC) and wait for the project manager to approve it.
    d. Escalate the problem to the project management office (PMO).

40. Why are teams with a shared understanding able to find solutions faster?
    a. The project vision makes it easier to see what resources are already available.
    b. Solutions are already provided for them with a value stream analysis.
    c. The project manager does not need to consult the project management office (PMO).
    d. The solutions are related to the project goals.

41. As opposed to a project vision, what does a project charter list?
    a. The amount of damage certain impediments will cost the company
    b. The overall goal of the project
    c. Various stakeholders, team members, and why the project is important
    d. Various tasks and how long they will take

42. If a team is facing the same problem continually, what is the next step the team should take?
    a. Tell team members to address their own impediments again.
    b. Determine the root cause with a root cause analysis.
    c. Use a RACI chart to address future impediments.
    d. Escalate to the product owner.

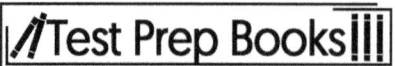

43. The Five Whys is a technique that helps to discover what?
    a. Skills that a team still needs to work on
    b. The causes and effects of a problem
    c. Financial damage that an impediment is causing
    d. The accountability for various deliverables

44. If a team member has a different opinion than others after planning poker, what is the next step the project manager should take?
    a. Ask them to explain their reasons for their decision.
    b. Bring the issue up to the project management office (PMO).
    c. Conduct a fishbone analysis.
    d. Wait until the end of the work period to address it.

45. What does the planning poker technique involve?
    a. Team members raise their fist into their air and vote about their agreement with a decision.
    b. Teams ask why a problem has been occurring multiple times until a solution is found.
    c. Team members pick a card that represents how much effort a task would take.
    d. Teams write down their favorite decision on cards and place it on the Big Visible Chart (BVC).

46. If a team reaches a consensus that the project manager personally disagrees with, what should the project manager do?
    a. Support the team.
    b. Ask the team to rethink their decision.
    c. Consult with the product owner.
    d. Perform a Five Whys analysis.

47. Why is an After-Action Review (AAR) useful for teams?
    a. It analyzes how tasks can be done better in the future.
    b. It assesses how transparent the team has been in its decision making.
    c. It functions similarly to daily meetings and is performed every day.
    d. It analyzes the root cause of a problem.

48. In order to help adapt to a virtual team environment, the team decides to use an instant messaging system as its primary form of communication. What kind of communication tool is this?
    a. Colocation
    b. Asynchronous tool
    c. Big Visible Chart
    d. Synchronous tool

49. The company has decided to invest in a large office space that includes things like team meeting rooms, computer labs, bulletin boards, and a small kitchen. What type of communication tool would this office space fall under?
    a. Synchronous tool
    b. Colocation
    c. Asynchronous tool
    d. Transparency

50. A remote team with members from all over the world has been suffering from decreased productivity because team members are unfamiliar with each other and have trouble communicating. What is one way to increase team members' trust in one another?
    a. Consult an external stakeholder.
    b. Perform a Myers-Briggs test.
    c. Engage in team building activities.
    d. Meet in the team's assigned colocation.

51. A company is creating its very first remote team to work on a project. What is one advantage that remote teams have over in-person teams?
    a. Ability for teams to expand quickly by adding remote workers
    b. Decreased use of technology for communication
    c. Faster onboarding process
    d. Simpler meeting coordination

52. A project manager wants to evaluate how effective their remote workers are and decides to use a statistical test to see if team members are doing adequate work by measuring the expected amount of work completed against the actual amount of work completed. What is this test called?
    a. DISC assessment
    b. Value stream analysis
    c. Burndown chart
    d. Variance analysis

53. The project manager notices that the remote team has started to favor using instant messaging systems instead of video conferencing as its main form of communication. How should the project manager respond to this observation?
    a. Ask an external stakeholder for their opinion.
    b. Adapt to the team's choice and include both of these tools as forms of communication.
    c. Stress that the team charter lists video conferencing as their main form of communication.
    d. Reject instant messaging as a form of communication.

54. Which is NOT a component of a team's ground rules?
    a. Tools the team uses for communication
    b. Meeting times and basic etiquette
    c. A list of the company's external stakeholders
    d. Procedures for voicing concerns and complaints

55. A longtime team member has repeatedly violated the ground rules and ignored advice from others. What action is appropriate in this situation?
    a. Wait for their feedback on the next team meeting.
    b. Remind them to refer to the team charter.
    c. Removal from the team
    d. Mentoring and guidance

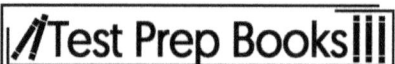

56. A new team member has started to wear strong perfume to work, and some people have complained about the smell to the project manager. What should the project manager do in this situation?
    a. Speak with the team member privately and work with them to find a solution.
    b. Remove the team member from the project.
    c. Immediately update the team charter without telling the team.
    d. Allow her to continue her behavior.

57. On the first day of a new project, two team members argue over whether the team requires cameras to be on during team meetings. What should the project manager do in this situation?
    a. Allow the team members to solve this problem on their own.
    b. Mention this incident during the quarterly review.
    c. Remove them from the project.
    d. Refer the team members to the team ground rules.

58. One thing that teams need to consider when creating ground rules is to make them simple enough that even external stakeholders can understand them. What roles do external stakeholders have in projects?
    a. They are involved with the formal training of new team members.
    b. They are only indirectly involved with the project but are affected by its results.
    c. They help teams create "generalized specialists."
    d. They are an integral part of the team and contribute to the project.

59. Before starting a project, a project manager wants to consult with their team to develop a set of ground rules. Why are ground rules beneficial for teams?
    a. Ground rules break down team impediments and how to address them.
    b. Ground rules unify teams and explain what behavior is and is not acceptable.
    c. Ground rules list the team's resources.
    d. Ground rules explain the team's different personality types.

60. Where should the team's ground rules be listed?
    a. In the team charter
    b. In a RACI chart
    c. In the After-Action Review
    d. In a synchronous tool

61. If a team member is underperforming and wants to improve, what is an appropriate step to address this situation?
    a. Remove the team member from the team.
    b. Inform the project management office.
    c. Provide mentoring and guidance.
    d. Report them to the project manager.

62. Mark has been angrily criticizing others on his team because he feels like they are not working fast enough. Which component of emotional intelligence does Mark need to work on?
    a. Empathy
    b. Self-awareness
    c. Motivation
    d. Self-regulation

63. After seeing a new team member become frustrated and upset that they are not doing as well as they should be doing, Emily approaches the new team member and tries to comfort them. She explains that she also felt the same way when she was new and understands what they are going through. She offers them advice. What component of emotional intelligence does this represent?
    a. Self-awareness
    b. Empathy
    c. Self-regulation
    d. Motivation

64. Which test classifies personality types as Analytical, Amiable, Driver, or Expressive?
    a. DISC assessment
    b. Keirsey Temperament Sorter (KTS)
    c. Merrill-Reid model
    d. Myers-Briggs Type Indicator (MBTI)

65. A project manager analyses their team members and determines most of them have a Driver personality. What might the team struggle with?
    a. Appearing unfriendly and uncooperative with each other
    b. Missing deadlines
    c. Taking too long to make decisions and overanalyzing situations
    d. Needing extra guidance and rules

66. Which personality might NOT function well in hectic and fast-paced environments?
    a. Driver
    b. Expressive
    c. Amiable
    d. Feeling

67. Jamal is described by his teammates as sociable, friendly, and fun. Which personality indicator describes him?
    a. Analytical
    b. Amiable
    c. Driver
    d. Expressive

68. Which of the following is NOT a benefit of using incremental delivery?
    a. Incremental delivery allows for feedback from customers earlier in the project process.
    b. Incremental delivery combats student syndrome—the propensity of individuals to wait until just before a deadline to begin work.
    c. Incremental delivery ensures that all members of the project team are on the same developmental stage of the project at the same time.
    d. Incremental delivery keeps stakeholders involved and engaged by presenting them with multiple deliverables throughout the project.

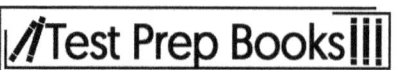

69. Under what set of circumstances would a project manager be most likely to use the minimum marketable feature (MMF) tool?
    a. Right before the execution phase of a predictive project management approach so that maximum value can be delivered quickly to both internal and external stakeholders
    b. Early in the planning phase of a predictive project management approach so that all members of the project team can be effectively informed about what the finished project deliverable should look like
    c. Early in the planning phase of an adaptive project management approach so that features of a deliverable can be tested and piloted in environments where that otherwise may be difficult
    d. Right before the execution phase of an adaptive project management approach so that the project team can be made aware of the minimum number of features expected for the product to be marketable

70. What are the factors by which Alistair Cockburn's Effectiveness of Communication Channels model evaluates communication methods?
    a. Stakeholder attitude and communication channel effectiveness
    b. Push communication channel effectiveness and pull communication channel effectiveness
    c. Project team size and communication channel effectiveness
    d. Communication effectiveness and richness of communication channels

71. Which of the following accurately describes the difference between push communications and pull communications?
    a. Push communications consist of any communication that is sent out to project stakeholders, whereas pull communications consist of any communication in which a project stakeholder is seeking out information on their own.
    b. Push communications consist of any communication in which a project stakeholder is seeking out information on their own, whereas pull communications consist of any communication that is sent out to project stakeholders.
    c. Push communications consist of any communication in which the target audience is existing stakeholders, whereas pull communications consist of any communication in which the target audience is new or potential stakeholders.
    d. Push communications consist of any communication in which the target audience is new or potential stakeholders, whereas pull communications consist of any communication in which the target audience is existing stakeholders.

72. Which of the following accurately describes the stages information passes through in Shannon and Weaver's Mathematical Theory of Communication model?
    a. Sender, Encoder, Channel, Recoder, Channel, Decoder, Receiver
    b. Sender, Encoder, Channel, Decoder, Receiver
    c. Channel, Encoder, Receiver, Decoder, Sender
    d. Receiver, Recoder, Channel, Decoder, Sender

73. Which of the following is NOT a benefit of risk-adjusted backlogs?
    a. Risk-adjusted backlogs allow project managers and project teams to measure the risk associated with not properly prioritizing something in the backlog.
    b. Risk-adjusted backlogs allow changes to be made earlier in the project life cycle, reducing the total cost of change.
    c. Risk-adjusted backlogs, once defined and established in the planning stages of the project, prioritize automatically.
    d. Risk-adjusted backlogs also include potential opportunities, which can prove especially helpful when identified early in the program.

74. Which three attributes are used to classify stakeholders in the Salience Classification model?
    a. Interests, expectations, and concerns
    b. Financial capacity, functional capacity, and physical capacity
    c. Power, legitimacy, and urgency
    d. Supportive, neutral, and unaware

75. Which of the following correctly describes the difference between a stakeholder register and a persona?
    a. A stakeholder register is primarily associated with predictive project management methods, whereas a persona is primarily associated with adaptive project management methods.
    b. A stakeholder register is primarily associated with adaptive project management methods, whereas a persona is primarily associated with predictive project management methods.
    c. A stakeholder register usually contains only negative reactions to a project and/or its deliverables, whereas a persona usually contains both positive and negative reactions to a project and/or its deliverables.
    d. A stakeholder register usually contains both positive and negative reactions to a project and/or its deliverables, whereas a persona usually contains only negative reactions to a project and/or its deliverables.

76. Which of the following is NOT a benefit of using a cost baseline?
    a. Because a cost baseline shows anticipated costs chronologically, it is easy for project members in any stage to know what the next upcoming expenditure will be.
    b. Because a cost baseline shows cumulative costs, it is easy for project managers to tell whether the project is above or below budget overall.
    c. Because a cost baseline displays all anticipated costs and their type, it is easy to gain a general sense of the project life cycle by looking at the cost baseline.
    d. Because a cost baseline can be used during the project, it can often provide valuable insights as to why one particular aspect of a project may be over or under budget.

77. Which of the following is NOT a disadvantage of bottom-up estimation?
    a. Bottom-up estimation is only possible once all aspects of a work breakdown structure (WBS) have been completed.
    b. Bottom-up estimation can be quite time-consuming to complete.
    c. Bottom-up estimation can be quite inaccurate, even if all low-level items can be identified.
    d. Bottom-up estimation is particularly difficult to complete in knowledge work projects.

78. Which of the following correctly describes the difference between traditional scheduling and agile scheduling?
    a. Traditional scheduling is recommended for small and large projects, whereas agile scheduling is only recommended for small projects.
    b. Agile scheduling is recommended for small and large projects, whereas traditional scheduling is only recommended for small projects.
    c. Traditional scheduling is based on a preliminary estimation, whereas agile scheduling is based on the data that emerge from the project process.
    d. Agile scheduling is based on a preliminary estimation, whereas traditional scheduling is based on the data that emerge from the project process.

79. Which of the following precedence relationships is NOT correctly described?
    a. Finish to Start—When activity 1 finishes, activity 2 begins.
    b. Start to Start—When activity 1 starts, activity 2 can begin as well.
    c. Finish to Finish—Activity 2 can only finish once activity 1 is finished.
    d. Start to Finish—Activity 2 cannot start until activity 1 finishes.

80. Which of the following accurately lists the forms of costs related to the cost of quality (COQ)?
    a. Control costs, adaptive costs, and reactive costs
    b. Success costs, expected costs, and failure costs
    c. Internal costs, external costs, and unexpected costs
    d. Prevention costs, appraisal costs, and failure costs

81. Which of the following accurately describes the difference between conformance and nonconformance?
    a. *Conformance* refers to project activities or results that are in line with organizational values and thinking, whereas *nonconformance* refers to project activities or results that are not in line with organizational values and thinking.
    b. *Conformance* refers to the costs associated with preventing quality issues, whereas *nonconformance* refers to the costs associated with project failures.
    c. *Conformance* means a project's scope is in line with regulatory statutes, whereas *nonconformance* means a project's scope exceeds regulatory statutes.
    d. *Conformance* refers to a project's budget being within 10% of expected variation, whereas *nonconformance* refers to a project's budget exceeding 10% of expected variation.

82. Which of the following is NOT a benefit of a work breakdown structure (WBS)?
    a. A WBS shows the hierarchy of the scope of the work, allowing for visualization of both high-level and lower levels of information.
    b. A WBS shows and enables the technique of project decomposition—the dividing of project work and scope into more manageable pieces.
    c. A WBS contains a WBS dictionary—a document listing project deliverables, activities, and scheduling information, as well as information about the specific tasks.
    d. A WBS contains a product backlog, which allows the project manager to rank tasks by their priority.

83. Which of the following mnemonics is helpful to remember in developing user stories?
    a. HOMES
    b. CARE
    c. INVEST
    d. LISTEN

84. Which of the following is NOT a plan contained within the overall project management plan?
    a. Scope management plan
    b. Feedback management plan
    c. Resource management plan
    d. Procurement management plan

85. What does the acronym CCB mean?
    a. Cost control budget
    b. Cost control board
    c. Change control board
    d. Collateral cost budget

86. Which of the following accurately describes the difference between industrial and knowledge work?
    a. Industrial work consists of specialized, structured work with tangible inputs and outputs, whereas knowledge work consists of holistic and changing work, often with intangible inputs or outputs.
    b. Industrial work consists of holistic and changing work, often with intangible inputs or outputs, whereas knowledge work consists of specialized, structured work with tangible input and outputs.
    c. Industrial work is completed during almost any project, whereas knowledge work is only completed in certain types of projects.
    d. Industrial work is only completed in certain types of projects, whereas knowledge work is completed during almost any project.

87. Budgets and project schedules are examples of what kind of project artifact?
    a. Baseline artifacts
    b. Hierarchy charts
    c. Logs
    d. Strategy artifacts

88. Which of the following best describes the difference between iterative and incremental development?
    a. Iterative development involves the same project members working on the same aspects of the project deliverables repeatedly, whereas incremental development involves every project member contributing something to each aspect or feature of the project deliverable.
    b. Iterative development involves every project member contributing something to each aspect or feature of the project deliverable, whereas incremental development involves the same project members working on the same aspect of the project deliverables repeatedly.
    c. Iterative development involves trying different ideas to clarify the approach, whereas incremental development involves the progressive development of different features.
    d. Iterative development involves the progressive development of different features, whereas incremental development involves trying different ideas to clarify the approach.

89. What do burndown charts depict?
    a. Burndown charts depict the rate at which stakeholders are leaving or disengaging from a project.
    b. Burndown charts depict the rate at which capital is being spent on a project.
    c. Burndown charts depict the rate at which changes are being made to a project document.
    d. Burndown charts depict the rate at which project deliverables are produced and accepted.

90. Which of the following accurately describes the difference between explicit and implicit knowledge?
    a. Explicit knowledge consists of easy-to-share information, such as facts and figures, whereas implicit knowledge consists of difficult-to-relate concepts, such as insights and experiences.
    b. Explicit knowledge consists of difficult-to-relate concepts, such as insights and experiences, whereas implicit knowledge consists of easy-to-share information, such as facts and figures.
    c. Explicit knowledge refers to knowledge that comes from within a project group or organization, whereas implicit knowledge refers to knowledge that comes from outside a project group or organization.
    d. Explicit knowledge refers to knowledge that comes from outside a project group or organization, whereas implicit knowledge refers to knowledge that comes from within a project group or organization.

91. A prototype for a project deliverable is a week late. If it becomes two weeks late, the senior management will be automatically informed. This example demonstrates which tool of project management?
    a. Stakeholder register
    b. Gantt chart
    c. Escalation paths and thresholds
    d. WBS

92. Which of the following is NOT associated with agile projects?
    a. Scrum
    b. MMF
    c. Persona
    d. Bottom-up estimation

93. Which of the following accurately lists the basic phases of the project management process?
    a. Planning, initiation, monitoring and controlling, executing, and closing
    b. Initiation, planning, execution, monitoring and controlling, and closing
    c. Opening, executing, learning, adapting, and closing
    d. Planning, deploying, learning, adapting, redeploying, and closing

94. In project management, what is meant by the term *assumption*?
    a. An assumption is any responsibility the project manager is assuming as a result of the project.
    b. An assumption is something assumed to be true about one or another aspect of a project.
    c. An assumption describes any sort of verbal agreement between a project manager and an organization.
    d. An assumption refers to any risk an organization may take on as a result of a project.

95. Which of the following accurately describes the difference between de facto regulations and de jure regulations?
    a. De facto regulations vary depending on the industry, whereas de jure regulations apply to all organizations.
    b. De facto regulations apply to all organizations, whereas de jure regulations vary depending on the industry.
    c. De facto regulations are legally sanctioned, whereas de jure regulations are widely accepted but not legally sanctioned.
    d. De facto regulations are widely accepted but not legally sanctioned, whereas de jure regulations are legally sanctioned.

96. Which of the following correctly pairs a type of communication with an example of that communication type?
    a. Formal written—reports
    b. Formal verbal—plans
    c. Informal verbal—briefings
    d. Informal written—casual conversations

97. Despite being told that a material is potentially toxic to the ocean, a company insists on using it due to its wide availability. What area of compliance is this company violating?
    a. Data security
    b. Environmental risk
    c. Social responsibility
    d. Ethics

98. It is important for companies to have team members from a variety of different backgrounds. This not only fosters teamwork, but also allows teams to look at problems from different angles. What category would this commitment be classified under?
    a. Technology
    b. Health and safety
    c. Market shifts
    d. Diversity

99. Who is responsible for making recommendations based on requested changes to a project?
    a. Change control board
    b. Steering committee
    c. Product owner
    d. Quality management plan

100. How should a company respond when new technology is available that could improve project progress?
    a. Make changes to the quality management plan.
    b. Consult with the change control board.
    c. Edit company compliance frameworks.
    d. Adjust project tolerance levels.

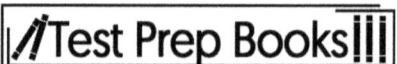

101. Which of the following factors affects the external business environment?
    a. Company culture
    b. Organizational structure
    c. Market performance
    d. Business practices

102. Why do companies need to be aware of geopolitics when conducting their business?
    a. Geopolitics affects the internal business environment.
    b. Geopolitics may cause an increased number of internal audits.
    c. Geopolitics may change existing laws about rules and regulations.
    d. Geopolitics does not majorly affect companies.

103. A company that fails to provide proper compensation for workplace injuries is violating which compliance category?
    a. Diversity
    b. Social responsibility
    c. Ethics
    d. Health and safety

104. What happens if a factor such as the budget exceeds a project's tolerance level?
    a. Further changes need approval from upper management.
    b. Project managers should make note of this in the quality management plan.
    c. The product backlog will be updated.
    d. The project completely shuts down.

105. Regarding changes to regulatory laws, who should the company consult to discuss how to prepare for upcoming changes?
    a. Project manager
    b. Product owner
    c. Corporate counsel
    d. Project scope

106. What best describes what companies must do during the rollout period?
    a. Develop a quality management plan.
    b. Begin drafting a project scope document.
    c. Actively monitor and make adjustments based on performance metrics.
    d. Calculate customer satisfaction using the net present value.

107. Someone who wants to work for a company that gives employees maximum independence and minimal interaction with upper management would be most comfortable in which organizational structure?
    a. Flat
    b. Projectized
    c. Matrix
    d. Functional

108. A new hire is touring a company and is informed that the company places strong emphasis on their project managers. The project managers have an expanded role in the company and can assign tasks and manage all resources. What kind of organizational structure is this?
   a. Flat
   b. Matrix
   c. Functional
   d. Projectized

109. Why would a product owner be concerned with a company's external business environment?
   a. Product owners contact change control boards to discuss external factors.
   b. Product owners pay attention to company culture to make recommendations on product backlog.
   c. Product owners are not concerned with the external business environment.
   d. Product owners are interested in relaying the needs of customers and stakeholders.

110. By what is project performance measured?
   a. The performance of the resources completing the work of the project
   b. The quality of the project deliverables compared to quality metrics established in the quality management plan
   c. The comparison of the actual costs and schedule against planned costs and schedule
   d. The effectiveness of the corrective actions taken to account for cost and schedule variances

111. Earned value refers to what?
   a. Value of how much profit the project will earn
   b. Value projected for the project to date and budget allocated for the work
   c. Work completed on the project to date and budget used for the work
   d. Value earned from applying lean and efficient principles to project

112. Planned value refers to what?
   a. Value projected for the project to date and budget allocated for the work
   b. Work completed on the project to date and budget used for the work
   c. Value the customer expects to gain from the project
   d. Value of the materials required to complete the project

113. The difference between the earned value and the planned value is which of the following?
   a. Cost variance
   b. Budget variance
   c. Schedule performance index
   d. Estimate to complete

114. Cost performance index refers to what?
   a. List of costs required to perform the work of the project
   b. Difference between the cost of high and low performing resources
   c. Amount of money required to complete the project at high performance
   d. Amount of work completed per dollar spent

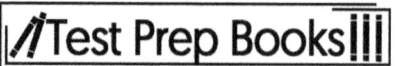

PMP Practice Test #1

115. To-complete performance index refers to which of the following?
   a. Projection of how much the project will cost to complete based on current project performance
   b. Difference between the amount of money spent and the amount of money allocated
   c. Prediction of how much money the project will lose if it continues at current performance
   d. Prediction of whether the project can be completed within the planned budget based on current performance

116. Which equation is used to calculate the variance at completion?
   a. EV-PV
   b. BAC-EV
   c. BAC-EAC
   d. (BAC-EV)/CPI

117. Change requests are used to make changes to which areas of the project?
   a. Scope
   b. Cost estimate
   c. Schedule
   d. All of these

118. Integrated change control focuses on what?
   a. Performing corrective actions to maintain quality
   b. Making decisions regarding changes to the project based on how it will impact other areas
   c. Coordinating changes to all areas of the project at the same time to limit impact
   d. Including all stakeholders in decisions regarding change requests

119. In a large organization, who typically makes decisions to approve or deny a change?
   a. Project manager
   b. Stakeholders
   c. Change control board
   d. Change control committee

120. What should occur before presenting a requested change to the change control board?
   a. Measure the impact of the change.
   b. Update project plans and documents.
   c. Decide whether to approve or deny the change.
   d. Communicate the change to the project team.

121. What does the project manager require in order to measure potential impacts?
   a. Project management software
   b. Realistic project plan
   c. Change request form
   d. Project performance evaluation

122. When measuring the impact of the change, the project manager examines which of the following?
   a. Risk to the project if the change is made
   b. Response the team will have to the project
   c. Effect the change will have on the schedule
   d. All of these

110

123. During what point in the project should the project manager perform quality control checks?
    a. When deliverables are complete
    b. Before work on the project starts
    c. When the first milestone has been reached
    d. Throughout the project lifecycle

124. Which of the following is used to analyze the current quality of the deliverables?
    a. Quality management plan
    b. Tests and evaluations
    c. Upper and lower control limits
    d. Data gathering

125. Which data gathering technique is used to determine if variances fall within the upper and lower control limits?
    a. Check sheets
    b. Control charts
    c. Statistical sampling
    d. Scatter plot

126. Which of the following refers to the maximum allowable variation in quality considered within control?
    a. Upper and lower control limits
    b. Tolerance threshold
    c. Mean
    d. Standard deviation

127. Which process analysis technique examines the complete process of the project, including the input into project, the guide that describes how and why to perform activities, the output of the activity, and the team member who performs the activity?
    a. Gap analysis
    b. Six Sigma
    c. Root cause analysis
    d. Value-added analysis

128. Which process analysis technique uses visual models to identify the flow of work to optimize processes?
    a. Value-added analysis
    b. Kanban
    c. Lean and efficient principles
    d. Pareto diagram

129. How does the continuous risk monitoring process improve project performance?
    a. Lessens probability of risks because they are constantly monitored
    b. Focuses on only the risk that continues to impact the organization
    c. Allows project managers to focus on other areas of the project because someone else is monitoring risk
    d. Helps to prevent monetary loss in the event of exposure because the project manager was prepared

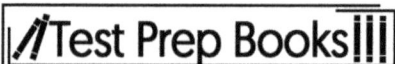

130. Which of the following risk monitoring tools indicates the current performance of the project?
    a. Periodic risk review
    b. Loss analysis
    c. Impact analysis
    d. Earned value analysis

131. Which data analysis technique is used to evaluate the team's competence?
    a. Technical performance analysis
    b. Work performance analysis
    c. Resource analysis
    d. Skills analysis

132. The risk monitoring process includes which of the following?
    a. Implement risk response strategies.
    b. Measure the impact of risks.
    c. Respond to risks using risk response strategies.
    d. Assess whether contingency reserves are sufficient to deal with identified risks.

133. To ensure all risk documents are up to date and accurate at all stages of the project, the project manager should perform what?
    a. Periodic risk review
    b. Risk register review
    c. Earned value analysis
    d. Reserve analysis

134. Reserves are used to do what?
    a. Respond to threats using prevention, transfer, or mitigation strategies.
    b. Offset risks that impact the project.
    c. Limit exposure to risks that impact the project.
    d. Verify risk response strategies.

135. Inconsistencies between what occurs during the course of the project and what was planned create which of the following?
    a. Variances
    b. Exposure
    c. Issues
    d. Impact

136. Which statement is true of issues?
    a. Issues represent the potential for negative impact.
    b. The approach to resolving issues is reactive.
    c. The approach to resolving issues is proactive.
    d. Issues represent the potential for positive impact.

137. Which statement is true of risks?
    a. Risks take the form of risk events that cause a negative impact.
    b. Risks can be prevented.
    c. Risks require an immediate resolution to prevent further impact.
    d. Risks are solved by the project manager or team member to which they are assigned.

138. The issue log is a component of which project management plan?
    a. Communications management plan
    b. Risk management plan
    c. Quality management plan
    d. Resource management plan

139. The issue log is used to do what?
    a. Help the project manager manage stakeholder expectations
    b. Help the project manager measure the impact of an issue
    c. Describe circumstances in the past that have led to issues
    d. All of these

140. In which circumstance is a change request required to resolve an issue?
    a. The issue is related to timing.
    b. The team can perform alternative activities to the activities that are delayed or blocked by the issue.
    c. The issue will delay milestones critical to the success of the project.
    d. The issue is permanent and cannot be resolved.

141. The project manager solicits insight from team members during which step of the learning management process?
    a. Analyze
    b. Record
    c. Identify
    d. Retrieve

142. Which step of the learning management process prioritizes and organizes the lessons learned?
    a. Record
    b. Store
    c. Retrieve
    d. Analyze

143. Where should the record of all the lessons learned during the project and past projects be maintained?
    a. PMIS
    b. Lessons learned register
    c. Lessons learned repository
    d. All of these

144. When should the project manager share lessons learned with the project team and stakeholders?
    a. During the planning stage of the project
    b. Each time a milestone is reached
    c. At the end of the project
    d. During each stage of the project

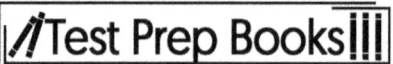

145. During which step in the learning management process must the lessons learned be organized, relevant, and complete?
    a. Retrieve
    b. Store
    c. Identify
    d. Record

146. Which of the following should be included in the leadership report of lessons learned?
    a. Categories of lessons learned by the team
    b. List of change requests
    c. Evaluation of the lessons learned
    d. Strengths and weaknesses of the project

147. Vendor performance is measured against what?
    a. Quality of deliverable
    b. Terms of the contract
    c. Statement of work
    d. Timely completion of deliverables

148. Correspondences, change requests, results of audits and inspections, invoices, and receipts should be included in which location?
    a. Procurement management plan
    b. Contract
    c. Procurement file
    d. Vendor performance review

149. Which term is used to describe disagreements between parties involved in a contract?
    a. Claim
    b. Conflict
    c. Dispute
    d. Violation

150. Which alternative dispute resolution method is legally binding?
    a. Hearing
    b. Arbitration
    c. Mediation
    d. Peer review

151. Which of the following is the project manager responsible for during claims administration?
    a. Acting as a mediator for disputes
    b. Acting as an arbitrator during arbitration
    c. Monitoring, documenting, and maintaining records
    d. Settling disputes between parties

152. The procurement process should result in which of the following outputs?
    a. Revised contracts
    b. Dispute settlements
    c. Formal acceptance of the project manager
    d. Closed procurements

153. Which requirements gathering technique features test users interacting with a mock-up of the deliverable?
   a. Focus groups
   b. Affinity diagram
   c. Prototyping
   d. Market research

154. Which type of requirement includes technical requirements, such as the performance of the project deliverable?
   a. Functional
   b. Non-functional
   c. Specific
   d. Non-specific

155. The requirements management plan defines what?
   a. What requirements are most important to stakeholders
   b. How to collect, assess, revise, and track requirements
   c. What work is required to meet the requirements of the project
   d. How to measure the success of deliverables to meet requirements

156. The process of deconstructing the work of the project into the work breakdown structure begins with which component of the project scope?
   a. Requirements management plan
   b. Traceability matrix
   c. Detailed description of deliverables
   d. Project scope statement

157. Which of the following techniques uses the formula *(optimistic + 4 x most likely + pessimistic) / 6* to estimate costs?
   a. Bottom-up
   b. Three-point
   c. Parametric
   d. Best average

158. Which of the following cost management techniques refers to adjusting the schedule of the project so activities are performed when funds are available to support them?
   a. Smoothing
   b. Cost aggregation
   c. Resource management
   d. Baselining

159. The resource management plan describes which of the following?
   a. How managers should treat team members
   b. What type and how many resources are required for each activity
   c. How to decide whether to make or buy resources
   d. How to allocate resources to support lean and efficiency principles

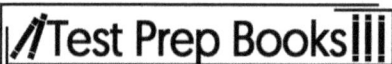

160. Which of the following elements of the project schedule graphically represents the sequence of activities and associated dependencies?
    a. Precedence diagram
    b. WBS
    c. Workflow
    d. Milestone chart

161. Lean and efficiency principles refer to what?
    a. Methods to keep employees healthy so they are more efficient
    b. Methods to identify and promote the most efficient employees
    c. Methods to decide which requirements can be disregarded to reduce spending
    d. Methods to identify and eliminate wasteful spending

162. Which of the components of the human resources plan describes the regulations associated with the resources?
    a. Organizational chart
    b. Risk register
    c. Staffing management plan
    d. Lean and efficiencies principles

163. Which type of communication method is used when a recipient extracts communication from an online repository?
    a. Decode
    b. Push
    c. Pull
    d. Interact

164. Which of the following tools and techniques for developing the communication management plan is used to represent the channels of communication available to the project team?
    a. Network model
    b. Channel diagram
    c. Communication model
    d. Distribution-node model

165. Which of the following solicitation documents is used when the primary criteria for selecting a vendor is the ability of the deliverable to meet the requirements of the statement of work?
    a. Request for quotation
    b. Request for proposal
    c. Request for bid
    d. Request for references

166. Which of the following types of contracts obligates the client to pay a fixed rate plus the cost of the work as long as it does not exceed a specified amount?
    a. Lump sum or fixed price
    b. Fixed price incentive
    c. Time and material
    d. Cost plus fixed fee

167. Which of the following basic quality tools measures the frequency of quality control variables in a vertical bar chart?
    a. Histogram
    b. Root cause diagram
    c. Check sheet
    d. Pareto diagram

168. Which of the following theorists proposed the zero defects approach to control the cost of quality?
    a. W. Edwards Deming
    b. Walter Shewhart
    c. Philip B. Crosby
    d. Joseph M. Juran

169. Scope creep is defined as which of the following?
    a. Unidentified risks that could disrupt the project
    b. Uncontrolled changes and additions to the project
    c. Anticipated resistance to changes within the organization
    d. Unexpected resistance to the project at the last minute

170. Which of the following tools to plan change management helps determine whether or not to approve a change by comparing the motivation for change to the resistance to change in the organization?
    a. Flowcharts
    b. Company culture
    c. Force field analysis
    d. Drive force analysis

171. Which of the following metrics used to assess the probability and impact of a risk refers to when the risk is likely to occur and how timely a response is required based on the impact of the risk?
    a. Probability and impact of risk
    b. Category of risk
    c. Urgency of risk
    d. Sensitivity of risk

172. Which of the following strategies is used to respond to unavoidable or high-impact risks?
    a. Mitigate or reduce the risk.
    b. Develop a fallback plan.
    c. Transfer the risk.
    d. Provide contingency funds to offset the impact.

173. The purpose of the project management plan is which of the following?
    a. Solve the problems of the other subsidiary plans.
    b. Describe each subsidiary plan in detail for the stakeholders.
    c. Summarize how the processes for each of the subsidiary plans contribute to the project goal.
    d. Introduce the new project goal based on the subsidiary plans.

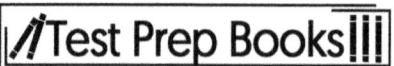

174. A project management information system is defined as which of the following?
    a. A process that assists the project manager to effectively apply information
    b. A system used to organize, plan, monitor, and execute a project
    c. A project management software system
    d. All of these

175. Which of the following is used to mark the end of the planning process and the beginning of the execution stage of the project?
    a. Kick-off meeting
    b. Push communication
    c. Milestone
    d. Brainstorming session

176. What is one of the purposes of the stakeholder management plan?
    a. Identify the roles and responsibilities of the stakeholders.
    b. Describe the strategies used to engage stakeholders.
    c. Determine which stakeholder will lead the other stakeholders.
    d. Describe the format in which to communicate with the stakeholders.

177. Which of the following tools and techniques to classify and organize stakeholders identifies the stakeholders that have the most influence?
    a. Salience model
    b. Power-interest grid
    c. Stakeholder engagement
    d. Social network analysis

178. HIPAA is an example of a compliance framework. What does HIPAA provide guidance on?
    a. Patient data
    b. Monitoring laws
    c. Health and safety
    d. Environmental protection

179. Companies should work not only for themselves, but also for others. For example, a company can support local communities and reduce their impact on the environment. What is this concept referred to as?
    a. Diversity
    b. Regulation
    c. Compliance
    d. Social responsibility

180. After testing a product multiple times, a project manager notices that the equipment used was incorrectly calibrated. What danger does this present to the company?
    a. The false data goes against compliance frameworks.
    b. The false data reduces a company's social responsibility.
    c. The false data could mislead the company about its compliance status.
    d. The false data affects the company's organizational structure.

Answer Explanations #1

1. B: Stewardship means that leaders are responsible for their actions and lead the team by example. Choice *A*, persuasion, is the ability to convince others to listen to the leader. Choice *C*, awareness, is when leaders understand that their actions affect others. Choice *D*, foresight, is the ability to make predictions based on data available to leaders.

2. C: Collaborative leaders make decisions with the support of the rest of the team and carefully consider everyone's opinion. Choice *A*, conceptualization, is incorrect because it is a tenet of leadership, not a style. Choice *B*, extroverted, is incorrect because it is one of the categories in the Myers-Briggs personality test, not a style of leadership. Choice *D*, the directive style of leadership, is incorrect because it is one in which leaders make their own decisions.

3. A: The Myers-Briggs Type Indicator (MBTI) breaks down a person's personality into four categories. The *T* represents *thinking*, indicating that this person uses logic when making decisions. Choices *B*, *C*, and *D* are not categories in the MBTI.

4. D: Collaborative leaders can take a long time to make decisions because they will constantly ask for everyone's opinion before making a decision. There are times when the leader needs to make a definitive choice quickly, which is why being flexible is important for a leader. Choice *A* is incorrect because collaborative leaders constantly speak with their team and get to know them. Choices *B* and *C* are incorrect because they are disadvantages of the directive style of leadership.

5. B: Team members should have the opportunity to grow their skills and advance in the company. Investing in professional development is worthwhile because it increases satisfaction and productivity. Choice *A* is incorrect because it can increase teamwork and improve relationships with team members, but it will not address their professional concerns. Choice *C* is incorrect because it would not increase team member satisfaction. Choice *D* is incorrect because this document lists team expectations; it does not explain how to receive professional training.

6. A: Human capital value added (HCVA) measures the financial worth of an employee and is one way to measure the team against performance indicators. Choice *B* is incorrect because it measures how much an employee cares about their work and how much motivation they have for the project. Choice *C* is incorrect because it measures how often employees are leaving the company. Choice *D* is incorrect because it measures the impact of an employee's absence from work.

7. D: Positive feedback increases the frequency of a behavior. Choice *A* is incorrect because it does not reflect the effect of positive feedback. Choices *B* and *C* are incorrect because they are features of negative feedback.

8. D: Critical feedback lists the negative aspects of an employee's work and does not give them advice on how to improve. Choice *A* is incorrect because it is feedback that is intended to decrease the frequency of a behavior. Choice *B* is incorrect because it is feedback that increases the frequency of a behavior. Choice *C* is incorrect because it is feedback that provides employees with advice on how to improve their performance.

9. B: Constructive feedback helps employees succeed by acknowledging their work and providing advice on how to proceed. Choice *A* is incorrect because it is critical feedback. Choice *C* is incorrect because it

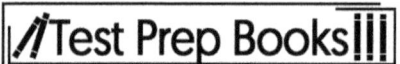

does not include advice on how the employee can improve their work or maintain their level of productivity. Choice D is incorrect because it is related to a burndown chart.

10. A: Burnup charts display the amount of work already done and help the team organize its progress. Choices B, C, and D are incorrect because they are not the appropriate times to use a burnup chart.

11. C: The Bradford Factor, also known as the Bradford Formula, is used to measure the effect an employee's absence has on the company. Choice A is incorrect because it measures how much motivation workers have to finish their work. Choice B is incorrect because it is the rate at which employees leave the company, with high turnover costing the company more in resources. Choice D is incorrect because it measures how much value, or work, a worker contributes to the company.

12. A: Peer reviews are helpful because they provide project managers with direct feedback and can function like interviews. Techniques like peer reviews are important for project management because they show if improvements made to the company or team are actually working. Choice B is incorrect because it involves employees rating themselves and giving their opinions on various matters. Choice C is incorrect because a burnup chart shows how much project work has already been completed. Choice D is incorrect because it is feedback that is harsh and not helpful to team members.

13. B: It is best to provide regular feedback during daily meetings and other scheduled events. Choices A, C, and D are not the appropriate times to give feedback because too much time has passed between the work and the feedback.

14. C: If feedback is given too late, the information may be outdated or not relevant to the current situation. Choices A and D are incorrect because they are not factors in providing feedback. Choice B is incorrect because feedback should be given at regular intervals.

15. B: A SWOT analysis is a technique to help a company understand its strengths and weaknesses. The *S* stands for *strengths*. Choices A, C, and D are incorrect because they are not part of the SWOT acronym.

16. C: The *O* in SWOT analysis stands for *opportunities*. This asks companies to think about ways that they can improve themselves. Choice A is incorrect because it represents *strengths*. Choice B is incorrect because it represents *weaknesses*. Choice D is incorrect because it represents *threats*.

17. A: RACI charts are used to determine who is responsible for what in project management. Different people and tasks are listed on a chart, and each person is assigned a letter based on what their role is concerning a deliverable. Choices B, C, and D are incorrect because they are not proper uses of a RACI chart.

18. D: The *I* in RACI stands for *informed*, which means that this person needs to be updated about a deliverable's status. Choice A is incorrect because it represents *responsible*, which means that this person does most of the work on the deliverable. Choice B is incorrect because it represents *accountable*, which means that this person is held accountable for the quality of the deliverable. Choice C is incorrect because it represents *consulted*, which means that this person is asked for advice on how to complete the deliverable.

19. A: Agile environments make use of sprints, or work periods, to deliver products. They are an appropriate time to ensure that tasks are being delegated and work is being done. Choices B, C, and D are incorrect because these time periods are too long for agile environments.

Answer Explanations #1

20. B: The *T* represents *threats*, or factors that are making it difficult for the company to succeed. A rival company with better results is worth researching in order to improve company performance. Choices *A*, *C*, and *D* are incorrect because they are not components of analyzing threats to a company.

21. C: Dot voting involves writing out all decisions that a team can make and asking team members to place a small dot or mark on their favorite decision. Choice *A* is incorrect because it involves asking teams to give a simple "agree" or "disagree" for a decision. Choice *B* is incorrect because it involves asking team members to put their thumbs up, down, or sideways to show their opinions about a decision. Choice *D* is incorrect because it involves asking team members to raise their fists in the air with one to five fingers raised, which shows their opinion about a decision.

22. B: Although simple voting is very fast, there are only two answers, which leaves no room for mixed opinions. Choices *A* and *D* are incorrect because they are not reflective of simple voting. Choice *C* is incorrect because simple voting can be used in a variety of work settings.

23. B: In Roman voting, a sideways thumb indicates mixed opinions. Choice *A* is incorrect because it is represented by a thumbs-up. Choice *C* is incorrect because it is not an option in Roman voting. Choice *D* is incorrect because it is represented by a thumbs down.

24. D: A skills gap analysis can help companies develop training programs because companies are more aware of what skills new members need to learn. Choice *A* is incorrect because human capital value added (HCVA) measures the effectiveness of workers. Choice *B* is incorrect because a RACI chart determines task accountability. Choice *C* is incorrect because a fist to five is used to see team members' opinions on a decision.

25. A: Formal training is developed specifically to train new hires and team members on the skills and knowledge necessary to work in a company. Classroom training is one type of formal training. Choice *B* is incorrect because it is experience and training in the field, such as with shadowing and internships. Choice *C* is incorrect because it is a type of project management environment. Choice *D* is incorrect because it is a type of experiential learning.

26. C: Mentorship is a type of experiential learning in which people can learn about a project directly through field work and training. Choice *A* is incorrect because it involves classroom training and courses. Choice *B* is incorrect because it is a type of formal training. Choice *D* is incorrect because it involves activities like watching videos online and reading books.

27. B: Informal training is not structured and includes an assortment of information sources that people can use. Choice *A* is incorrect because it is a type of project management environment. Choice *C* is incorrect because it involves training in the field. Choice *D* is incorrect because it is a type of experiential learning.

28. A: One component for developing training is considering the costs of creating and maintaining the training. Choice *B* is incorrect because it is a skills gap analysis. Choice *C* is incorrect because it is feedback from team members. Choice *D* is incorrect because it is usually performed by a company before developing a new project.

29. C: Employees have an interest in seeing the project succeed and should contribute their skills to help complete the project. Appraising the skills of employees prior to hiring helps create teams of people that can work effectively. Choice *A* is incorrect because it is a method to determine how team members feel

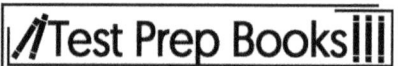

Answer Explanations #1

about a decision. Choice B is incorrect because it is performed to determine necessary resources and does not assess stakeholder skills. Choice D is incorrect because it is a decision making technique.

30. A: T-shaped individuals have deep knowledge on one subject but are also knowledgeable enough about general business practices. They are an asset to a team because of their flexibility. Choices B, C, and D are not the correct terms for this type of individual.

31. B: A skills matrix organizes the skills that teams have available to them. It makes it easier to see where teams are strong and where they may need improvement. Choice A is incorrect because it is a focus group. Choice C is incorrect because a skills matrix is not part of formal training. Choice D is incorrect because a generalized specialist is a type of person that can work well in many different team environments.

32. D: Estimating the project cost by dividing it into smaller components and combining the costs is a very detailed way to make estimates. Choice A is incorrect because it is analogous estimating. Choice B is incorrect because it is a project resource breakdown. Choice C is incorrect because it is a skills gap analysis.

33. C: Project managers need to constantly assess their team's skills and provide opportunities for them to develop their skills professionally. Choices A, B, and D are incorrect because they are not related to maintaining and developing skills.

34. A: Analogous estimating can be done with very little information because the technique uses historical data about completed projects to make estimates. Although fast, it may not be the most accurate estimate of project costs. Choice B is incorrect because it is very detailed and requires analyzing every component of a project to obtain estimates. Choice C is incorrect because, although it is similar to analogous estimating, it uses statistics to acquire more detailed estimates. Choice D is incorrect because it is a breakdown of all available project resources.

35. C: Impediments should be addressed as soon as possible in order to quickly work on finding a solution. Choices A, B, and D are incorrect because they are not the best times to address an impediment.

36. D: Teams and companies can sometimes have different priorities. For a company, prioritizing one impediment saves time and money that would have been spent on less important impediments. Choice A is incorrect because it does not address the company's concerns. Choice B is incorrect because it is analogous estimating. Choice C is incorrect because it is only important if companies need to update their training methods.

37. B: Team members constantly update the list of tasks that they have completed. If a task has not received updates for a long time, it would be useful to perform a task age analysis to learn why the tasks are not making progress. Choice A, a value stream analysis, analyzes how much work is being accomplished. Choice C, a skills gap analysis, analyzes the skills a team is missing. Choice D, a SWOT analysis, analyzes the strengths and weaknesses of a company.

38. C: Project management offices are a central location for teams to access. They can provide guidance and help to ensure that projects meet company standards. Choice A, assigning financial values to impediments, is a method for determining the severity of an impediment and is performed by the company. Choice B, organizing resources into a Big Visible Chart (BVC), is usually performed by agile

Answer Explanations #1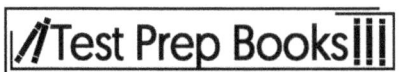

teams and is not a specific concern of a project management office. Choice D, addressing individual team members' impediments, is usually performed by a project manager.

39. A: If team members can solve their own problems, it saves time and resources and can prevent future impediments from happening. Choices B and C both involve waiting; these methods take too long to address impediments. Choice D, escalating the problem to the project management office (PMO), is an option only when teams are unable to fix their impediments.

40. D: Teams that are unified in their decision making find solutions faster because all of the solutions are related to the project goal. Choice A is incorrect because it is part of the project plan, not the project vision. Choice B is incorrect because it is not the purpose of a value stream analysis. A value stream analysis measures what actions are making or impeding progress. Choice C is incorrect because it is something teams can do if they cannot reach a solution after discussing all of their options.

41. C: The project charter lists stakeholders, team members, and project importance. Choice A is incorrect because it is assigning a financial value to an impediment. Choice B is incorrect because it is the project vision. Choice D is incorrect because it is a project plan.

42. B: If a problem has not been fixed yet, the team needs to find out why the problem keeps occurring. This can be done with a root cause analysis. Choice A is not effective because the problem will keep occurring, and the team will need to spend time and resources to fix it again. Choice C is not what a RACI chart is used for. RACI charts help to determine accountability for tasks. Choice D is an option only after teams have tried to solve their problems on their own.

43. B: The Five Whys is a technique that helps teams perform a root cause analysis. Choice A is incorrect because it is a skills gap analysis. Choice C is incorrect because it is a way for companies to measure how severe an impediment is. Choice D is incorrect because it is a RACI chart.

44. A: Project managers should ask team members for their viewpoint if their decision differs greatly from other team members. Choice B is incorrect because it refers to speaking to the PMO for advice regarding project standards and for other help. Choice C is incorrect because it is a root cause analysis. Choice D is incorrect because it is not the appropriate time frame; team members should be asked about their opinion as soon as possible.

45. C: Planning poker is a technique for teams to reach a consensus about decision making. Different cards are listed with numbers on them, representing how much effort the team member thinks the task will take. Choice A is incorrect because it is fist to five. Choice B is incorrect because it is a root cause analysis using the Five Whys. Choice D is incorrect because it is not what a BVC is used for. Instead, BVCs are a centralized place where team members can easily see project progress.

46. A: Team consensus is extremely important because each team member is unified in what they believe is important. Project management teams should accept the teams' decision and work with them to meet project goals. Choice B is incorrect because it does not promote a shared understanding. Choice C is incorrect because it should be performed if teams need additional guidance. Choice D is incorrect because it is used to determine why problems are happening.

47. A: After-Action Reviews were created to help future team members with solving tasks by drawing upon the experience of people who have already done it. Choices B, C, and D are incorrect because they are not what After-Action Reviews are used for.

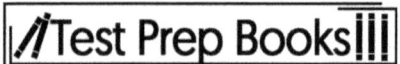

Answer Explanations #1

48. D: Synchronous tools let teams communicate in real time and mimic in-person meetings as much as possible. Choice *A*, colocation, is incorrect because it involves placing all of a project's resources into one place, like an office building. Choice *B*, an asynchronous tool, is incorrect because it is an unscheduled tool that anyone can access at any time, like message boards. Choice *C*, a Big Visible Chart, is incorrect because it is another way for teams to communicate with each other and is an area that team members can easily access and view project progress.

49. B: Colocation is placing all of a project's resources in one single area, which improves communication among team members and improves relationships and productivity. Choice *A*, the synchronous tool, is incorrect because it is a tool that mimics in-person meetings. Choice *C*, an asynchronous tool, is incorrect because it is a tool that can be accessed at any time without scheduled meetings. Choice *D*, transparency, is incorrect because it is the concept of being truthful and clear about project progress.

50. C: Team building is especially important in remote teams because team members are usually located far away from each other and are not able to meet in-person. Team building activities include having social hours, playing games, and telling stories. Choice *A* is incorrect because it is not involved with the company. Choice *B* is incorrect because it is a personality test and would not explain how to improve team communication. Choice *D* is incorrect because it is not an option for remote teams. A colocation is usually a physical location.

51. A: Remote teams can hire from around the country or even the world, which can quickly expand teams. Choice *B* is not an advantage because remote teams rely heavily on technology to function and communicate. Choice *C* is not an advantage because the onboarding and training process can take longer when conducted remotely. Choice *D* is not an advantage because remote teams can consist of team members in different time zones, which makes finding the best time for everyone to meet more difficult.

52. D: Variance analysis is a statistical test that measures expected work against actual work completed. Choice *A* is incorrect because it is a type of personality test. Choice *B* is incorrect because it is a measure of how much value certain activities bring to projects. Choice *C* is incorrect because it is a chart that measures how much work is left to do.

53. B: Teams should be flexible and adapt to the many tools that are available for remote teams. Choice *A* is not involved with the company or team. Choice *C* is incorrect because team charters can be updated. Choice *D* does not value the team's opinions.

54. C: A list of external stakeholders is not a component of a team's ground rules. Ground rules establish how teams should behave and what to do in certain situations. Choices *A*, *B*, and *D* are components of ground rules.

55. C: Serious violations against the team's rules warrant a reprimand or removal from the team. Choice *A* is incorrect because this situation needs to be dealt with as soon as possible. Choices *B* and *D* will not work if the team member has been consistently violating team rules.

56. A: It is important to treat team members with respect and to work with them to find solutions. Teams need to have excellent communication and a positive work environment to succeed. Choice *B* is incorrect because it is an option only after repeated examples of not following the rules. Choice *C* is incorrect because team charters should be updated with input from the team. Choice D is incorrect because it does not address the issue and creates problems with team trust.

57. D: Explanation about the team's policies can be found in the ground rules. Ground rules should be followed and updated as needed. Choice A is incorrect because arguments decrease the team's productivity. Choices B and C are incorrect because they are too extreme and not necessary for the team.

58. B: External stakeholders do not participate directly within the company but are affected by the results of projects. Examples include customers, the government, and the general public. Choices A, C, and D are incorrect because they do not describe the roles of external stakeholders.

59. B: Ground rules establish order and set a standard that the team should follow. Choices A, C, and D are incorrect because they are not the reasons that teams create and follow ground rules.

60. A: Ground rules should be located in a place that is easily accessible to everyone, like in the team charter. The team charter is a document that lists the project's tasks, goals, rules, and more. Choice B is incorrect because it is a chart to help determine accountability. Choice C is incorrect because it is an explanation of what went well and what did not go well when doing a task. Choice D is incorrect because it is a tool that lets teams meet in real time.

61. C: Team members should be given time to improve themselves and be provided with the tools that they need to succeed. Only serious violations warrant actions like removal. Choices A, B, and D are incorrect because they are actions taken after repeated rule violations or continuing underperformance.

62. D: Self-regulation is important because that represents how people are able to control their emotions and act respectfully in the workplace. Choice A is incorrect because it involves understanding how other people feel. Choice B is incorrect because it is how to recognize what one is feeling. Choice C is incorrect because it is a reason for a person to do something.

63. B: Empathy is the ability to relate to others. By recognizing how others are feeling, team members can share in their emotions and develop better relationships. Choice A is incorrect because it is the ability to recognize one's emotions. Choice C is incorrect because it is the ability to control one's emotions and act appropriately. Choice D is incorrect because it is how much willingness a person has to finish their work.

64. C: The Merrill-Reid model breaks down personalities into Analytical, Driver, Amiable, and Expressive types. Choices A, B, and D are incorrect because these tests do not use the categories in question.

65. A: Driver personalities are serious and excel at finishing work, but they may be uncompromising and appear unfriendly. Choices B and D are incorrect because they are reflective of Expressive personalities. Choice C is incorrect because it is reflective of Analytical personalities.

66. C: Amiable personalities set their own pace and work better in calm, relaxed situations. They may have difficulty in a very fast-paced environment. Choice A is incorrect because this type would struggle with appearing stubborn and unfriendly. Choice B is incorrect because this type may need guidance on meeting deadlines and keeping up with work. Choice D is incorrect because it is a personality type from the Myers-Briggs Type Indicator. There is no indication that an individual with a feeling type might not succeed in a fast-paced environment.

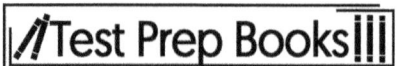

Answer Explanations #1

67. D: Expressive personalities have excellent social skills and easily fit into teams. Choice *A* is incorrect because it is a personality that uses data to make decisions. Choice *B* is incorrect because it is a personality that emphasizes harmony and calm. Choice *C* is incorrect because it is a personality that is determined and serious about work.

68. C: Incremental delivery is a strategy project managers can use to deliver value to the customer over the course of the project rather than all at one point. By breaking down the project life cycle into multiple, smaller deliveries, incremental delivery has many benefits, including allowing for early feedback, combatting student syndrome, and keeping stakeholders engaged. However, due to the very nature of incremental delivery, it is impossible to have all members of the project working on the same stage at the same time. Naturally, some members will be engaged in evaluating the success of one delivery while others are already beginning to design and develop the next delivery.

69. C: An *MMF,* or *minimum marketable feature,* refers to the smallest independent feature that can be added in quickly to deliver value to the user. *MMF* is a term used specifically early in adaptive projects and often serves as a quick way to pilot and test potential project deliverables.

70. D: Alistair Cockburn's Effectiveness of Communication Channels model is used, as the name implies, as a method to measure the effectiveness of various communication channels through which a project manager may want to engage with stakeholders. The richness of communication channels is on the *x*-axis of the model, whereas communication effectiveness is on the *y*-axis.

71. A: Push and pull communications both describe methods of communication by which the project manager communicates and shares information with stakeholders. *Push communications* specifically refer to any communication that is sent out to project stakeholders—they are *pushed* onto stakeholders. Conversely, *pull communications* refer to any instance in which a stakeholder is seeking information—they *pull* the information they are seeking from one source or another.

72. B: Shannon and Weaver's Mathematical Theory of Communication model lists five stages that describe the flow of information, starting with the first stage of sender and ending with the receiver stage. In between, information is encoded, sent through a channel, and decoded by the receiver. There is no stage of this model concerned with recoding information.

73. C: Risk-adjusted backlogs can be defined as any backlog that contains information relating to potential project risks, opportunities, and the activities needed to minimize risk and maximize opportunity. With risk-adjusted backlogs incorporated, it becomes easier for project managers and teams to identify and minimize potential risks early and invest early on potential opportunities. Risk-adjusted backlogs, however, are still prioritized by the product owner, who may choose to prioritize based solely on the magnitude of potential risk or opportunity or some other metric.

74. C: The Salience Classification model is a triple Venn diagram meant to represent the potential interactions between three key stakeholder attributes. These three attributes are power (defined as their authority), legitimacy (defined as how appropriate their involvement is in the project), and urgency (the stakeholder's immediate need).

75. A: Stakeholder registers and personas are both valuable tools for identifying the wants, expectations, and concerns of potential project stakeholders. Personas are usually less detailed than stakeholder registers and are more commonly seen in adaptive project environments, whereas stakeholder registers are more detailed and associated with predictive project environments. However,

Answer Explanations #1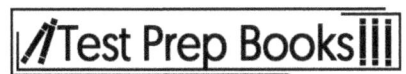

both personas and stakeholder registers contain positive and negative reactions to a project and/or its deliverables.

76. D: A cost baseline is an approved and time-phased budget. It is structured chronologically and lists all individual expenditures as well as cumulative expenditures. Although it can be used to help identify areas in which the project is running over or under budget, it cannot be used to determine why this change has occurred.

77. C: Bottom-up estimation is a form of cost estimation in which the estimates for all work packages are added up to create the total estimate. Bottom-up estimation is often quite time-consuming and requires a WBS to work. However, once all these elements are identified, bottom-up estimation can be quite accurate.

78. C: Traditional and agile scheduling are two forms of project scheduling. Traditional scheduling (also referred to as *predictive planning*) outlines scheduling through a management plan developed at the beginning of the project. Agile scheduling, on the other hand, is useful for agile projects and uses the data gathered from the project process to alter and improve the scheduling framework and process.

79. D: Precedence relationships describe the logical relationships that can form between two project activities. They are written so that the first part of the relationship describes what needs to occur to the first activity in order for the second part of the relationship to occur to the second activity. Start to Finish relationships occur when activity 2 cannot finish until activity 1 starts.

80. D: The cost of quality (COQ) is the overall expenditure made on a project to ensure that project deliverables fulfill requirements. There are three major kinds of costs associated with COQ: prevention costs (related to the prevention of poor quality); appraisal costs (related to testing and auditing); and failure costs (related to nonconformance).

81. B: Conformance and nonconformance are both associated with the COQ, generally defined as the costs related to ensuring quality project deliverables. Conformance costs are incurred during the project to avoid failure, whereas nonconformance costs are incurred during and after the project, attributable to a project failure.

82. D: A work breakdown structure (WBS) represents a hierarchical view of the scope of the work required for the project goals to be reached and the deliverables to be created. It is more commonly used in traditional projects and is typically created early in the project and referenced throughout the project process. It does not contain a product backlog, which is only used in agile projects.

83. C: INVEST (standing for Independent, Negotiable, Valuable, Estimable, Small, and Testable) is a mnemonic designed to help teams remember how to write user stories. User stories are customer-centric views of the project deliverable created by project members, with the goal of creating and implementing features that are valuable and useful.

84. B: The project management plan should describe how the project will be conducted, monitored, controlled, and ended. There are a number of subsidiary plans, including a scope management plan, a resource management plan, and a procurement management plan. However, there is no such thing as a feedback management plan, and any feedback received on the project would most likely fall under the stakeholder engagement plan or the communications management plan.

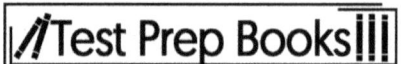

Answer Explanations #1

85. C: CCB stands for change control board. A change control board is a chartered group tasked with reviewing and ruling on proposed changes to the project.

86. A: Kinds of work can be differentiated by their form, with industrial work (factory based) and knowledge work (knowledge based) denoting the two most common forms of work in developed nations. Industrial work is tangible and specialized, places the emphasis on running things, and consists of more structure with fewer decisions. Knowledge work, on the other hand, is intangible and holistic, places the emphasis on improving things, and consists of less structure with more decisions. Despite the fact that many projects may primarily consist of one form of work or another, it is also likely that any project will consist of some work that is industrial based and some that is knowledge based.

87. A: Budgets and project schedules are both examples of baseline artifacts. Baseline artifacts are the approved version of a product or plan. Baselines are usually not updated past their initial creation so that they can be compared to later results.

88. C: Iterative and incremental development both represent developmental styles that attempt to incorporate more adaptive systems. In both types of development, there is a period of active project deliverable development and then a period when data and feedback are gathered regarding the changes. However, with iterative development, each new development cycle entails trying different ideas to clarify the approach, whereas with incremental development, each new developmental cycle entails adding progressively more and more features onto the project deliverable.

89. D: Burndown charts depict the rate at which work is getting done on a project, which is also referred to as the *project team velocity*. Specifically, burndown charts measure the rate of progress toward the project deliverables.

90. A: *Explicit* and *implicit knowledge* both refer to different forms of knowledge, with the key difference being the kind of information conveyed. Explicit knowledge consists of things that can be easily known or derived, whereas implicit knowledge consists of more esoteric concepts and specifically relates to information that cannot be easily broken down and related to others.

91. C: *Escalation paths* and *thresholds* refer to any automated system whereby a certain variance in cost or schedule will result in the delay or issue being automatically relayed to upper management.

92. D: Agile projects use adaptive methods to complete quality project work in an ever-changing environment. Agile project tools include scrum, MMF, and persona. Bottom-up estimation, on the other hand, is a much more time-intensive tool and requires prior work that is simply not possible with many agile projects.

93. B: In a traditional project life cycle, there are five phases: initiation, planning, execution, monitoring and controlling, and closing.

94. B: An assumption is anything that is assumed to be true about a project or an aspect surrounding the project environment. Identifying and keeping track of assumptions made during a project is another responsibility of the project manager.

95. D: Regulations are any requirement imposed by a government body. *De jure regulations* refer specifically to officially sanctioned regulations, whereas *de facto regulations* are widely accepted but not actually officially sanctioned by any government body.

Answer Explanations #1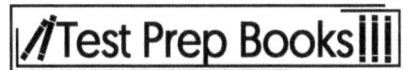

96. A: It can be helpful for project managers to consider the kind of communications they send along two axes—formal versus informal and written versus verbal. Formal written communications include plans and reports, and formal verbal communications include updates and briefings. Informal written communications include emails and texts, and informal verbal communications include casual conversations.

97. B: Companies are required to adhere to environmental laws to reduce harmful effects on the environment. Choice *A* is concerned with protecting the company from data breaches and handling sensitive information. Choice *C* is the company's responsibility to not only improve the company, but also the community around them. Choice *D* handles ethical concerns, such as policies regulating fraud.

98. D: Diversity expands a team's potential by including a wide variety of team members. Companies need to be inclusive and in compliance with diversity initiatives. Choices *A* and *C* are factors that affect how businesses operate. Choice *B* describes a company's commitment to protect employees and provide a clean working environment.

99. A: The change control board is responsible for analyzing and recommending actions based on changes and product challenges. Choice *B* describes who is responsible for general leadership in a company. Choice *C* refers to a member of an agile team that helps teams organize their workload. Choice *D* is a document that highlights how a company will maintain high product quality.

100. B: The change control board handles most requests to analyze the effects of a new change on a company, including the effects of technology. Choices *A* and *D* can be handled by a project manager and do not affect the company's implementation of technology. Choice *C* is usually edited in response to new laws or regulations based on industry standards.

101. C: Market performance affects the company's external business environment because companies do not have direct control over market demands. Choices *A*, *B*, and *D* affect a company's internal business environment.

102. C: Companies constantly need to pay attention to geopolitics because all companies must follow local, state, and federal government regulations. An area's geopolitical situation might also cause companies to reconsider their position if the government is not stable. Choice *A* is incorrect because geopolitics does not affect the internal business environment, but it does have an effect on the external business environment. Choice *B* is incorrect because geopolitics does not affect the number of internal audits. Choice *D* is incorrect because geopolitics can affect companies.

103. D: Workplace injuries fall under health and safety compliance. Companies need to have a plan for when injuries occur. Choices *A*, *B*, and *C* do not address workplace injury.

104. A: Project tolerance levels are determined before a project begins. Further changes beyond the tolerance level need approval from upper management since an aspect of the project is moving beyond acceptable limits. Choices *B*, *C*, and *D* are not the correct steps to take after tolerance levels are exceeded.

105. C: A corporate counsel handles all legal matters for a company and can research new laws. Choices *A*, *B*, and *D* do not directly involve legal matters.

106. C: The rollout period is important because the product is now released into the market. Companies need to monitor product performance using a performance metric of their choosing. Choices *A* and *B*

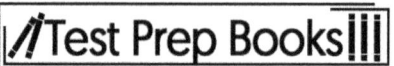

Answer Explanations #1

should be done before and during a project. Choice D is not the correct usage of the net present value. Net present value calculates cash flow and profitability.

107. A: Flat companies place more emphasis on regular employees than on management. Workers are largely independent. This is mostly seen in smaller companies with relatively few employees. Choice B is for larger companies and gives project managers more influence. Choice C is a mixed structure where employees do both regular projects and work in a department. Choice D is based around departments that work together to finish projects.

108. D: Projectized companies give greater influence to project managers and have them oversee more aspects of each project. Choice A is a structure that emphasizes little to no upper management and more employee autonomy. Choice B is a mixture of functional and projectized structures. Choice C places people into specialized departments to finish projects.

109. D: Product owners pay attention to the external business environment because they relay the concerns of customers and stakeholders. Choice A is not among a product owner's responsibilities. Choice B does not affect the external environment, although it does affect the internal business environment. Choice C is incorrect because product owners are concerned with the external business environment.

110. C: Project performance is calculated using several equations, including earned value compared to planned value and cost to complete against budget to complete. The performance of resources completing the work, Choice A, and the quality of the project deliverables compared to quality metrics, Choice B, are not measures of project performance. While the effectiveness of corrective actions, Choice D, may be a measure of quality control when measuring processes, it is not a measure of project performance.

111. C: Earned value is measured against the planned value, the value projected for the project to date and the budget allocated for the work (Choice B). It is also used to calculate variances and performance indexes for the project. Choice A, the value of how much the project will earn, and Choice D, the value earned from applying lean and efficient principles to the project, are not measures of project performance.

112. A: Planned value is projected in the cost management plan. The work completed to date, Choice B, is the earned value. Choice C, the value the customer expects to gain, and Choice D, the value of the materials required, are not measures of project performance.

113. B: The budget variance is calculated as EV−PV, while the schedule performance index (SPI), Choice C, is calculated as the product of EV and PV. The estimate to complete, Choice D, is the estimate of how much will be required to complete the project. Cost variance, Choice A, is not a variance discussed in Task 1.

114. D: The cost performance index is calculated as the product of EV and AC. The list of costs required to perform the work, Choice A, is part of the cost management plan, while the difference between the cost of high and low performing resources, Choice B, and the amount of money required to complete the project at high performance, Choice C, are not measures of project performance.

115. D: The to-complete performance index (TCPI) also predicts whether the project can be completed at the new estimate to complete (ETC). The projection of how much the project will cost to complete based on current project performance, Choice A, is the ETC, a measure of the TCPI. The difference

Answer Explanations #1

between the amount of money spent and the amount allocated, Choice *B*, is a cost variance, while the prediction of how much money the project will lose at the current performance rate, Choice *C*, is a result from calculating the cost performance index, not the TCPI.

116. C: Variance at completion is calculated as BAC-EAC. EV-PV (Choice *A*) is cost variance, BAC–EV (Choice *B*) is the estimate to complete, and the BAC–EV/CPI (Choice *D*) is how to calculate the TCPI when performance variances are expected to continue.

117. D: Change requests are used to make any changes to scope (Choice *A*), cost estimate (Choice *B*), or schedule (Choice *C*).

118. B: Integrated change control also includes communicating changes to the team and implementing and evaluating the change. Choice *A* is incorrect because performing corrective actions is a focus of project performance and/or quality control. Choices *C* and *D* are incorrect because coordinating changes to limit impact and including stakeholders in decisions regarding change are not focuses of integrated change control.

119. C: In larger companies, a change control board is made up of the project manager, stakeholders, project sponsors, customers, SMEs, etc. Choice *A* is incorrect because project managers are often the decision-makers in smaller companies and for smaller issues, but they do not typically have the authority to approve or deny major changes in larger companies. Choice *B* is incorrect because stakeholders can be part of the change control board, but they do not typically make decisions independently.

120. A: Before presenting the change to the board, the project manager should know the impact of the requested change to offer insight into whether it should be approved or denied. Choice *C* is incorrect because the change control committee makes decisions about whether to approve or deny the change after it's presented by the project manager. Choices *B* and *D* are incorrect because updating project plans and documents and communicating changes are done after the decision is made.

121. B: The project manager must have a realistic plan against which to measure how the change will impact the scope, cost, and schedule. Choice *A* is incorrect because project management software is not required, but it can help make data analysis easier. Choice *C* is incorrect because a change request form is required to request a change but not to measure impact. Choice *D* is incorrect because the project performance evaluation is not required for change control.

122. D: Risk to the project (Choice *A*), the response the team will have (Choice *B*), and the effect the change will have on the schedule (Choice *C*) are measured against a realistic project plan to predict the impact.

123. D: The project manager should perform quality control processes throughout the project lifecycle in order to measure and correct quality variances as they appear. Choice *A* is incorrect because if the project manager waits until deliverables are complete, the team will be unable to prevent defects as they appear and will have to re-do the work. Choice *B* is incorrect because the quality control plan is made before the work starts. Choice *C* is incorrect because, though the first milestone may be a good time to schedule a quality check, it is not the only time to perform quality control checks.

124. B: Tests and evaluations help to determine trends in defects or variance, while data gathering (Choice *D*) includes testing and evaluations as only one part of collecting data about defects. Choice *A* is incorrect because, while the quality management plan contains metrics, it is not a tool to analyze

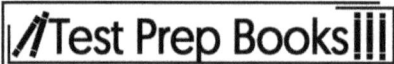

Answer Explanations #1

deliverables. Choice C is incorrect because the upper and lower control limits are data points within which to measure quality control.

125. B: Control charts are a data representation technique that visualize data points between control limits. Choices A, C, and D are incorrect because check sheets are used to identify frequency of quality control metrics, statistical sampling evaluates a sampling of deliverables to collect the data visualized in the control chart, and a scatter plot is used to identify correlations between independent and dependent variables.

126. B: Deliverables are considered acceptable if they do not cross the tolerance threshold. Choices A and C are incorrect because the upper and lower control limits are data points within which results must fall to remain in control, while the mean is the average of the variance between upper and lower control limits. Choice D is incorrect because standard deviation is the common range of deviation from the mean for a group of data points.

127. A: Gap analysis is used to reveal gaps in all the project processes and components. Choices B and C are incorrect because Six Sigma is a data-driven process analysis technique that is used to determine where and why rework is occurring in a process, while root cause analysis uses diagrams to identify the cause of problems. Choice D is incorrect because value-added analysis examines activities in a process to determine if they contribute to the project goals.

128. B: The Kanban technique typically uses sticky notes and a whiteboard to identify the work to do, the work in progress, and the work completed. Choices A and C are incorrect because value-added analysis examines activities in a process, while lean and efficient principles are used to eliminate efficiencies in processes that use unnecessary time, money, and resources. Choice D is incorrect because Pareto diagrams display the top causes of quality variances in order of importance by frequency over time.

129. B: Continuous risk monitoring also helps identify new unknown risks that could be impacting the project, but it does not lessen the probability of risk (Choice A). Choice C is incorrect because the project manager should be the one monitoring risk rather than assigning someone else to do it, though other team members might perform some or all of the steps of the process. Choice D is incorrect because less monetary loss is a measure of how well the response strategies are working rather than a direct result of continuous monitoring.

130. D: Earned value analysis indicates the current performance of the project, while impact analysis (Choice C) is performed in risk management planning as a way to measure the impact of a risk, not the performance of a project. Choice A is incorrect because periodic risk review is a tool to monitor risk, not improve performance. Choice B is incorrect because loss analysis is not a tool to measure project performance.

131. A: Technical performance analysis measures the team's success using technology, equipment, and material. Choices B, C, and D are incorrect because work performance analysis is an output of risk monitoring and encompasses all work on the project, while resource analysis and skills analysis are not tools of risk monitoring.

132. D: Assessing contingency reserves is part of monitoring. Choices A, B, and C are incorrect because implementing risk response strategies and measuring the impact of risk are part of planning, while responding to risks using response strategies is part of executing.

133. A: The project manager should schedule periodic risk reviews regularly to ensure the risk register is up to date. Choices *C* and *D* are incorrect because earned value analysis is used to measure project performance, and reserve analysis is used to assess if reserves are sufficient. Choice *B* is incorrect because risk register review is not a tool of monitoring risk, though risks in the register are reviewed throughout the process.

134. B: Contingency reserves are a risk response strategy used to offset the impact of risks that are unavoidable or insignificant. Choice *A* is incorrect because preventing, transferring, or mitigating risks are risk response strategies. Choice *C* is incorrect because limiting exposure to risks is done through risk response strategies. Choice *D* is incorrect because verifying those strategies is part of the risk monitoring process.

135. C: Issues occur frequently as a result of variances (Choice *A*), which are the inconsistencies between what occurs and what was planned. Choice *B* is incorrect because exposure is quantifiable loss due to a risk. Choice *D* is incorrect because impact is the potential for loss, damage, or missed deadlines.

136. B: The approach to solving issues is reactive because issues are already impacting the project when they are discovered. Choices *A*, *C*, and *D* are incorrect because risks represent the potential for negative or positive impact, and the approach to solving risk is proactive because response strategies are planned ahead of time to deal with them.

137. B: Risk can be mitigated, transferred, or prevented using response strategies, not solved by the project manager or a team member (Choice *D*). Choices *A* and *C* are incorrect because issues take the form of risk events and require an immediate resolution. Risks are mitigated, transferred, or prevented using response strategies.

138. A: The issue log is a component of the communications management plan because the log must act as a tool to communicate issues identified by team members or stakeholders, assign issues to team members, and track issues to resolution.

139. A: The issue log helps the project manager manage stakeholder expectations, prevent greater impact from lack of reporting, and ensure transparency in processes. Choice *B* is incorrect because the risk management plan helps the project manager measure the impact of an issue by including methods to measure impact. Choice *C* is incorrect because the lessons learned register includes information about the circumstances in the past that have led to issues.

140. C: If the issue will delay milestones, a change request is required to take corrective action to resolve the issue. If the issue is related to timing, Choice *A*, it will typically resolve itself. Choice *B* is incorrect because the team can perform alternative activities without a change request. Choice *D* is incorrect because no corrective action will solve a permanent issue and a change request is not required.

141. C: During the identify step, project teams meet to discuss their experiences and ask questions to identify and share lessons learned.

142. D: During the analyze stage, the lessons are analyzed for priority and organized so they can be stored in such a way that they can be found during the retrieval step.

143. D: A PMIS, or project management information system, contains all the records and documents within the project, including the lessons learned, in an online knowledge base or in physical files. The lessons learned register is a document such as a spreadsheet used to maintain the records. A lessons

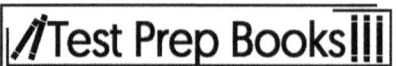

learned repository is a database of lessons learned that might be too large for a single document, or it might be a knowledge management system with keyword searches for easy retrieval.

144. D: The project manager should share lessons learned with the project team and stakeholders during each stage of the project, including during the planning stage (Choice *A)*, each time a milestone is reached (Choice *B)*, and at the end of the project (Choice *C)*.

145. A: If the team is unable to retrieve the lessons learned from where they are stored, they are unable to benefit from them.

146. D: The leadership report for lessons learned should include the strengths and weaknesses of the project; the gains and setbacks; and the issues, solutions, and proposed solutions. It is meant to be a brief overview, and therefore the categories of lessons learned (Choice *A)*, the evaluation of the lessons learned (Choice *C)*, and the list of change requests (Choice *B)* fall outside the scope, though some brief notes about these items might be included if they are irrelevant.

147. B: The terms of the contract outline the obligations of each party, while the statement of work (Choice *C)* is the statement upon which the terms of the contract are based. Choices *A* and *D* are incorrect because the quality and the timely completion of the deliverable are measures of how well they have met the terms of the contract.

148. C: The procurement file is where all the documents related to procurement should go, including contracts (Choice *B)* and vendor performance reviews (Choice *D)*. Choice *A* is also incorrect because the procurement management plan is the plan for how to manage procurement and includes how to handle these documents, not the documents themselves.

149. C: A dispute is resolved through alternative dispute resolution methods or litigation. Choices *A*, *B*, and *D* are incorrect because a claim is the term used to describe when one party claims that the other party violated the terms of a contract, while a conflict is not a term associated with claims administration.

150. B: During arbitration, the parties in disagreement present their arguments to a disinterested party who makes a legally binding decision to solve the dispute. Choice *C* is incorrect because during mediation, the mediator facilitates open conversation to negotiate a compromise but does not make any decisions. Choices *A* and *D* are also incorrect because hearings and peer reviews are not alternative dispute resolution methods.

151. C: As the claims administrator, the project manager must monitor, document, and maintain all records related to claims. Choices *A*, *B*, and *D* are incorrect because project managers do not settle disputes between parties when disagreements escalate and require a mediator or an arbitrator.

152. D: When a procurement has been closed, it has been completed per the terms of the original, revised, or new contracts, and it has been reviewed, accepted, and paid for. Choices *A*, *B*, and *C* are incorrect because revised contracts, dispute settlements, and formal acceptance by the project manager are part of the closed procurement.

153. C: A prototype is a mock-up or test version of a product with limited features and functionality with which test users can interact and give feedback to the project team. Choice *A* is incorrect because focus groups are sessions in which focused groups of SMEs, stakeholders, and end users share their experiences and provide feedback about a product. Choice *B* is incorrect because an affinity diagram is a

Answer Explanations #1

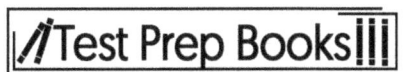

diagram that organizes ideas and feedback into groups of related ideas. Choice D is incorrect because market research is not a requirement gathering technique.

154. B: Non-functional requirements include the technical requirements, such as performance and user experience, while functional requirements (Choice A) are the specific features of the product. Choices C and D are incorrect because specific and non-specific are not terms used to describe the types of requirements for a project.

155. B: The requirements management plan defines the processes by which to collect, assess, revise, and track the requirements for the project. Choice A is incorrect because the requirements most important to stakeholders could be noted in the detailed requirements documentation, the stakeholder register, and the stakeholder management plan. Choices C and D are incorrect because the work required to meet the requirements of the project and the criteria by which to measure the success of the deliverables to meet the project requirements are defined in the project scope.

156. D: The process of deconstructing the work of the project begins with the project scope statement that establishes the project baseline, which is then broken down into individual deliverables, which are described in detail (Choice C) in the project scope statement. Choices A and B are incorrect because the requirements management plan describes how to manage requirements and includes a traceability matrix that visually represents tracing, or the process of following a test case backwards to the requirement, which is not included in the WBS.

157. B: The three-point technique uses this formula to calculate the estimated cost based on the optimistic, most likely, and pessimistic costs. Choices A and C are incorrect because the bottom-up approach calculates the sum of the estimated cost of each individual activity, while parametric estimation is based on historical and statistical information. Choice D is incorrect because the best average is not a cost estimation technique.

158. A: Smoothing is the term used to describe adjusting the project schedule to perform activities when the funding is available to support them. Choice B is incorrect because cost aggregation is also known as bottom-up, which includes determining the budget based on the sum of all the estimated costs. Choices C and D are incorrect because resource management and baselining are not cost management techniques.

159. B: The resource management plan describes the type and quantity of human and material resources required for each activity using the same techniques used to create the WBS. Choices A and C are incorrect because the way managers should treat team members is not a topic for project management, and the way to decide whether to make or buy resources is a procurement management topic. Choice D is incorrect because the way to allocate resources to support lean and efficiency principles is a topic for the human resource management plan.

160. C: A workflow or flowchart visually represents the sequence of activities and associated dependencies. Choices A and B are incorrect because a precedence diagram is used to identify dependencies within the WBS. Choice D is incorrect because a milestone chart is not an element of a project.

161. D: Lean and efficiency principles are applied to project management to identify activities, resources, and processes that are unnecessary or inefficient in order to eliminate wasteful spending in a project. Choices A, B, and C are incorrect because methods to keep employees healthy, identify and

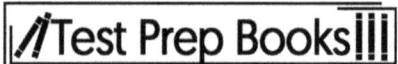

promote employees, and decide which requirements can be disregarded are not included in the scope of the project plan.

162. C: The staffing management plan includes information about how to acquire resources, when resources will be available, how they will be released and trained, and what regulations are associated with resources to maintain compliance. Choices A and B are incorrect because the organizational chart represents the hierarchy of the project team, while the risk register describes the risks associated with the project. Choice D is incorrect because lean and efficiency principles are applied to eliminate waste in a project.

163. C: Pull communication is used when the recipient extracts or pulls communication from an online repository, while push communication, Choice B, is used when a sender transmits or pushes one-way communication to a receiver. Choice D is incorrect because interactive communication occurs between two parties who act as both senders and receivers. When a communication is received, the recipient decodes, or reads, the message, so Choice A is incorrect.

164. A: A network model graphically represents the lines or channels of communication from the source to the distribution and access nodes. The communication model, Choice C, defines the elements of the basic communication process. Choices B and D are incorrect because channel diagrams and distribution-node models are not techniques associated with project management.

165. B: A request for proposal (RFP), or request for information (RFI), is used when the primary criteria to select a vendor is not money but rather factors, such as their ability to meet the requirements of the SOW, their production capacity, their reputation, their management approach, etc. A request for quotation (RFQ) (Choice A) or a request for bid (ROB) (Choice C) is used when the primary concern is cost. A request for references (Choice D) is not a solicitation document used to select a vendor.

166. B: A fixed-price incentive contract states the client will pay the costs and a fixed fee only if the vendor guarantees the cost of the project will not exceed a specified amount, while a cost plus fixed contract fee, Choice D, states that the customer will pay the costs and a fixed fee, but the contractor does not guarantee a maximum cost. Choice A is incorrect because a lump sum/fixed price contract states the contractor will pay all costs, while the customer will pay a specified fixed price. Choice C is incorrect because time and material contracts specify a fixed price for time and material or units of work, and the client pays the sum total.

167. A: A histogram measures frequency of quality control variables in a bar chart, while a root cause diagram, Choice B, traces quality control issues to their root cause. A check sheet, Choice C, measures occurrences of quality control variables in real time using tally or check marks, and a Pareto diagram, Choice D, uses a bar chart to identify the few key causes of quality issues.

168. C: Philip B. Crosby proposed that to lower the cost of quality control, one should prevent defects during the production process. W. Edwards Deming (Choice A) theorized that management is responsible for 85% of the cost of quality, and Walter Shewhart (Choice B) developed the plan-do-check model. Joseph M. Juran (Choice D) presented the idea that grade is the category of a deliverable, and while low quality is unacceptable, low grade can be acceptable depending on the requirements.

169. B: Scope creep is defined as continuous uncontrolled changes and additions that cause the project to grow in scope.

170. C: Force field analysis compares the driving force motivating change against the likely resistance to the change in the organization to inform decisions on whether or not to approve a requested change. Flowcharts, Choice *A*, graphically represent a sequence of activities. Company culture (Choice *B*) and drive force analysis (Choice *D*) are not change management tools.

171. C: The urgency of the risk is a metric used to qualify the impact of a risk based on how soon the risk is likely to occur, how timely the response to the risk must be, and how much impact the risk will have. Probability and impact, Choice *A*, are based on how likely it is the risk will occur and what the damage or benefit will be, while the category of risk, Choice *B*, describes the type of risk to determine how it will affect the organization. Choice *D* is incorrect because sensitivity is not a metric used in the qualitative analysis.

172. B: Develop a fallback plan to deal with a risk that is unavoidable and could have a powerful impact on the organization. Fallback plans are used when mitigating (Choice *A*) or transferring (Choice *C*) the risk is not feasible. Choice *D* is incorrect because contingency funds are used to offset accepted risks.

173. C: The project management plan summarizes the subsidiary plans of the project and describes how the processes established in each plan contribute to the overall goal. Choices *A*, *B*, and *D* are not included in any project plan.

174. D: A PMIS is a system used to organize, plan, monitor, and execute a project using project management software and/or processes that assist the PM to effectively apply the information collected during the planning process.

175. A: The kick-off meeting is conducted at the end of the planning phase and includes key stakeholders, the project manager and team, executive leadership, etc. The purpose of the meeting is to summarize the project goals and the work to be done to achieve them, as well as to gain support and enthusiasm for the project. Push communication, Choice *B*, is a type of communication, and a milestone, Choice *C*, is a major accomplishment achieved during the course of the project. Brainstorming sessions, Choice *D*, are a technique used to generate ideas during the planning stage.

176. B: The stakeholder management plan describes the strategies to engage stakeholders and manage their expectations. Choice *A* is incorrect because the stakeholder register identifies their roles and responsibilities. Choice *C* is incorrect because project management plans do not determine which stakeholder will lead the others. Choice *D* is incorrect because the communication management plan describes the format in which to communicate with stakeholders.

177. D: A social network analysis is used to identify organizational, functional, and social links between stakeholders with influence over the others. A salience model, Choice *A*, is used to classify stakeholders into eight groups based on three points: power, legitimacy, and urgency. The power-interest grid, Choice *B*, classifies stakeholders based on their power over and interest in the project. Stakeholder engagement, Choice *C*, is a result of applying stakeholder management strategies rather than a tool to classify and organize stakeholders.

178. A: Companies need to be in compliance with HIPAA if they are working with patient data. HIPAA protects patient data and maintains confidentiality. Choices *B*, *C*, and *D* are not handled by HIPAA.

179. D: Social responsibility is how a company can use its resources to not only increase its wealth but to also benefit its community. Choice *A* describes when companies try to maintain teams made up of people from different backgrounds. Choice *B* is the set of laws and rules that companies need to follow.

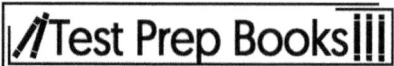

Choice *C* makes sure that the company is following both their own internal standards and industry standards.

180. C: False data can mislead companies because they might believe their products are compliant with regulations when in reality they are not. Choices *A*, *B*, and *D* are not areas affected by the false data from this particular product.

PMP Practice Test #2

1. While working on a project, when should you deliver work to the customer?
   a. Once early in the project and once toward the end
   b. When the project is complete
   c. At frequent, regular intervals, regardless of completion status
   d. At specific, predetermined intervals designated by completion status

2. Which of the following behaviors is representative of student syndrome?
   a. A team member asks for an extension on a project deadline.
   b. A team member waits until the last minute to start working on a project.
   c. A customer is unresponsive to your attempts to contact them.
   d. A customer oversteps in micromanaging the project.

3. In a predictive project life cycle, which of the following steps is taken first?
   a. Design
   b. Development
   c. Testing
   d. Analysis

4. Which of the following is NOT a meaningful type of business value?
   a. Growth capability
   b. Risk success rate
   c. Environmental benefits
   d. Social benefits

5. Which of the following is a product road map that shows each individual group's major deliverables through a predetermined time period?
   a. Technology stack road map
   b. Now-next-later road map
   c. Team-centric road map
   d. Released-based product road map

6. Which of the following is NOT one of the twelve agile principles?
   a. Simplicity is essential.
   b. Working software is the primary measure of progress.
   c. Attention to technical excellence and good design increases agility.
   d. Sponsors, developers, and users should do the most work on a rotational schedule.

7. In project management, what does MMF stand for?
   a. Minimum metric frequency
   b. Most malleable factor
   c. Mandating message frequency
   d. Minimum marketable feature

8. Which of the following should you do when communicating with stakeholders?
    a. Set rigid and clear communication cycles for all stakeholders and stress the importance of adhering to them.
    b. Identify the most important stakeholder and engage in more regular communication with them.
    c. Meet with each stakeholder and learn their individual communication needs.
    d. Avoid in-depth conversations with stakeholders until you have marketable features to present.

9. Which of the following does NOT need to be on a quality communications management plan?
    a. The work schedules of your stakeholders
    b. A glossary of commonly used terminology with each person and their company
    c. Information flowcharts
    d. Guides for escalating priority on issues that need more visibility

10. What should you do when determining what means you should use to reach out to a stakeholder?
    a. Always use the most detailed communication medium available to both you and the stakeholder.
    b. Determine the priority and expected length of the communication and use an appropriately involved medium.
    c. Always use the stakeholder's listed preferred medium of communication.
    d. Send a weekly email asking the stakeholder how they would prefer to touch base.

11. When using a hybrid or agile model, how should you share passive information such as status reports and meeting minutes with stakeholders?
    a. Email or otherwise individually message them with the information.
    b. Share the information when you privately meet with them.
    c. Post a file in the shared meeting space when all involved people are on a call together.
    d. Post the information in easily accessible places, such as project sites and digital team spaces.

12. What is the most effective way to communicate the progress of a project with stakeholders?
    a. A detailed and formal written report
    b. A live demonstration
    c. Easily understood charts and graphics
    d. A verbal progress report

13. Which of the following is the last step in the risk management process?
    a. Planning risk responses
    b. Performing quantitative risk analysis
    c. Monitoring risks
    d. Performing qualitative risk analysis

14. In which type of process might a team create a risk list instead of a risk management plan?
    a. Agile process
    b. Hybrid process
    c. Predictive process
    d. You should never only make a risk list.

15. Which type of risk is NOT actively managed in most teams?
    a. Low impact, high probability
    b. High impact, low probability
    c. Neither needs to be managed.
    d. Both must be managed.

16. How do predictive project management styles manage risk?
    a. By identifying all possible risks at the beginning of the project life cycle and managing them all before engaging in the project
    b. By dedicating a single team member to the management of each risk that arises
    c. Predictive project management styles have minimal risk by their nature and do not need to manage risk.
    d. By using clearly defined risk management techniques and deliberate documentation and deliverables dedicated to managing risk

17. How do agile project management styles manage risk?
    a. By dedicating a specific group of team members to manage risks until all risks are adequately managed
    b. With many small risk management practices, such as short iterations, feedback gathering, and regular customer demos
    c. By outsourcing risk management to other teams
    d. Agile project management styles manage risk in the same way as predictive project management styles.

18. Which of the following steps is NOT repeated in iterative risk management?
    a. Risk management planning
    b. Risk identification
    c. Risk response implementation
    d. Qualitative risk analysis

19. There is a new competitor that poses a threat to the success of your project. Which of the following would NOT be a proper risk response?
    a. Transferring risk
    b. Avoiding the root cause of the risk
    c. Exploiting the risk
    d. Avoiding the risk

20. It is usually sufficient to simply prioritize keeping which type of stakeholder satisfied?
    a. Low influence, high interest
    b. High influence, low interest
    c. Low influence, low interest
    d. High influence, high interest

21. In agile projects, what is a persona?
    a. A point person that handles the majority of communication with all stakeholders
    b. A given set of speech patterns and terminology that is tailored to engaging with stakeholders
    c. A written description of a stakeholder or customer that gives core reminders of their wants, needs, regular issues, and opportunities
    d. A stakeholder register with more detailed and tailored project requirements and impact scores

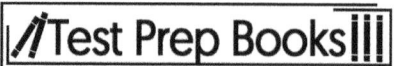

22. Why might someone integrate hybrid communication strategies into an otherwise agile project?
    a. Agile communication methods may not always be accessible or of interest to stakeholders.
    b. Agile communication methods use technology that is too complex for some stakeholders.
    c. Having a fully agile project could communicate unreliability to stakeholders.
    d. You should not alter usual agile communication strategies at all.

23. Which of the following is a direct cost?
    a. IT equipment
    b. Services
    c. Facilities
    d. Materials

24. Which of the following is NOT an approach used to estimate costs?
    a. Parametric estimation
    b. Convergent estimation
    c. Bottom-up estimation
    d. Analogous estimation

25. How should you use various cost estimation methods?
    a. Use more than one method and look for where their ranges converge.
    b. Decide on a method at the beginning of the project and adhere to it.
    c. Rotate between methods every time cycle for maximum risk coverage.
    d. Use the method preferred by the majority of your shareholders.

26. When going through the stages of budget evolution, which of the following is added to the budget first?
    a. Cost baseline
    b. Control accounts
    c. Contingency reserve
    d. Management reserve

27. What is the approved project budget minus any management reserves called?
    a. Activity cost estimate
    b. Cost baseline
    c. Control accounts
    d. True budget

28. An ideal cost baseline chart should look like which of the following?
    a. As straight of a diagonal line going upward as possible
    b. A bell curve
    c. As straight of a horizontal line as possible
    d. An S curve

29. Who needs to be in agreement regarding what "done" looks like at all times?
    a. The project manager
    b. The project manager and interested stakeholders
    c. The project manager, all project team members, and all interested stakeholders
    d. Everyone involved in the project

30. When is it appropriate to consult the team for potential solutions to a problem?
    a. Any time you feel that their task execution experience would be of value
    b. Only if you cannot think of a satisfactory solution on your own by the next deadline
    c. Only when the problems are a significant threat to the project
    d. It is never okay to bother the team with your own work problems.

31. Which of the following is a cost estimation approach that uses formulaic and data-driven methods to approximate cost?
    a. Analogous estimation
    b. Objective estimation
    c. Parametric estimation
    d. Bottom-up estimation

32. When should you take direct control of a cost that is overrun due to overspending?
    a. During the next regularly scheduled all-hands meeting
    b. Immediately upon the overspend
    c. Preemptively upon seeing costs reach a certain threshold from the current maximum
    d. When expenditures dip into the management reserve

33. How do predictive projects tend to primarily create a project schedule?
    a. A Gantt chart
    b. Tracking the team's velocity
    c. A schedule management plan
    d. Multiple road maps

34. How do agile projects tend to primarily create a project schedule?
    a. Release of burndown graphs
    b. A product backlog
    c. Milestone charts
    d. Featuring workshops

35. What does WBS stand for?
    a. Weekly backlog stand-up
    b. Working board of shareholders
    c. Weekly benchmark setting
    d. Work breakdown structure

36. What is the purpose of a feature workshop in the agile process?
    a. To establish a significant majority of the project's expected features
    b. To familiarize every member of the team with each other's strengths and weaknesses in production
    c. To create a full, comprehensive list of every feature that could possibly be in the project, over-anticipating if necessary
    d. To explore the scope of the project

37. How many steps in predictive activity estimation should occur only once in the process?
    a. One
    b. Two
    c. Four
    d. Six

38. At most, how many steps in predictive activity estimation should occur in cyclical repetition?
    a. One
    b. Two
    c. Four
    d. Six

39. Which of the following would NOT be used in a predictive process as an organizational process asset (OPA)?
    a. Published industry benchmarks
    b. Plans from earlier projects
    c. Risk and issue logs from earlier projects
    d. Anticipated team productivity rates through the life of the project

40. In agile projects, what does progress velocity measure?
    a. The rate at which team members are expected to increase their productivity
    b. A real-time measurement of team productivity in a predetermined period of time
    c. The ratio of on-schedule projects to behind-schedule projects
    d. The amount of time you dedicate for the team to complete a specific amount of work

41. Which of the following is a visual representation of a project schedule that shows both activity deadlines and activity interrelationship?
    a. Network diagram
    b. Gantt chart
    c. Milestone chart
    d. Critical path

42. Which of the following is the precedence relationship that allows activity x to begin upon the start of activity y?
    a. Finish to start (FS)
    b. Start to start (SS)
    c. Finish to finish (FF)
    d. Start to finish (SF)

43. Which of the following plans in an agile product road map is the most "big picture" and encompasses the smaller tasks within it?
    a. An iteration
    b. A release
    c. A feature
    d. A user story

44. In an ideal project life cycle, work item sizes are which of the following?
    a. Larger at first and decrease with time
    b. Smaller at first and increase with time
    c. Smallest in the middle of the life cycle, with spikes at the beginning and end
    d. As evenly and equally divided as possible

45. Which approach often uses earned value management (EVM) to track their progress?
    a. Agile
    b. Hybrid
    c. Predictive
    d. All approaches

46. Which approach often uses cumulative flow diagrams (CFDs) to track their progress?
    a. Agile
    b. Hybrid
    c. Predictive
    d. All approaches

47. Which of the following schedule modification techniques would work best with a predictive approach?
    a. Assigning the product owner to be their own change control board (CCB)
    b. Progressive elaboration
    c. Frequent retrospectives
    d. Shortening planning cycles

48. Little's Law states that the completion time of individual tasks in a queue increases as:
    a. The quantity of people working on a single task decreases.
    b. The queue shrinks in quantity.
    c. The queue grows in quantity.
    d. The task sizes increase.

49. If your agile team has a current average velocity of 15 points and has been working on their project for five iterations, each lasting three weeks, how long should it take for them to complete the 105-point project?
    a. Five weeks
    b. Eight weeks
    c. Two weeks
    d. Six weeks

50. What is the longest acceptable timeline through a network diagram called?
    a. Danger zone
    b. Critical path
    c. Dead line
    d. Red zone

51. Which of the following is NOT a standard quality management process?
    a. Retrospectives that aid in managing quality for future projects
    b. Translating a plan into performable quality activities
    c. Assessing performance by monitoring quality management activity results
    d. Identifying required quality levels for the project

52. Which of the following is the minimum benchmark of quality in a project's field?
    a. Regulation
    b. Product floor
    c. Standard
    d. Deliverable

53. Which of the following is NOT a core part of a project's cost of quality (COQ)?
    a. Failure costs
    b. Appraisal costs
    c. Prevention costs
    d. Anticipatory costs

54. Which quality management tool breaks a single problem down into many smaller cause categories?
    a. Root cause analysis
    b. Sampling
    c. Fishbone diagram
    d. Audit reports

55. How should a good agile approach handle waste?
    a. Record noticed waste and present it at the end of the project life cycle for future reference.
    b. Make noticed waste as visible as possible, as quickly as possible, for course correction.
    c. Keep noticed waste between the project manager and the teammate(s) causing the waste so as not to alarm other team members.
    d. Push forward; there is nothing to be done about waste after the planning phase.

56. Which subsection of the project management plan acts as the perimeter for project activities?
    a. Scope management plan
    b. Quality management plan
    c. Requirements management plan
    d. Benchmarking

57. How is scope explored and built upon in agile projects?
    a. Built scope evaluations
    b. Product backlog refinements
    c. Box vision design
    d. Feature workshops

58. Which of the following techniques would be a poor approach to monitoring scope on a predictive project?
    a. Trend analysis
    b. Scope validation
    c. Variance analysis
    d. Iteration reviews

59. What does the project management plan do?
    a. Documents how the project's schedule will be developed and controlled
    b. Integrates every type of management plan into a single master plan
    c. Lays out the schedule, budget, and constraints for all of a given company's project managers
    d. Provides a hands-off means of letting the project mostly run itself

60. Project management information systems (PMIS), such as Azure and DevOps, are more colloquially referred to as which of the following?
    a. Project trackers (PTs)
    b. Information aides (IAs)
    c. Digital project managers (DPMs)
    d. Project management tools (PMT)

61. Which of the following is a collection of procedures, usually computerized, that serve to monitor and report on various project aspects?
    a. Electronic project tracker (EPT)
    b. Master monitor network (MMN)
    c. Configuration management system (CMS)
    d. Control change board (CCB)

62. Which of the following approaches does NOT allow for effective change management in dynamic projects beyond the team level?
    a. Change management plan
    b. Disciplined agile
    c. Scaled agile framework
    d. Scrum of scrums

63. Predictive projects manage compliance through what process?
    a. Control change boards
    b. Backlog reprioritization
    c. A contingency protocol
    d. Integrated change management

64. How do you set up a project to experience little to no changes?
    a. Project changes are never fully avoidable.
    b. Run a project with a predictive model to anticipate and adjust for potential changes.
    c. Use a control change board.
    d. Only accept simple projects at first and work your way up.

65. What strategy do hybrid projects normally use to handle change?
    a. Focusing on only the most immediately project-threatening changes that arise
    b. Using lightweight versions of usually intensive predictive planning artifacts
    c. Reprioritizing their backlog
    d. Escalating to the control change board

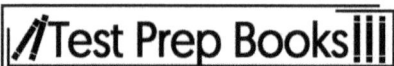

PMP Practice Test #2

66. In which circumstance should an agile project team make decisions on its own without consulting the control change board (CCB)?
    a. Never. The CCB should always be consulted; it's what they're there for.
    b. Only when the change is of minimal severity and can be easily facilitated
    c. When the nature of the change pertains to the project manager's specialty
    d. Only when the change needs to be addressed more quickly than it would take to consult the CCB

67. When using an agile approach, who is responsible for determining responses to changes?
    a. The project's control change board
    b. The project manager
    c. The product owner
    d. The shareholders

68. Which of the following factors does NOT need to be included when performing a make-or-buy analysis for a product?
    a. Product's learning curve
    b. Ongoing need for the product's value
    c. Team's ability to build rather than buy
    d. Number of competitors who also bought the product

69. Which strategy would be most effective in communicating with external vendors and suppliers for a project?
    a. Adding them to your project's communications management plan
    b. Weekly email updates on your project's process
    c. Identifying a primary vendor contact and engaging primarily with them
    d. Providing all required information up front and keeping necessary interaction lengths to a minimum

70. What is the primary downside of a time-and-materials (T&M) contract type?
    a. The actual total costs are unknown.
    b. No incentive for finishing early can result in overruns.
    c. It requires the seller to have extensive estimations and to pad their budget.
    d. There is no way to determine whether materials will run out.

71. Which of the following contract types is designed specifically for agile approaches?
    a. Incremental delivery
    b. Fixed-price
    c. Time-and-material
    d. Cost-reimbursable

72. You find out that a seller with whom you have an active non-compete agreement is now providing their services to another company in your field. Which course of action is most appropriate?
    a. Make the seller sign a waiver that consents to lower pay than the contract initially stipulated.
    b. Send the seller a cease-and-desist letter and inform the competitor of the seller's previous agreement.
    c. Inform the seller of an official breach of contract and invoke the contract's appropriate consequence.
    d. Remove the seller from the project and terminate all communications with them.

148

73. What is a project artifact?
    a. A design related to managing a project
    b. A document related to managing a project
    c. A model related to managing a project
    d. All of the above

74. Which of the following project artifacts is heavily associated with agile project approaches?
    a. Deficit reports
    b. Product backlogs
    c. Risk logs
    d. Acceptance criteria

75. Which of the following statements is NOT always true of project artifacts?
    a. They are stored privately and securely within the project team.
    b. They are stored in company project records to be referred to in the future.
    c. They can be accessed by select approved stakeholders.
    d. Version control systems track their changes.

76. In the modern, software-driven business landscape, which of the following is the best model for executing most projects?
    a. There is no single best model.
    b. Agile method
    c. Predictive method
    d. Hybrid method

77. It is estimated that approximately four out of five jobs in developed nations fall under which work form?
    a. Industrial work
    b. Agricultural work
    c. Government work
    d. Knowledge work

78. What is the ideal approach for managing a project with a low change likelihood; a newer, smaller team; and less access to the customer?
    a. Agile
    b. Agile-leaning hybrid
    c. Predictive
    d. Predictive-leaning hybrid

79. Who makes the final decision regarding what type of management approach a project will have?
    a. The shareholders
    b. The project manager
    c. The project management office
    d. The holder of the final say varies from group to group.

80. What is project governance?
    a. The authority held by the project manager over their project
    b. An individual organization's set work structure
    c. The framework of a project's work practices built from multiple sources of structure within the organization
    d. The chain of authority by which the product owner's word supersedes regular team members, the project manager supersedes the product owner, and so on

81. A review point between phases on a predictive project, also called a governance gate or kill point, is called what?
    a. Phase gate
    b. Checkpoint
    c. Roundtable
    d. Reconfiguration

82. What is the first thing you should do when encountering a risk that has become an issue?
    a. Be on the lookout for more issues.
    b. Promptly record the issue in the project's issue log.
    c. Resolve or minimize its impact as quickly as possible.
    d. Engage your team in issue resolution dialogue.

83. If you and your team go through the issue resolution steps and cannot find a proper resolution, what should you do?
    a. Transfer the issue to another team working on the same project.
    b. Restart the issue resolution process from the beginning.
    c. Record the issue as unsolved in the issue log and move forward with the project.
    d. Escalate the issue to the project sponsor.

84. Which of the following agile projects is most likely to be used if the team does NOT have an official issue log?
    a. Weekly stand-ups
    b. A dedicated issues resolution team member
    c. An impediment board
    d. An issues backlog

85. Which piece of knowledge would an agile team call tacit knowledge?
    a. The project manager agreed to dip into management reserves yesterday.
    b. The team has an unspoken agreement to not hold meetings in the morning.
    c. Two equally ranked team members are being paid considerably different amounts.
    d. The phone number of the primary shareholder

86. How often is it useful to hold lessons learned review workshops in a predictive project?
    a. After each project phase
    b. At the end of the project
    c. After the first project phase and at the end of the project
    d. Lessons learned review workshops belong only in agile projects.

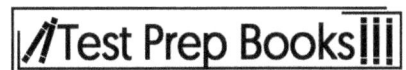

87. Knowledge transferring can be simpler for remote teams because everyone receives information in the same way at the same rate. How can knowledge transferring be more difficult for remote teams?
    a. There is no way to verify that everyone is properly intaking the knowledge.
    b. People's working hours may be drastically different.
    c. Different locations have different internet and cellular connectivity speeds.
    d. It is harder to communicate tacit knowledge remotely.

88. At which point during a project's life cycle should you close contracts?
    a. Upon total completion of the project, unless a contractor's work is still needed due to unforeseen changes
    b. As soon as the agreed-upon work is completed, whenever that may be
    c. At the end of the project's current phase to ensure that the agreed-upon work is properly done
    d. Once every primary stakeholder has agreed that the contractor's work is no longer needed

89. Which of the following is NOT an effective definition of *complete* for a piece of work?
    a. The team member has put in a full 40-hour work week.
    b. All functional tests have been passed.
    c. All code has been successfully documented.
    d. Refactoring has been fully completed.

90. What is the correct first step if you learn that your project is getting canceled?
    a. Close out all your project's procurements and payments.
    b. Inform the project's stakeholders.
    c. Follow designated closure guidelines.
    d. Identify the cause of the cancellation and attempt to solve it.

91. Which level of Speed Leas' five levels of conflict involves personal attacks directed at other team members, as well as self-protecting language?
    a. Level 1: Problem to Solve
    b. Level 2: Disagreement
    c. Level 3: Contest
    d. Level 4: Crusade

92. While solving a problem, the team discusses which tool might work best. Which statement is the most concerning and would require immediate intervention?
    a. "Tool A is much simpler than Tool B, so I think that is the best option."
    b. "I don't care what we choose. Either one will probably work fine."
    c. "He can be so indecisive. We should make a decision before he joins the call."
    d. "I disagree. Tool B has aspects we may need to incorporate in the future."

93. Assume you are using the confronting/problem-solving approach to resolve a conflict between two team members. What would be the first step toward resolving the conflict?
    a. Seek a win-win solution.
    b. Define the problem.
    c. Clarify the issue.
    d. Explore and evaluate alternatives.

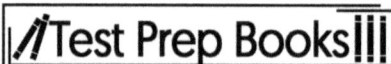

94. According to the five dysfunctions of a team pyramid model developed by Patrick Lencioni, which dysfunction immediately follows the lowest level, an absence of trust?
    a. Fear of conflict
    b. Lack of commitment
    c. Avoidance of accountability
    d. Inattention to results

95. Regarding the five levels of agile conflict, which of the following de-escalation tactics would be best suited for a conflict that has recently escalated to Level 3: Contest?
    a. Look for a win-win opportunity through collaboration.
    b. Offer support and empower teammates to resolve the conflict between themselves.
    c. Take whatever action needed to prevent team members from hurting each other.
    d. Negotiate with both sides by getting the facts of the situation.

96. During a sprint you overhear one of your team members say to another while alone in a conference room, "I know we're on the same team, but it's us against them. We can't let those people win." What level of conflict does this most likely indicate?
    a. Level 2: Disagreement
    b. Level 3: Contest
    c. Level 4: Crusade
    d. Level 5: World War

97. Which of the following is NOT a benefit of supporting diversity and inclusion?
    a. Improved customer empathy
    b. More accurate decision-making
    c. Improved risk management
    d. Larger blind spots

98. The project management office (PMO) lead suggests you implement a Theory Y approach when working with your team after a big deadline has passed. This means you should provide the team with ____.
    a. more autonomy
    b. stricter guidelines
    c. lower production goals
    d. more rewards

99. What is the recommended management style for stakeholders who possess low interest but high power in terms of the power/interest grid?
    a. Keep informed
    b. Keep satisfied
    c. Manage closely
    d. Monitor

100. At the onset of a new project, you decide that designing the product box will lead to a clearer vision of what is ahead. Which of the following is the key first step of this exercise?
    a. Small-group ideation and brainstorming
    b. Logo design
    c. Scheduling and task assignment
    d. Team presentations and a lengthy discussion

101. Regarding the four stages of psychological safety, which of the following defines the third stage, contributor safety?
   a. The innate desire to be accepted by a group is fulfilled, and the team member feels safe being themselves.
   b. Instead of holding on to their work until it is deemed perfect for fear of negative feedback, the team member feels comfortable presenting their work and receiving criticism.
   c. The team member feels supported in their growth and experimentation with new approaches, asking questions along the way.
   d. The team member feels safe going against the status quo and speaking up when they believe something could be done differently in the future.

102. Ensuring that the team is free of interruptions, eliminating blockers as they arrive, consistently delivering a clear vision, and fueling growth are all key aspects of which value mindset?
   a. Empathy
   b. Servant leadership
   c. Supporting diversity and inclusion
   d. Net contribution

103. What can you assume if a project is reporting a schedule performance index (SPI) of .85?
   a. The project is ahead of the planned schedule.
   b. The project is coming in under the projected budget.
   c. Eighty-five percent of the project is completed.
   d. The project is behind the planned schedule.

104. Which of the following is NOT attributed to the acronym SMART?
   a. Time-bound
   b. Specific
   c. Achievable
   d. Manageable

105. A PMO member has suggested that you set an objective and key result (OKR) for your team's upcoming project. If the objective is to become the market leader in digital therapy, which of the following would NOT be a suitable key result?
   a. Gain a 15% increase in market share.
   b. Acquire 50,000 new customers before the end of the year.
   c. Hire enough licensed therapists to work with the influx of new customers.
   d. Reduce cancellations to 10%.

106. Simple qualitative descriptions designed to inspire the team and illustrate the end goal of a project are known as ___.
   a. objectives
   b. key results
   c. key performance indicators (KPIs)
   d. lagging metrics

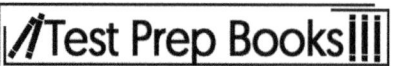

107. If the cost performance index (CPI) of a traditional project you are managing is 0.9, and the schedule performance index (SPI) is 1.1, what can you deduce about the project?
    a. The project is over budget and ahead of schedule.
    b. The project is over budget and behind schedule.
    c. The project is under budget and ahead of schedule.
    d. The project is under budget and behind schedule.

108. What are the three most essential elements to include when creating an agile team charter?
    a. Team practices, values, and reporting structures
    b. Team values, agreements, and practices
    c. Team agreements, scope statements, and practices
    d. Team values, agreements, and RACI matrix

109. An empowered team tends to have ____ motivation and will often engage in ____ arguments and debates compared to non-empowered teams.
    a. more; more
    b. as much; fewer
    c. more; fewer
    d. fewer; as many

110. You are the project manager for an agile team that needs to choose one of three technical solutions, all of which cost about the same. What is the recommended approach?
    a. Allow the project manager to make the final decision.
    b. Calculate the expected monetary value of each option.
    c. Dot voting
    d. Simple voting

111. Since the onset of a project, your team has been debating a simple two-choice decision at great length. While this is a constructive debate, you know the team must come to a decision quickly to avoid falling behind schedule. What technique can you employ to ensure a decision is made?
    a. Highsmith's decision spectrum
    b. Simple voting
    c. Dot voting
    d. Fist to five

112. Your new agile team has been reluctant to engage in constructive debate and prefers to make quick decisions that end up being suboptimal. What should you do for the next decision to be made?
    a. Simple voting
    b. Decide on the best choice without consulting the team.
    c. Bring in a subject matter expert to make all remaining decisions.
    d. Highsmith's decision spectrum

113. Which type of training would shadowing and peer-to-peer coaching fall under?
    a. Formal training
    b. Informal training
    c. On-the-job (experiential) training
    d. Safety training

114. You decide to offer diversity training to a global team you manage after hearing that a few team members are using insensitive language and unintentionally offending others. What is the most effective format for this upcoming training?
    a. Instructor-led and locally sourced training
    b. Online locally sourced training
    c. Synchronous instructor-led training
    d. Standardized online on-demand training

115. You decide to provide your team with a book and recommend listening to an industry-specific podcast at the onset of a new project. What type of training is this?
    a. Experiential training
    b. Informal training
    c. Formal training
    d. On-the-job training

116. You need to determine whether or not your team needs training before an upcoming project. Of the following tools, which would NOT be an effective way to determine the level of training the team might require?
    a. Reviewing the WBS task analysis
    b. Having team members complete a survey
    c. Running a skills gap analysis
    d. Conducting a SWOT analysis

117. A new team member lacks the required knowledge surrounding AI for the current project. What would be the most effective form of training for this new team member?
    a. An up-to-date book about AI
    b. A podcast discussing the possibilities of AI
    c. Synchronous group virtual learning
    d. Shadowing the most knowledgeable team member

118. Suppose you are recruiting new talent and are looking for someone who is T shaped rather than I shaped concerning their expertise. What general skill set are you looking for?
    a. Expertise in one area with broader skills in other areas
    b. Mastery in one area without any knowledge of others
    c. A broad but shallow skill set in many areas, with no real expertise
    d. A shallow skill set in only one domain

119. Which of the five stages within the Tuckman model is characterized by team members attempting to find their place within a team where they can work best and have the most to offer?
    a. Performing
    b. Norming
    c. Storming
    d. Forming

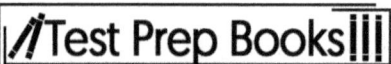

120. A new team member has just been recruited to join your team, and you need to assess their skill levels in a few areas relating to the current project. What is the most effective way to do so?
   a. Structured interviews
   b. Attitudinal surveys
   c. Ability tests
   d. Focus groups

121. Your team, which had previously entered the performing stage of the Tuckman model, just lost a team member unexpectedly and must reconfigure the group dynamic. What stage will they most likely re-enter?
   a. Adjourning
   b. Forming
   c. Norming
   d. Storming

122. When creating a RACI matrix, a stakeholder who is assigned to do the work to complete a task can be considered ___, whereas a person who is required to sign off on a completed task is deemed ___.
   a. responsible; consulted
   b. informed; consulted
   c. responsible; accountable
   d. accountable; responsible

123. Your team has been producing desired results while engaging in effective collaboration on a project for the past week. What stage of the Tuckman model has the team entered?
   a. Performing
   b. Norming
   c. Storming
   d. Forming

124. Which of the following would NOT be a common source for identifying impediments within your team?
   a. Lessons learned workshop
   b. Project kickoff meeting
   c. Retrospective meeting
   d. Daily standup

125. Actively seeking out issues that slow down progress or make the project unnecessarily difficult and working with your team to find a solution describes what crucial process?
   a. Value stream mapping
   b. Gemba walk
   c. Impediment removal
   d. Backlog assessment

126. The PMO at your organization suggests that you increase awareness of project and task blockers by implementing techniques designed to visualize impediments. Which of the following is the best tool for visualizing impediments?
    a. Task board
    b. Burndown chart
    c. Release roadmap
    d. Network diagram

127. The process of locating problems that make progress unnecessarily difficult and working with the team to find a solution can be referred to as ___.
    a. project management
    b. performing
    c. task age analysis
    d. impediment removal

128. A task assigned to one of your remote team members was scheduled to take one day to complete; however, it is still unfinished after three days. You want to reach out to your team member to see if there may be something blocking their progress. Which of the following is most likely to yield existing impediments?
    a. "Are you done with task X yet?"
    b. "This was only supposed to take one day—what's taking you so long?"
    c. "Is there anything I or other team members can do to support you with task X?"
    d. "How long will it take you to complete task X?"

129. Which stage of the agreement negotiation life cycle is characterized by understanding the problem, defining goals, and building relationships?
    a. Deciding to negotiate
    b. Preparing
    c. Negotiating
    d. Executing

130. What happens to the formality of an agreement as separation from your team or core group increases?
    a. The formality increases.
    b. The formality remains the same.
    c. The formality decreases.
    d. A verbal or informal agreement may be used.

131. You have been asked to create agreements for multiple stakeholder groups on an upcoming project you are managing. Whereas the agreement with your own team may be ___, the agreement you are designing for an outside vendor should be ___.
    a. informal (verbal or written); formal (written)
    b. formal (written); formal (written)
    c. informal (verbal or written); legal (written)
    d. legal (written); informal (verbal or written)

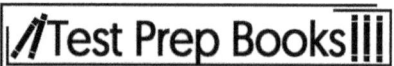

132. What stakeholder group would an individual fall into if they are the person funding an update to an existing product?
    a. Suppliers and vendors
    b. Sponsors and executives
    c. Customers and users
    d. Business representative

133. Which of the following are the three primary common project constraints, also known as the project management triangle or triple constraints?
    a. Cost, scope, and time or schedule
    b. Risks, quality, and resources
    c. Cost, scope, and resources
    d. Schedule, resources, and quality

134. Which of the following stakeholder groups would vendors, customers, and team members most likely be a part of?
    a. Hopefully positive
    b. Initially neutral
    c. Interested
    d. Likely negative

135. Ensuring that stakeholders are engaged and that their business needs are consistently validated can effectively ___ the possibility of substantial change requests or rejection further into the project life cycle.
    a. eliminate
    b. increase
    c. decrease
    d. maintain

136. You are the project manager of a new team in the early stages of the project life cycle, and one of the first things you need to do is identify all stakeholders involved. Which of the following would NOT be an effective way to gather a list of stakeholders?
    a. Look to the stakeholder register of an older but similar project.
    b. Gather the team and ask them what stakeholders may be involved.
    c. Deliver a survey to known stakeholders.
    d. Pull contact information from lead and lag time calculations.

137. Which of the following tools is the most effective at helping team members move fluidly from one portion of the project to the next without confusion or interruption?
    a. Product box
    b. Task board
    c. Project charter
    d. Stakeholder register

138. Of the following, what information is LEAST likely to be contained in the stakeholder register?
    a. Stakeholder name and contact information
    b. Project role and requirements
    c. Impact and influence scores
    d. Task assignments and schedule

139. You are worried that the majority of your team members are too heavily influenced by the most experienced stakeholder when asked to make difficult decisions. Which of the following methods is LEAST likely to succumb to the halo effect?
   a. Roman voting
   b. Fist to five
   c. Wideband Delphi estimation
   d. Focus groups

140. Which exercise is best suited for identifying the root cause of a problem?
   a. Wideband Delphi estimation
   b. Five whys
   c. Planning poker
   d. After-action review (AAR)

141. If the project charter focuses on the details of why, how, with who, and by when, which document illustrates the ultimate *where* of a project?
   a. Project vision
   b. Project plan
   c. The fishbone analysis
   d. Product box

142. While making a decision with your team, you employ the fist-to-five method to reach an agreement. What is the main benefit of this technique?
   a. The team will make a decision as quickly as possible.
   b. The project manager will have the final input.
   c. All disagreements will be heard throughout the decision-making process.
   d. The team will reach the best decision collaboratively.

143. A short, simple story that reads parallel to the product being built, with the purpose of aligning the team around a singular view, is also known as a(n) ___.
   a. product box
   b. XP metaphor
   c. task board
   d. project vision

144. Virtual teams tend to progress through the Tuckman stages of group development ___ compared to traditional in-person teams.
   a. almost immediately
   b. faster
   c. at the same pace
   d. more slowly

145. Which of the following is the most effective check-in statement when reaching out to a team member you have not heard from in a short while?
   a. "What have you been doing today?"
   b. "When do you expect to be done with your portion of the assignment?"
   c. "Is there anything I can do to help?"
   d. "How much progress have you made this morning?"

146. Your team has recently transitioned to a fully remote setting, and you are asked if an agile approach is still possible. What is the most appropriate response?
   a. With minimal modifications and added technological support, an agile approach is still plausible.
   b. No, a virtual team has too many barriers that prevent an agile approach from being effective.
   c. Yes, no changes are needed to apply an agile approach in a fully remote workplace.
   d. While a few agile approaches may remain, we will have to implement mostly traditional values and practices moving forward.

147. If possible, what is the best point in the project life cycle to bring the team together for an in-person meeting?
   a. Once the project has been completed
   b. After all major checkpoints
   c. Around the halfway point
   d. For the first team meeting

148. Your organization has recently transitioned from a traditional office to an all-remote workplace. Which of the following is NOT an advantage of this transition?
   a. Innovation increases
   b. Freedom for staff to travel
   c. A larger pool of talent to hire from
   d. Smaller overhead

149. As the project manager of an all-remote team, you will have to focus ___ on team member engagement compared to a traditional in-person team.
   a. the same amount
   b. less
   c. more
   d. all your efforts

150. When a new team is formed, it is crucial to set a list of ground rules that guide the way team members interact on a daily basis. Who should be in charge of defining these ground rules?
   a. The project manager only
   b. All team members, including the project manager
   c. The project manager and PMO only
   d. All team members, excluding the project manager

151. Effective ground rules can be a catalyst for psychological safety within teams. A team member who is starting to feel safe asking questions is exhibiting what stage of psychological safety?
   a. Inclusion safety
   b. Learner safety
   c. Contributor safety
   d. Challenger safety

152. Which two axes define the stages of the psychological safety chart?
   a. Communication and conflict
   b. Respect and knowledge
   c. Respect and permission
   d. Comfortability and permission

153. During a heated discussion, Henry, a more vocal team member, repeatedly interrupts and talks over quieter teammates, not allowing them to fully contribute and violating the ground rules the team set together. Ideally, who should be the first to recognize and act against this violation?
   a. Henry
   b. The other team members
   c. The project manager
   d. The HR department

154. What is the most effective way for a project manager to create a team working environment that fosters respect and allows the team to comfortably adhere to ground rules?
   a. Constantly reminding the team of ground rules
   b. Always allowing team members to settle disputes amongst themselves
   c. Removing team members who violate any of the ground rules
   d. Modeling the desired behavior

155. During an agile team sprint, at what point is individual coaching and mentoring most likely to surpass whole-team coaching?
   a. At the onset of the sprint
   b. At the midpoint
   c. At the finale of the sprint
   d. Whole-team coaching will always be more prevalent.

156. What is the most effective approach to improving project performance or team production?
   a. Adding new tools to the team's repertoire
   b. Implementing new techniques
   c. Mentoring and coaching that focus on team capability
   d. Reprimanding team members who exhibit below-average performance

157. An outside project that your team is relying on is underperforming, and you have been asked to assist the project manager in coaching and mentoring. Of the following, which would NOT provide insight into prior coaching practices?
   a. The communications plan
   b. The mentoring and training plan
   c. Team assessments
   d. The training schedules

158. How does whole-team coaching compare to individual coaching at the beginning of a sprint?
   a. Individual coaching is of the utmost importance, as team members must all be capable of delivering their portion of the project.
   b. Whole-team coaching is most prominent at the start of the sprint since team members need to build trust and develop shared commitments.
   c. Coaching does not occur on an individual level or as a team until all the planning is complete and everyone has begun work on their assigned tasks.
   d. The team will need to be coached both individually and as a whole before beginning the sprint.

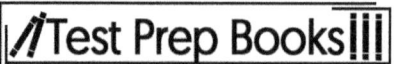

159. Allowing other team members and stakeholders to participate in the role of coaching and mentoring can effectively increase ___ within the team.
    a. profits
    b. productivity
    c. empowerment
    d. technological capabilities

160. Effective project managers must possess a good psychological understanding of themselves and others. Which term encompasses this quality?
    a. Conflict management
    b. Emotional intelligence
    c. Agile mindset
    d. Empowerment

161. The four quadrants of emotional intelligence (EQ) can be defined as ___ and ___, both personally and interpersonally.
    a. empathy; motivation
    b. action; awareness
    c. emotions; actions
    d. self-regulation; social skills

162. Of the following skills, which one would best fit in the social skills quadrant?
    a. Optimism
    b. Adaptability
    c. Leveraging diversity
    d. Leadership

163. Which of the four quadrants is defined by actions on a personal level?
    a. Empathy
    b. Motivation
    c. Self-regulation
    d. Social skills

164. The fourth quadrant, empathy, is found at the intersection of ___ and ___.
    a. interpersonal skills; actions
    b. personal skills; actions
    c. personal skills; awareness
    d. interpersonal skills; awareness

165. Awareness of the emotions and context of a conversation and the ability to take to heart what's being conveyed, both directly and indirectly, defines which key skill?
    a. Active listening
    b. Internal listening
    c. Empathy
    d. Understanding others

166. What is the process in which information is consistently gathered and analyzed throughout the project to determine, address, and align expectations?
   a. Project requirements
   b. Interviews
   c. Stakeholder analysis
   d. Focus groups

167. What is the document that is a reference of authority for the future of a project?
   a. Gnatt chart
   b. Process document
   c. Project management plan
   d. Project charter

168. What is the name of the requirements that define how an end user will interact with the product or service?
   a. Transitional requirements
   b. Functional requirements
   c. Technical requirements
   d. Operational requirements

169. Who is responsible for conducting a benefits analysis?
   a. Stakeholders
   b. Customers
   c. Project team
   d. Project manager

170. What is the correct formula to calculate the present value (PV) of money?
   a. $PV = FV/(1+i)^n$
   b. $PV = NPV/FV = 1$
   c. $PV = FV/(1+i)$
   d. $PV + FV/(1-i)$

171. Which project has the lowest benefit-cost ratio (BCR)?
   a. Project A had a cost of $200,000 and benefit of $150,000.
   b. Project B had a cost of $100,000 and benefit of $120,000.
   c. Project C had a cost of $250,000 and benefit of $100,000.
   d. Project D had a cost of $500,000 and benefit of $300,000.

172. Referencing question 171, which project will most likely be *approved* by the organization based on the benefit-cost ratio?
   a. Project B
   b. Project D
   c. Project A
   d. Project C

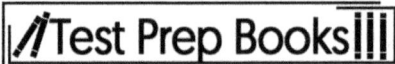

173. When performing a stakeholder analysis, what does it mean when the stakeholder has high importance and low influence on the project and falls into the *meet their needs* quadrant on the matrix?
    a. Stakeholders are involved in the decision making and should be engaged regularly throughout the project, as they are most critical.
    b. Stakeholders are helpful in formulating opinions and decisions and should be engaged.
    c. Stakeholders are non-supportive.
    d. Stakeholders should be engaged and kept informed in the low-risk areas of the project.

174. Which is NOT considered a way to resolve conflicting requirement issues amongst the stakeholders?
    a. Set up a meeting with the stakeholder groups and have them reiterate the project goals and objectives.
    b. Set up a meeting with the stakeholder groups and include an unbiased mediator who has knowledge geared towards higher level business goals.
    c. Create a prototype or mockup of each conflicting requirement issue and conduct a walkthrough with a small user group to determine which one works well.
    d. Ask all the project team members for their input on which requirement to choose.

175. As project manager you are responsible for developing the project plan. Included in the plan are the key deliverables and milestones that have been identified based on the business requirements in order to manage customer expectations and direct the achievement of business goals. Which of the following validation activities is considered a deliverable and NOT a milestone?
    a. Final user acceptance testing complete (UAT)
    b. Project acceptance
    c. Tested system based on specifications
    d. Go-live

176. What is the present value (PV) of $2,000 dollars to be received in two years with an interest rate of 15% per year and a late fee of $500?
    a. $1,890.36
    b. $609.64
    c. $2,499.64
    d. $2,300.00

177. What is an example of a high-level risk based on the choices below?
    a. The project team will be released to attend training.
    b. Fixed budget of $500,000
    c. Website and pages
    d. Two resources assigned to the project are simultaneously working on another project.

178. A project manager has suggested that the company's working culture could use improvements. Which of the following is a component of company culture?
    a. Product roadmaps
    b. Incentive programs
    c. Kanban boards
    d. Matrix organizational structure

179. What is the benefit-cost ratio for a system implementation project charging $215,000 that will generate $320,000?
   a. 0.67
   b. 1.49
   c. 68.8
   d. 105

180. What kind of information does the net present value (NPV) give to companies?
   a. The number of audits a company has received
   b. A summary of the costs of all resources in a project
   c. The total value of an investment that a company has made
   d. The total number of workers available for a project

Answer Explanations #2

1. C: Choice C is correct because a frequent, regular delivery pattern creates a culture of accountability, and projects do not need to be completed to show a customer your progress. Choices A and B are too infrequent, and Choice D can vary frequently in time.

2. B: Choice B is correct because *student syndrome* is the tendency for team members to procrastinate and only begin earnestly working on a task when the deadline is near. Choices A, C, and D are all problems in their own right, but they are not the definition of *student syndrome*.

3. D: Choice D is correct because the order of a predictive project's life cycle is: plan, analysis, design, development, testing, and then deployment. Choices A, B, and C are all later in the life cycle.

4. B: Choice B is correct because risk success rate is not a business value; it's a metric that could lead to any number of business values. Choices A, C, and D are all positive business values.

5. A: Choice A is correct because this question specifically describes a technology stack road map. Choices B and D are different types of road maps, and Choice C is not an actual project management term.

6. D: Choice D is correct because it is not in line with principle eight of the agile manifesto, which is that sponsors, developers, and users should be able to keep up a constant pace indefinitely. Choices A, B, and C are all among the 12 agile principles.

7. D: Choice D is correct because a minimum marketable feature (MMF) is an important and often used term for a quickly developed, self-contained feature that delivers worthwhile value to recipients. Choices A, B, and C are all made-up terms that are not related to project management.

8. C: Choice C is correct because being able to communicate with stakeholders reliably and respectfully is a high priority, and each stakeholder will have different communication needs and preferences. Choices A, B, and D are all unreliable, ineffective, or immoral ways to handle communicating with stakeholders.

9. A: Choice A is correct because work schedules do not completely dictate communication availability, and knowing a stakeholder's work schedule does not ensure that you know their availability. Choices B, C, and D are all things that should be on a good communications management plan.

10. B: Choice B is correct because quick questions do not always mandate something as in-depth as a full video call, but more serious conversations may be too dynamic and complex for a text or email exchange. Choices A, C, and D are incorrect, primarily because a single hard and fast communication approach is never a good idea when communicating with real people.

11. D: Choice D is correct because hybrid and agile models work best with maximum information transparency so that all members can readily access the same information whenever they individually need it. Choices A and B put too much priority on individually communicating with stakeholders, and Choice C is not always accessible after a call ends.

Answer Explanations #2

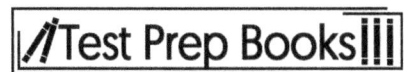

12. B: Choice *B* is correct because demonstrations are not only more tangible and easily understood, but they are solid proof that progress is where you say it is. Choices *A*, *C*, and *D* can all be situationally useful, but none of them are as concretely effective as a proper demo. "Show, don't tell."

13. C: Choice *C* is correct because monitoring the effectiveness of the risk process is the final step in risk management. Choices *A*, *B*, and *D* are all steps that occur earlier in the process.

14. A: Choice *A* is correct because small agile projects will often simply create a risk list and accept whatever risk management approach is outlined in the project charter. Choices *B* and *C* are too rigid to make do without a proper risk management plan, and Choice *D* is incorrect because some small agile projects only make a risk list.

15. D: Choice *D* is correct because the only type of risk that is occasionally safe to not actively manage is a low impact, low probability risk. Choices *A*, *B*, and *C* all ignore likely and/or dangerous risks.

16. D: Choice *D* is correct because risk management is a dedicated and premeditated activity in predictive approaches. Choices *A* and *C* are impossible, and Choice *B* is a significant waste of team member time.

17. B: Choice *B* is correct because agile approaches use these strategies to constantly prioritize risk reduction in their backlogs, avoiding risks before they become proper threats. Choices *A* and *C* are wastes of resources, and Choice *D* is blatantly untrue.

18. A: Choice *A* is correct because every step in iterative risk management is performed cyclically except for planning the risk management, which happens once at the beginning of the time cycle.

19. C: Choice *C* is correct because exploiting risk is an opportunity response, not a threat response. *A*, *B*, and *D* are all valid threat response tactics.

20. B: Choice *B* is correct because high power, low interest stakeholders need to only be kept happy and don't need to be brought into the regular minutia of the project. Choice *A* should always be kept informed, Choice *C* needs to only be monitored, and Choice *D* should be regularly engaged and consulted.

21. C: Choice *C* is correct because agile projects will often keep less detailed records of every stakeholder and keep a more qualitative record of them in what is called a persona. Choice *A* is ineffective, Choice *B* is the definition of *code switching*, and Choice *D* is not in line with an agile strategy.

22. A: Choice *A* is correct because agile communication strategies often involve demos that people may not be able to attend or a video with far more information than certain stakeholders are interested in engaging with. Choices *B* and *C* assume truths that do not exist, and Choice *D* is not appropriate.

23. D: Choice *D* is correct because materials are accumulated only as a direct result of beginning a project. Choices *A*, *B*, and *C* are all things that your team could have existing access to, making them indirect costs.

24. B: Choice *B* is correct because the three primary approaches to cost estimation are analogous, parametric, and bottom-up estimation. Choice *B* is based on the principle of combining these three methods but is a made-up term.

Answer Explanations #2

25. A: Choice A is correct because checking the overlap between various estimation methods indicates forecast accuracy quite well. Choices B, C, and D are needlessly rigid.

26. C: Choice C is correct because contingency reserves are added in step two of budget evolution. Choices A and D are added in step four, and Choice B is added in step three.

27. B: Choice B is correct because the question describes the cost baseline. Choice A is in the first step of budget evolution, Choice C is the individual accounts that comprise the cost baseline, and Choice D is not an actual term.

28. D: Choice D is correct because the S-curve graph is the intended shape of a visualized cost baseline. Choices A, B, and C exhibit unrealistic or inefficient project work patterns.

29. D: Choice D is correct because a project-wide agreed-upon definition of *done* is among the most critical points of communication for resource management and many other factors of the project life cycle.

30. A: Choice A is correct because asking the team for advice is potentially beneficial to the project, as it acknowledges the team's intelligence and strengths and displays your respect for their own specialties. Choices B, C, and D are needless and potentially harmfully restrictive.

31. C: Choice C is correct because this question describes the parametric estimation technique. Choices A and D are different estimating techniques, and Choice B is not an actual term.

32. B: Choice B is correct because action should be taken as soon as you expect a cost overrun to occur. Choices A and D only allow the problem to worsen, and Choice C is overcareful.

33. C: Choice C is correct because schedule management plans follow the predictive method of laying out as many meaningful details of a project plan as possible, as early as possible. Choice A is a tool that might be used in a schedule management plan, Choice B is a way that agile projects handle scheduling, and Choice D are tools frequently used in agile release plans.

34. B: Choice B is correct because a product backlog follows the agile method of tackling portions of a project in a more fluid and adaptable order than a traditionally predictive order of operations. Choice A is designed for project schedule monitoring, Choice C is a generic outline of a project schedule, and Choice D is a style of activity estimation.

35. D: Choice D is correct because the frequently used abbreviated term WBS stands for work breakdown structure, a method of project deconstruction that breaks work down into smaller deliverables for the sake of scope management. Choices A, B, and C are made-up terms.

36. A: Choice A is correct because feature workshops follow the agile method of informed yet dynamic and fluid development patterns. Choices B and D should have already happened before a feature workshop, and Choice C is wasteful, short-sighted, and uselessly thorough for agile approaches.

37. C: Choice C is correct because you only need to review the scope of (1) the management plan, (2) the project constraints and assumptions, (3) the external factors, and (4) the organizational process assets (OPAs) once. Choices A, B, and D are incorrect values.

38. C: Choice C is correct because you should be (1) breaking down work packages, (2) consulting any necessary subject matter experts, (3) evaluating any of the package's activity constraints, and (4) recording activity estimates in a regular cycle once OPAs have been reviewed until all planned activities are completed. Choices A, B, and D are incorrect values.

39. D: Choice D is correct because predicting the productivity of team members uses anticipatory knowledge, and OPAs in predictive approaches use historical information to make schedules. Choices A, B, and C are all good examples of predictive OPAs.

40. B: Choice B is correct because project velocity is a live-kept record of how much progress a team can make per period. The ever-shifting average velocity is then used to set expectations going forward. Choice A stands in contrast with the mercurial nature of agile processes, Choice C is a fully unrelated metric, and Choice D is just the definition of a *project time period*.

41. A: Choice A is correct because the question gives the definition of a *network diagram*. Choices B, C, and D are all other ways to create a project schedule.

42. B: Choice B is correct because this question gives the definition of *start to start (SS) precedence relationships*. Choices A, C, and D are all different existing precedence relationships.

43. B: Choice B is correct because releases are the largest category in agile product road maps. Choices A, C, and D are all smaller plans that are separated into releases.

44. D: Choice D is correct because consistent work sizes make it easier to predict your team's output realistically and reliably. Choices A, B, and C are indicative of a very unbalanced schedule.

45. C: Choice C is correct because earned value management (EVM) provides effective comparative scoring to the more extensive, predetermined schedules of a predictive approach. Choices A, B, and D involve processes that are not always reliable enough in their plan to make use of an EVM.

46. A: Choice A is correct because cumulative flow diagrams (CFDs) show fluid completion rates and scope growth rates to accommodate for the malleable structure of agile plans. Choices B, C, and D involve processes that can be too rigid in their planning to make use of CFDs.

47. B: Choice B is correct because it simply involves adding more details to plans as more information arises, which does not interfere with existing structure, making it ideal for predictive approaches. Choice A does too much unplanned outsourcing, Choice C interferes with established plans, and Choice D is impossible in predictive approaches because the planning stage is not cyclical.

48. C: Choice C is correct because Little's Law states that a project's completion time is directly proportional to the length of its backup queue. Choice A is relative to the project, Choice B is untrue, and Choice D, although influential of a metric in Little's Law, is not a metric of Little's Law itself.

49. D: Choice D is correct because the average velocity of a team represents how many points they earn per cycle on average. So, if a three-week cycle averages 15 points and the team has been working on it for five cycles, they're currently at 75 points. That means it would presumably take them two more cycles (six weeks) to hit 105 points. Choices A, B, and C are all incorrect values.

50. B: Choice B is correct because the longest acceptable timeline through a network diagram is called the critical path. Choices A, C, and D are all made-up terms in the context of project management.

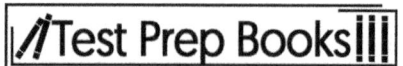

51. A: Choice *A* is correct because, for many projects, retrospectives are only helpful in managing future quality, not current quality. Choices *B, C,* and *D* consist of the three primary high-level quality management processes.

52. C: Choice *C* is correct because standards are quality benchmarks set by either competition, authority, or the general public consent. Choice *A* is a legal requirement, Choice *B* is made up, and Choice *D* describes a portion of a product to be presented to shareholders or customers.

53. D: Choice *D* is correct because the cost of quality (COQ) generally consists of prevention, appraisal, or failure costs or any combination of the three, which are Choices *A, B,* and *C*. If you are setting aside costs that anticipate low quality, your planning is already not where it should be.

54. C: Choice *C* is correct because a quality management tool that breaks a single problem down into many smaller cause categories is a fishbone diagram. Choices *A, B,* and *D* are all other quality management tools.

55. B: Choice *B* is correct because agile approaches rely on constant and clear information intake that can be frequently acted upon. Choices *A* and *D* do not reflect agile project techniques, and Choice *C* goes against the agile approach's ideal open flow of information.

56. A: Choice *A* is correct because the scope management plan serves to describe the development, monitoring, control, and validation of a project's scope, effectively setting the project's functional perimeter. Choice *C* is the other subsection of the project management plan, and Choices *B* and *D* are not project management plan subsections at all.

57. C: Choice *C* is correct because the box vision exercise is designed to allow stakeholders to ideate and add specifications on the scope of agile projects in the early stages. Choices *A, B,* and *D* are all steps that occur too late in the project life cycle to be exploratory.

58. D: Choice *D* is correct because iteration reviews are most helpful when many people involved in the project are working fluidly on their own, and touching base is critical to simply maintain expectations. This is not helpful to predictive approaches in which a majority of the team should be on the same page that was established early in the process. Choices *A, B,* and *C* are all good techniques for predictive projects to monitor scope.

59. B: Choice *B* is correct because the project management plan is the highest level of a master document for a given project. Choice *A* is a schedule management plan, and Choices *C* and *D* are functionally impossible.

60. D: Choice *D* is correct because *PM tools* is the commonly used term for what the PMP exam calls project management information systems (PMISs). Choices *A, B,* and *C* are all made-up terms in the context of project management.

61. C: Choice *C* is correct because a collection of procedures that serve to monitor and report on various project aspects is a configuration management system (CMS). Choices *A* and *B* are made up, and Choice *D* is related to action, not analysis.

62. A: Choice *A* is correct because a change management plan is too rigid and organized to reliably be of aid to more dynamic projects. Choices *B, C,* and *D* are all effective approaches in high-change environments.

Answer Explanations #2

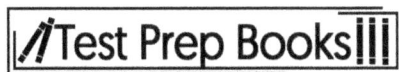

63. D: Choice D is correct because traditional, predictive projects use integrated change management to manage both project compliance and project changes. Choice A is a group of people used in more than just predictive approaches, Choice B is specifically an agile approach, and Choice C is not an actual project management term.

64. A: Choice A is correct because trying to fully avoid changes in a project is a fool's errand. Choice B is good for predicting and preparing for changes, but they cannot fully avoid them. Choice C is a group specifically designed to handle changes that do occur. Choice D is often not possible in a workplace and cannot be relied upon; even if it could be, it would not be an effective means of avoiding change.

65. B: Choice B is correct because lighter versions of traditional artifacts, such as scope statements and vision statements, are most effective at accommodating small changes at minimal cost, which is important when balancing a hybrid combination of project management styles. Choice A is incredibly destructive, Choice C is an agile-specific method, and Choice D only occurs if changes to a hybrid model have the potential to defy the project's scope plan.

66. D: Choice D is correct because change control boards (CCBs) should always be consulted if there is time to do so, regardless of change severity, but with agile projects, changes that demand immediate action occasionally occur. Choices A, B, and C all ignore this rule.

67. C: Choice C is correct because agile approaches appoint the product owner to head change management, often on their own with considerably less documentation than a traditional integrated change management approach might have. Choice A is a group that should always be consulted by the product owner whenever possible, but they are not in charge of change management. Choices B and D are simply without basis and are incorrect.

68. D: Choice D is correct because comparing your own process to your competitors puts an unhelpful amount of faith and priority in the goings-on of teams and work processes that you don't fully know. Choices A, B, and C are all valid metrics by which a PM can decide whether to make or buy a product.

69. A: Choice A is correct because it integrates the sellers and vendors into your project communication cycle as seamlessly as possible, leaves an open line of communication, and gives them access to most of the information they would want to know. Choice B is overbearing, and Choices C and D close off communication channels where it may be necessary to keep them open.

70. B: Choice B is correct because a time-and-materials (T&M) contract builds a seller's profit into an hourly rate, encouraging longer work times for the seller. Choice A is a downside of cost-reimbursable contracts, Choice C is a downside for fixed-price contracts, and Choice D is simply an untrue statement regarding T&M contracts.

71. A: Choice A is correct because incremental delivery contracts are broken down into smaller agreements of separate work packages to considerably reduce misestimation risks, which are higher in agile approaches. Choice B actively conflicts with agile approaches, and although Choices C and D could work in an agile project, they were not tailor-made to fit the agile approach.

72. C: Choice C is correct because the specific consequence of breaking the non-compete agreement, which should be specified in the contract, should be designed to mitigate or lessen the damages caused by the agreement's breach. Choice A is redundant when considering Choice C, and Choices B and D do not collect on agreed-upon penalties for the breach of contract.

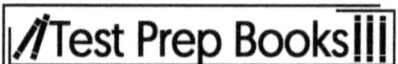

73. D: Choice D is correct because project artifacts are defined as any fluid internal product related to the management of a project, including documents, models, and designs, which will likely see many iterations throughout a project's life cycle.

74. B: Choice B is correct because the product backlog is one of the cornerstone aspects of every agile project, to the point where projects with backlogs are effectively synonymous with agile projects. Choices A, C, and D can all appear on other project types.

75. B: Choice B is correct because accessibility for future endeavors is not a universal requirement for project artifacts. Choices A, C, and D should always be true when interacting with project artifacts.

76. A: Choice A is correct because every project has varying levels of uncertainty, timelines, stakeholder needs, and other factors that prevent one single approach from dominating project management.

77. D: Choice D is correct because 80% of modern jobs in developed nations are categorized as knowledge work; thus, modern project management revolves around managing knowledge work. Choices A and B were dominant work types in the past, and Choice C is a type of employer, not a categorization of work.

78. C: Choice C is correct because projects with little expected change, smaller teams with less established trust, and little customer access are all severe red flags for anything approaching an agile methodology—so much so that even hybrid models are likely to be more dynamic than is useful for this project.

79. D: Choice D is correct because the values and skill sets of every organization are different, and there is no standardized rule regarding who gets the final say regarding the project management approach.

80. C: Choice C is correct because project governance is simply the amalgamation of all key elements that aid in the project's work structure. Choices A and D have nothing to do with work structure, and although individual companies might have set project governance tendencies, Choice B falsely implies that project governance is fixed within an organization, when actually it can be tailored from project to project.

81. A: Choice A is correct because a governance gate or kill point is also called a phase gate. Choice B, although also a potentially accurate term for a phase gate, is not the correct name. Choices C and D have nothing to do with phase review.

82. B: Choice B is correct because the issue log is critical for ensuring that everyone in the project who needs to know about issues is made aware as soon as possible; communication is priority. Choice A ignores the issue in front of you, and Choices C and D, although absolutely necessary, do not take precedence over an issue log.

83. D: Choice D is correct because the issue must still be considered and worked on, but going through the same steps with no changes is spinning your wheels and wasting project time in the long run. Choice A interferes with the other team's work and only laterally shifts responsibility. Choice B is a waste of time, and Choice C is often unacceptable for any issue of real significance.

84. C: Choice C is correct because impediment boards and lists are the primary replacement for an issue log in agile projects. Choice A will not be dedicated to issue resolution, Choice B is a waste of resources, and Choice D is a single part of an impediment board.

85. B: Choice *B* is correct because *tacit knowledge* is defined as unwritten expertise that helps a team member intuitively function in the team's workflow. Choices *A*, *C*, and *D* are all official and recorded pieces of information and are thus not tacit.

86. A: Choice *A* is correct because lessons learned review workshops are a simple and useful way to turn experiences on a project phase into useful knowledge for upcoming work, including future phases in the current project. Choices *B* and *C* miss out on a potential trove of useful knowledge during the project life cycle, and Choice *D* is a false statement.

87. D: Choice *D* is correct because tacit knowledge requires experience, familiarity, and a sense of nuance regarding the project and the team, and unwritten "helpful tidbits" are often not a part of official knowledge transfer practices. Choice *A* is incorrect because a team member's performance remains indicative of how knowledgeable they are regarding the project. Choices *B* and *C* can be avoided by circumventing or properly planning around such factors.

88. B: Choice *B* is correct because contracts may be closed out at any time, regardless of where in the project life cycle you are, and it is good practice to close contracts as soon as work is done in order to avoid any needless additional costs. Choices *A* and *C* are incorrect because a contractor's definition of *complete* should be clearly legislated and quantified in the contract, and keeping a contractor around for additional work would require reworking the contract's definition of *complete*. Choice *D* is incorrect because managing contractors is not the stakeholders' job.

89. A: Choice *A* is correct because the purpose of a definition of *complete* is to understand when it is acceptable to close or move forward with a project. Choice *A* might be a valid reason for a team member to be personally done for the week, but it still does not signify the work itself as *complete*. Choices *B*, *C*, and *D* are objective benchmarks of progress that can situationally serve as a definition of *complete*.

90. C: Choice *C* is correct because cancellation is just another cause for project closure and should not be treated differently than standard project closure. Choices *A* and *B* are also both steps you should take, but they should be outlined in the project closure guidelines in the appropriate order. Choice *D* is often a waste of time if you are already in this position because the decision has often already been finalized.

91. C: Level 3: Contest is the correct answer choice because Level 2 precedes conflict that involves personal attacks. Level 1 is a more friendly and productive form of problem-solving that abstains from personal attacks or the need for defensive language. A crusade-level conflict, on the other hand, moves past language and can be characterized by team members choosing sides and dividing amongst themselves.

92. C: This statement involves a personal attack or slight directed at another team member and does not discuss the problem. Choices *A* and *D* are focused on finding the best solution, and they provide facts and arguments about the tool rather than anything personal about a teammate. Choice *B* shows a fear of conflict, and possibly a lack of commitment, but it would fall under *problem to solve* rather than the upper four levels of conflict.

93. B: Defining the problem is always the first step when using a confronting/problem-solving approach. Step two, exploring and evaluating alternatives, cannot be done until the initial conflict has been acknowledged, shared goals are established, and the problems have been separated from the people.

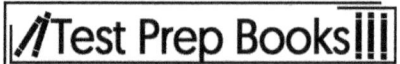

94. A: The absence of trust between team members often leads to a fear of conflict and a subsequent lack of unfiltered passionate debate. Choice B, lack of commitment, is a product of not engaging in healthy disagreements and leads to team members agreeing to decisions they don't believe in. The top two tiers of the model, avoidance of accountability and inattention to results, are both illustrated by individuals who work for their own good and put individual goals ahead of the team vision due to a lack of trust and camaraderie within the team.

95. D: The key point of this answer choice is to get all the facts. By doing so, the project manager can effectively take the conflict from a personal situation to a factual disagreement, halting progress through the five levels of conflict and ideally resolving the argument. Choice C is an extreme response and would be better suited for a more drastic disagreement. A conflict that has escalated into a contest has likely gone too far for a win-win situation. Allowing team members to resolve the conflict on their own may not be the best course of action if the threat of a higher-level conflict is more likely than not.

96. D: This statement would indicate that the highest level of conflict is on the horizon because of the divided and combative language used without one part of the team present. While the context of this statement would be necessary to fully understand which stage this conflict has entered, it has clearly surpassed a disagreement or contest. Divided language is also a hallmark of a crusade-level conflict; however, the secrecy and refusal to speak to the other team members described in this question indicates the highest level of conflict.

97. D: Choice D is the correct answer because a more diverse team can discuss a broader range of viewpoints, which leads to fewer areas uncovered and a smaller chance that a previously unaccounted-for problem arises.

98. A: While Theory X in Douglas McGregor's theories of management and motivation refers to a more authoritarian style with tighter control, Theory Y is a more liberating theory of management where teams are given more responsibility and are empowered through continuous improvement.

99. B: During the stakeholder analysis portion of a project, you identify any conflicts that may arise with stakeholders and the level of effort required for each one. Once you determine that a stakeholder has a high level of power but low interest in the project, the best course of action is to keep them satisfied rather than consistently making sure they are well-informed.

100. A: Small-group work is a key first step in this exercise because it supports early collaboration between team members and outside stakeholders. Logo design is an optional portion of designing the product box and while it may be one of the first things a group discusses, it is usually not the most important. Scheduling and task assignment occur after the product vision has been clarified and teams have made presentations. Group discussion is always the last portion of this exercise, where everyone comes together to decide on aspects like features and project requirements.

101. B: Contributor safety is defined by the feeling of safety that allows early, frequent contributions without fear of negative feedback. Choice A illustrates inclusion safety, the first stage of the process. Choice C describes learner safety, and Choice D describes the final stage, challenger safety.

102. B: Servant leadership is the idea that project managers, as the leaders of a project, should facilitate from behind and work for their team rather than expecting the team to work for them. This mindset certainly requires empathy and the support of diversity and inclusion; however, these do not define the

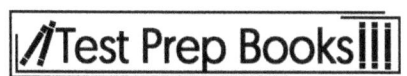

Answer Explanations #2

entire value system. The net contribution of all team members can increase with a good servant leader, but this term is more of a metric than a value mindset.

103. D: SPI is an acronym for schedule performance index, which is calculated by comparing the current project schedule to the originally planned schedule. An SPI does not factor into a project's budget, and the index value has no correlation to the percent of the project completed. A value above 1.0 indicates the project is ahead of schedule, while anything below 1.0, such as .85, shows that the project is behind schedule.

104. D: While goals should be manageable, the acronym SMART stands for specific, measurable, achievable, relevant, and time-bound. Choice *D* is the only word not included.

105. C: Key results can be defined as quantitative metrics used to track a team's progress on the objective. Since they are quantitative metrics, they must include a number, and Choice *C* is the only answer that does not include a specific value. Choices *A*, *B*, and *D* all include quantitative values that are in line with the original objective, which makes them suitable key results.

106. A: Objectives are often short phrases such as, "Become the market leading online menswear distributor." They are designed specifically to engage team members and ensure the vision of a project remains in sight. Key results attach achievable numbers to the objective, giving the team a more actionable direction toward project goals. A key performance indicator is a specific metric designed to track any aspect of a project, and lagging metrics are measurements of what has happened in the past over a substantial period of time.

107. A: Both CPIs and SPIs are calculated so that any number below one indicates that the project is over budget or behind schedule. Since this question is asking about a project with a CPI of .9, you can infer that each dollar spent is yielding 90 cents in practice. Similarly, an SPI of 1.1 shows that the project is moving 10% faster than originally planned.

108. B: A team charter defines how a team should collaborate effectively over the course of a project and typically addresses values, agreements, and practices. Reporting structures are usually in effect prior to the creation of a team charter. A RACI matrix defines individual responsibilities, and scope statements may evolve over time, so both would be irrelevant to the team charter.

109. A: The more empowered a team is, the higher their motivation will be since they have some autonomy in deciding how to move forward. An empowered team also leaves more room for debate since they must decide among themselves what the best course of action is.

110. C: Since this decision is about technical solutions, it would be best to allow team members to decide amongst themselves rather than defer to the project manager, who may not have as strong of a grasp on the subject matter. The expected monetary value may not provide much insight since the solutions all have a similar cost. Dot voting is better suited than simple voting for decisions with more than two options, so dot voting is the best approach here.

111. B: Simple voting is the best technique to ensure that teams decide on one of two choices without further debate. Highsmith's decision spectrum, dot voting, and fist to five all leave room for debate, while simple voting requires a simple "for" or "against" from each team member.

112. D: Because this is an agile team, you should encourage autonomy and make sure the team feels empowered to make the best decision. Deciding on your own or bringing in a single expert to choose

175

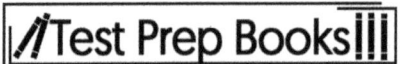

Answer Explanations #2

would result in a loss of autonomy that the team may come to resent. Simple voting will likely lead to the lack of spirited debate continuing. Highsmith's decision spectrum, Choice D, would be the best decision here, as it will force team members to flesh out their opinions and come to the best solution as a unit.

113. C: Choice C is the best answer because shadowing and peer-to-peer training would both occur while at work. Formal training involves methods like virtual learning and individual training, while informal training refers to books, podcasts, conferences, and other less rigid styles of training.

114. D: Since your team members are in different places around the world, it would be unfair to require everyone to be present for training at the same time. Additionally, any locally sourced training is going to be somewhat biased toward local standards and customs. Choice D is the best option since the training will be equally helpful to everyone involved, and team members may complete it at a convenient time.

115. B: Books, podcasts, blogs, or even discussion forums all fall under the category of informal training. Formal training involves activities such as classroom training or virtual learning. On-the-job and experiential training fall under the same category and involve techniques like shadowing and mentoring.

116. A: While a WBS task analysis may be a useful tool for determining what skills the team requires for this project, it is the only choice that doesn't directly assess what skills team members have or do not have. Surveys can fall victim to team members over- or underestimating the skills they possess, but it is still a useful tool if you have a trusted team. Skills gap and SWOT analyses are designed specifically for this task and should be effective for deciding what training is required.

117. D: Shadowing would be the most effective training for this new team member since their learning will take place during work hours. Books and podcasts can be great tools; however, forcing only one team member to complete extra work outside of the office can lead to them feeling overwhelmed and ostracized. Group virtual learning might feel redundant if only one team member requires the training, so Choice D is the best answer.

118. A: Choice B best defines a person who is I shaped, with deep knowledge of one area but a lack of other skills. Choice A is correct because T-shaped people have mastery of one area in addition to broader skills in a few other key areas.

119. D: Choice D, forming, is the correct answer because it is the first stage where team members meet each other, get to know everyone, and find their place. Storming is characterized by initial competition and conflict in trying to establish roles, followed by norming, where team members settle into their roles before the fourth stage, performing, when team members are at ease and can effectively collaborate with each other.

120. C: Ability tests are the most common type of assessment for newly recruited team members since they are objective and provide accurate data about the individual's skill set. Interviews, surveys, and focus groups can all be useful tools for appraising skills as well, but they can be more difficult to conduct when dealing with an unfamiliar team member who may want to embellish their skills to seem competent.

121. D: When a key team member is subtracted, the remaining group must figure out once again how they work together best and establish a new hierarchy moving forward. Adjourning occurs when the work is finished, and the team goes their separate ways. Forming has already occurred with the team members that remain. A perfect team could, in theory, return to norming unphased by the loss of a team member, but since no team is perfect, this is unlikely. Other individuals will have to fill in any gaps left behind, so that leaves Choice D, storming, as the best answer.

122. C: In a RACI matrix, the person responsible for a task is the one doing the work, while the person who signs off and marks it done is accountable for the task. Stakeholders who are consulted may be asked to give their input but won't be doing most of the work and do not have the authority to deem a task completed. Informed individuals should be given regular progress updates but will not require input on every task or decision to be made.

123. A: When a team can collaborate to work toward a common goal, it is operating in the performing stage. Each teammate has found their place within the system and settled down as a hierarchy has been established, and everyone knows how the other team members tend to work best.

124. B: While it is good to be on the lookout for potential blockers that may arise, the team is unlikely to be able to identify any impediments during an initial kickoff meeting, so Choice A is correct. Lessons learned workshops, daily standups, and retrospectives are all good times to ask your team about anything that might be impeding their workflow.

125. C: Value stream mapping, Gemba walks, and backlog assessments are all useful tools in the impediment removal process. However, Choice C is the best answer here because impediment removal refers to the entire process of identifying blockers and eliminating them so that the team can continue to make progress without interruption.

126. A: A task board will often show items on which progress has been slowed or stopped completely due to a variety of possible impediments, so it's a good way to find issues visually. Release roadmaps and network diagrams may provide some insight into existing blockers; however, they are less interactive and therefore less likely to include the most up-to-date obstacles affecting your team. Similarly, burndown charts may illustrate impediments on a larger scale by showing how much work has been completed and how much remains, but they are unlikely to provide insights about what specifically has been slowing down progress.

127. D: Impediment removal is the key process of finding and solving issues that block the team from progressing on a task. Choice C, task age analysis, is a useful tool in the process of impediment removal, but it does not describe the entire process. Performing is the final stage of the Tuckman model, in which impediment removal may play an important role in the team's success, and project management encompasses much more than impediment removal alone. That leaves Choice D as the best answer.

128. C: Without the face-to-face interactions that occur consistently in a traditional in-person office, identifying impediments that halt team members' progress can be more difficult. When checking in with your team, it is best to be empathetic and ask about the individual and what they might need rather than asking about the work directly, as that can make people defensive and less likely to be honest about blockers they are facing.

129. B: The initial stage, deciding to negotiate, is when issues are first identified and problems can be defined. Once problems are identified and it is deemed in everyone's best interest to negotiate, the next step is to prepare (Choice B) by gaining a better understanding of the issues at hand and building relationships with the other party. Negotiation cannot take place until this is done, at which point agreements can be put in writing, and your team can begin to execute.

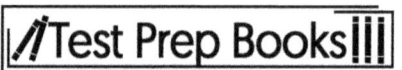

Answer Explanations #2

130. A: The formality of an agreement has a direct relationship with the separation from your team. Formality increases as the separation from your team increases since trust is likely to decrease when dealing with external parties or even other departments. While informal or verbal agreements may be suitable when only co-workers are involved, it is best to exhibit caution when dealing with outside parties by documenting all agreements and creating a legally bound contract.

131. C: The level of formality of an agreement increases as the distance from your team increases, so it's best to plan for the worst-case scenario and draw up a legally binding agreement with a third-party vendor. If you're working with a team that you trust and know well, a verbal agreement should suffice. Even if you decide to write the agreement out and provide your team with a concrete copy, it is unlikely that a legal document will be required on your team's side.

132. B: Sponsors and executives commission your team or organization to create a new product or update an existing one. Suppliers and vendors are third-party groups that often work on a portion of the project. Business representatives are the project's subject matter experts and help by providing feedback and explaining what the sponsor needs. Customers are anyone who will use the finished product.

133. A: The three constraints listed in Choice *A*—cost, scope, and time or schedule—are the three constraints commonly depicted as a golden triangle. Risks, quality, and resources make up the silver or iron triangle, meaning they are still important and need to be acknowledged in the process of project planning and management.

134. A: The types of people listed in the question will likely share a common goal and thus will have a positive outlook on the project. Stakeholder groups such as competitors or protestors would be more likely to have negative feelings, whereas the media and similar groups will initially have neutral feelings, likely to be swayed by further output.

135. C: It is crucial to check with stakeholders periodically to make sure that their needs are met through every checkpoint of a project. Doing so will not eliminate the possibility of a major interruption or course change, but it will certainly decrease the chances of something unexpected occurring within stakeholder groups.

136. D: Document analysis of past projects, questionnaires, and surveys, as well as simply asking the team, are all valid and effective means for identifying stakeholders. Lead and lag time calculations don't usually include contact information and thus would not be a useful way of identifying new stakeholders.

137. B: Whether it's digital or low-tech, a highly visible task board helps break down the barriers between tasks, allowing the team to move forward more effectively. While a project charter can also be useful in maintaining a shared vision while moving through the project life cycle, it is a higher-level document that is less interactive and may not provide the same assurance about what's up next. Product boxes also provide some vision regarding the end goal of a project, but they do not include information on specific tasks to be completed. The stakeholder register is not related to the project schedule or task assignments, so it's unlikely that team members would find any direction within this deliverable.

138. D: The purpose of a stakeholder register is to compile all information about every stakeholder in one document. This includes, but is not limited to, name and contact information, role and

Answer Explanations #2

requirements, as well as impact and influence scores. Task assignments and scheduling are more likely to be found in documents like a task board or project charter.

139. C: The halo effect occurs when the most respected person in the group exhibits a significant amount of pull over the others' decision-making. Wideband Delphi estimation is a technique that requires each team member to submit their own estimates, without others' knowledge, before combining the results and discussing them. Roman voting and fist to five can easily fall victim to the halo effect since everyone has full knowledge of all opinions that are posed before their own. Focus groups, if conducted correctly, can avoid the dangers of the halo effect; however, they pose the same issue of every group member being aware of the others' opinions.

140. B: While an after-action review can be useful in analyzing a participant's actions and how they lead to a positive or negative outcome, the five whys is the best choice because it is designed specifically to move past the obvious problems and identify the root cause-and-effect. Wideband Delphi estimations and planning poker are both useful exercises in reaching a consensus, but they do not assist in identifying a problem.

141. A: The vision, charter, and plan of a project all work together to build a shared understanding of the project goals and how they will be achieved. Choice A, the project vision, is the best answer because its main mission is to help stakeholders understand the end goals or destination of a project.

142. D: While fist to five is not the slowest way to make a decision, it is not the quickest either, so Choice A does not provide the full answer. The project manager may act as another participant in this method; however, they will not have the full authority to make the final decision because it is in their best interest to reach an agreement in a collaborative fashion. Therefore, Choice B is not correct. Fist to five can be a good way to surface disagreements; however, other methods do this just as well, if not more efficiently, so Choice C is not the best answer. Fist to five allows the team to talk through different viewpoints and collaborate to arrive at the best decision possible, so Choice D is the best answer.

143. B: An XP metaphor is a metaphor explaining the product in a simple way that unites the whole team around a singular perspective. Product boxes and task boards can also have a similar effect on individuals contributing to a project; however, they are not written as stories. The project vision also has the purpose of uniting the team around a single vision of the product, but this is not the best answer here.

144. D: Teams that only interact digitally tend to move from forming to storming to norming at a slower pace due to meeting less often and needing to overcome the barrier of technology. Team members also may be less likely to confront others and face problems head-on since it is much easier to withdraw and avoid than it would be in a face-to-face setting.

145. C: Choice C illustrates the most effective way to check in because it exhibits empathy and a willingness to help, as opposed to a check-up or check-on that only serves to evaluate progress and ensure that work is being done. The purpose of a virtual check-in is to provide the support that is often lacking in remote teams. The other three answer choices leave no room for personal connection.

146. A: Choice A illustrates the most appropriate response because the most drastic change will be the need for more tech support. Most agile practices will only need minimal changes. Choice B illustrates a pessimistic point of view. Although barriers to communication will make an agile approach more complex, recent technological updates have made it possible to continue with an agile mindset even if

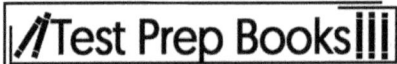

the team is globally distributed. Choice *C* is incorrect because remote work will require some level of adjustment. Choice *D*, while not entirely inappropriate, illustrates too drastic of a switch to traditional values.

147. D: If team members' individual locations allow for it, an in-person meeting is most useful at the onset of a project. Allowing everyone to meet face-to-face even once can ease tension down the line and break down some of the barriers to virtual communication.

148. A: While the transition to a remote workplace requires some creative problem-solving to ensure everyone feels comfortable and empowered, innovation can be stifled due to a lack of daily conversations that occur in a traditional office. Remote work does provide the advantage of a staff that is able to travel more often, a wider talent pool during recruiting, and a smaller overhead without the cost of office space.

149. C: While it is unrealistic that you would have to focus all your effort on making sure your team members are engaged on a daily basis, maintaining engagement certainly requires more effort to bring individuals together when everyone is working remotely. If you assume that team members will be equally engaged on a remote team, you will likely lose out on input from less outspoken stakeholders since remote teams often lack daily informal conversations and general rapport with one another.

150. B: While the project manager will often lead or begin the discussion on defining ground rules, everyone who is going to be abiding by them should be involved in their conception. The most effective ground rules are ones that all team members agree with, including the project manager, so deciding on rules individually or without consultation would likely cause some level of disagreement.

151. B: Learner safety is the second stage and is defined by a feeling of security when posing questions to the rest of the team. It is preceded by inclusion safety, which is the feeling of belonging to a team with common goals in mind. Contributor safety follows, which is the stage where team members can feel safe asking for feedback on their work. The final stage is challenger safety, which is when team members are comfortable disagreeing with the group's ideas.

152. C: Ground rules that promote respect in conjunction with steadily increasing permission due to positive experiences with the team lead to higher levels of perceived psychological safety. Communication is a key aspect of any well-run team, and conflict is inevitable; however, these two metrics do not directly define the stages of psychological safety.

153. A: In an ideal situation, Henry would immediately recognize that he has been disrespectful and apologize to remedy the situation. If not, a strong team would be able to identify and call out this behavior before an intervention from the project manager is necessary. Finally, if all else fails and this behavior continues, the HR department is a last line of defense against ground rule violations.

154. D: Rules that are broken by the project manager are less likely to be respected by the rest of the team. Choice *D*, modeling the desired behavior, is the best answer here. A simple reminder of the established ground rules can be effective if they are broken, but constantly preaching them can seem overbearing and condescending. While team members should be able to settle some disagreements on their own, failure to intervene when needed can lead to a degrading culture and a lack of respect for ground rules. Team members who consistently defy ground rules may need to be removed; however, doing so over any little infraction can hurt the psychological safety of the rest of the team.

155. B: During the middle of the sprint, individual team members are more likely to have questions and problems regarding smaller portions of the project that they are working on and will require more coaching. Whole-team coaching will be most prevalent at the beginning, when everything needs to be planned, and at the end, when the team must evaluate what worked well and what didn't.

156. C: A common mistake among project managers is the belief that simply adding new tools or techniques for the team to put into practice will immediately lead to better performance. It is usually much more effective to focus on individual team members' capabilities and coach them on more effective methods, so Choice C is the correct answer. Making it known that a team member or the whole team is underperforming is useless without establishing a path forward that allows for growth.

157. A: While the communications plan is a crucial part of any successful team, it would not give you any insight into the coaching practices that have been in place. Team assessments, training schedules, and the mentoring plan would all provide you with relevant information and allow you to better understand what the coaching practices might be lacking.

158. B: Whole-team coaching is the most prominent at the beginning and end of a sprint, first to build shared values and a unified vision and then to engage in retrospectives and dig deeper into what worked and what didn't. Individual coaching will still take place on an as-needed basis for those who may be lacking in required skills prior to the sprint; however, most of the individual mentoring will take place during the middle stages of the project when team members are most likely to encounter problems and setbacks in their work.

159. C: The biggest advantage of allowing other team members to coach one another is promoting empowerment within the team. It is unlikely that the project manager is the most knowledgeable team member on every aspect of a project, so allowing others to become the expert and help those who are less knowledgeable promotes the idea that they are the ones who own the work. This process is unlikely to have a direct increase in profits; it can increase productivity, but that is not the main benefit. Technological capabilities can increase if they are the aspect team members are being coached on, but this is not the best reason for sharing the role of coaching.

160. B: Emotional intelligence is the psychology of understanding others as well as oneself. This includes regulating emotions and personal feelings and the ability to work well with others.

161. B: Action, also referred to as management, and awareness define the four quadrants of EQ, with half relating to personal issues and the other half to interpersonal issues. Motivation and empathy do fit in both quadrants of awareness, as do self-regulation and social skills for action, but they do not define the overall matrix.

162. D: While all these skills have an influence on the people around you, leadership is the best answer because it requires action at an interpersonal level. Optimism and adaptability are both personal subsets of emotional intelligence, and leveraging diversity, while it is an interpersonal skill, has more to do with awareness than action.

163. C: Self regulation involves skills such as self-control, conscientiousness, and adaptability. Empathy is defined by interpersonal awareness, whereas motivation is in the EQ quadrant at the intersection of personal intelligence and awareness. Actions on an interpersonal level can also be referred to as social skills, which is the upper right-hand quadrant.

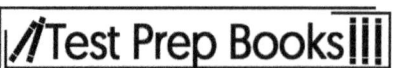

164. D: The traits that fall into the category of empathy require awareness within interpersonal skills. Some examples of these skills are understanding others and leveraging diversity. Interpersonal actions labeled as social skills include traits such as collaboration, team building, and leadership. The other side of the matrix relates to personal actions and awareness and is defined by self-regulation and motivation/self-awareness.

165. A: Active listening is a skill that requires empathy and a real interpersonal connection. It is the process of understanding what is being said in addition to what might be omitted in the physical and emotional context of a conversation. Internal listening is the lowest level of listening and means looking only for words or ideas that concern yourself. Understanding others is a subset of empathy, both of which are required to undergo true active listening.

166. C: Stakeholder analysis is the process in which information is consistently gathered and analyzed throughout the project to determine, address, and align expectations. Getting to know the stakeholders, keeping an open line of communication, and making them feel like part of the process is critical to a project's success.

167. D: The project charter is the document that officially authorizes the project. The charter is developed in the initiating process of the project and formally approves the work of the project to begin as well as names the project manager.

168. B: Functional requirements are the behavior requirements of what a product will achieve. They describe the necessary capabilities of a system in business terms and the features required for the end user.

169. D: The project manager is responsible for conducting the benefits analysis. The analysis determines if the value of the benefits of the project outweigh the cost. The result supports the organization's decision to either buy the product or develop it themselves. Once the project manager has the results, the stakeholders are informed and will form their final decision to move forward or abandon the project.

170. A: The correct formula to calculate present value (PV) is $PV = FV/(1+i)^n$. The formula calculates the current worth of future money that may be paid out over a specific period of time. The calculation is broken down as such:

$$PV = Present\ value$$

$$FV = Future\ value$$

$$i = Cost\ of\ capital\ or\ interest\ rate$$

$$n = Number\ of\ time\ periods$$

171. C: Project C has the lowest benefit-cost ratio and would be a project an organization would abandon, as the cost outweighs the benefit. The formula to calculate the ratio is benefit/cost. 100,000/250,000 = .4. The result of .4 indicates that only 40 cents are earned for each dollar spent, meaning there is no profit.

172. A: Project B will likely be approved by an organization to move forward, as the benefit outweighs the cost to produce. 120,000/100,000 = 1.2. Most organizations approve projects with a 1.2 ratio to move forward, as this result indicates the profit is $1.20 on each dollar spent.

Answer Explanations #2

173. B: Stakeholders who formulate opinions and decisions and should be engaged on the project fall into the *meet their needs* quadrant on the matrix. These stakeholders are categorized as high importance and low influence. They do not require a lot of information to keep them satisfied, but they need just enough as to not make them bored with the message.

174. D: Asking the project team members for their input on which requirements to choose should there be a conflict in stakeholder requirements is the correct answer, as the question asked for the answer that was not considered a way to resolve conflicting requirements. It is critical to project success to meet with the stakeholders and have them reiterate the goals and objectives of the project, individually in the group setting. It will become obvious when this approach is taken that not everyone understands the business case for the project as well as the goals and objectives.

175. C: Tested system based on specifications is considered a deliverable and not a milestone. A deliverable is not a task or an activity; it's a measurable outcome that meets the project requirements. They are specific outputs that have to be produced for project completion.

176. A: The present value is $1,890.36. Present value tells you the current worth of a future sum of money. The future value in this example is $2,500 ($2,000 invoice fee + $500 late fee), with a two-year payback term and 15% cost of capital. Although $500 is received in late fees, $609.64 is lost in present value in this example.

$$PV = \frac{\$2{,}500}{(1 + .15)^2}$$

$$PV = \frac{\$2{,}500}{(1.15)^2} = \frac{\$2{,}500}{1.3225}$$

$$PV = \$1{,}890.36$$

177. D: Having two resources assigned to the project simultaneously working on another project is a high-level risk on the current project. A full-time dedicated resource should be assigned to the project because the project schedule could be delayed should they be pulled onto another project simultaneously.

178. B: Company culture is a collection of values that describe what a company thinks is important to its business practices. Choices *A* and *C* are used in agile environments to track work progress and do not play a role in company culture. Choice *D* is a type of organizational structure, not an aspect of culture.

179. B: 1.49 is the benefit-cost ratio for a system implementation that charges $215,000 (cost) and generates $320,000 in value (benefit). The result of 1.49 means for every $1.00 of cost, there is $1.49 of benefit, concluding the investment is worth the benefit.

$$\frac{Benefit}{Cost} = Ratio$$

$$\frac{\$320{,}000}{\$215{,}000} = 1.49$$

180. C: The net present value is an indicator of profitability. A higher NPV is better than a lower NPV. It is calculated as future predicted cash flow minus the initial investment costs. Choices *A*, *B*, and *D* are not what the NPV calculates.

PMP Practice Test #3

To keep the size of this book manageable, save paper, and provide a digital test-taking experience, the 3rd practice test can be found online. Scan the QR code or go to this link to access it:

testprepbooks.com/online387/pmp

The first time you access the tests, you will need to register as a "new user" and verify your email address.

If you have any issues, please email support@testprepbooks.com.

Dear PMP Test Taker,

Thank you for purchasing this study guide for your PMP exam. We hope that we exceeded your expectations.

Our goal in creating this study guide was to cover all of the topics that you will see on the test. We also strove to make our practice questions as similar as possible to what you will encounter on test day. With that being said, if you found something that you feel was not up to your standards, please send us an email and let us know.

We would also like to let you know about other books in our catalog that may interest you.

ASP

This can be found on Amazon at: amazon.com/dp/1637750986

Six Sigma

This can be found on Amazon at: amazon.com/dp/1637751591

CHST

This can be found on Amazon at: amazon.com/dp/1637753683

We have study guides in a wide variety of fields. If the one you are looking for isn't listed above, then try searching for it on Amazon or send us an email.

Thanks Again and Happy Testing!
Product Development Team
info@studyguideteam.com

Online Resources

Included with your purchase are multiple online resources. This includes the practice tests in an interactive format and a convenient study timer to help you manage your time.

Scan the QR code or go to this link to access this content:

testprepbooks.com/online387/pmp

The first time you access the page, you will need to register as a "new user" and verify your email address.

If you have any issues, please email support@testprepbooks.com.

Thank you for letting us be a part of your studying journey!